THE MODERN HISTORY OF LEBANON

THE MODERN HISTORY OF LEBANON

KAMAL S. SALIBI

CARAVAN BOOKS

DELMAR, NEW YORK

First Edition 1965
First Caravan Books printing 1977
Second Caravan Books printing 1993
by arrangement with Weidenfeld and Nicolson

Published by Caravan Books, Delmar, New York 12054

Printed in Lebanon by Heidelberg Press–Lebanon

Library of Congress Cataloging in Publication Data

Salibi, Kamal Suleiman, 1929–
The modern history of Lebanon.

Reprint of the ed. published by Weidenfeld & Nicolson, London.
1. Lebanon—History—1516– I. Title.
DS84.S25 1977 956.92 77-15054
ISBN 0-88206-015-5

CONTENTS

MAPS

PREFACE

I WISH to thank Professor Bernard Lewis for asking me to write this history of Lebanon, and for suggesting important revisions in the first part.

Professor Nabih Faris read and made useful comments on all the chapters. Also helpful in a variety of ways were my colleagues Ralph Crow, John Gulick, Malcolm Kerr, Walid al-Khalidi, Joseph Malone, and Richard Yorkey. I further owe thanks to Mr Michel Asmar of the Cénacle Libanais, Mr Jibran Bikhazi of our University Library, Dr Georges Borgi, Mr Dominique Chevallier, Mr Antoine Medawar, Mr Shafik Muharram, Aref Bey al-Nakadi, and Mr Pierre Roccalve for advice and assistance.

I owe particular gratitude to Mr Frank Stoakes, formerly of St Antony's, Oxford, for reading my complete manuscript, often in more than one draft, and offering invaluable suggestions on style and content. My colleagues Dr David Gordon and Mr Glen Balfour-Paul read the last chapter and were also extremely helpful.

K. S. SALIBI

American University of Beirut
18 March, 1964

INTRODUCTION

LEBANON, ON the eastern shores of the Mediterranean, is today a small republic stretching approximately one hundred miles along the Phoenician coast, with a total area of 4,015 square miles and a population scarcely exceeding one-and-a-half million. Her territory, mostly rugged mountain, is dominated by the parallel ranges of the Lebanon and the Anti-Lebanon, and bounded on the north by the Eleutherus river (Nahr al-Kabīr), on the east by the crest of the Anti-Lebanon, and on the south by a line across the highlands of Galilee. The Lebanon and Anti-Lebanon ranges run north-east to south-west, following the slant of the coast, and between them lies the rift valley of the Biqāʿ. West of the Biqāʿ, the Lebanon range runs so close to the coastline that in places it falls directly to the sea, its rocky promontories dividing the narrow coastal plain into a number of isolated strips. Beirut, the capital of modern Lebanon, is located in one of the broader coastal strips, almost exactly mid-way down the coast.

It was on 1 September 1920 that France, as mandatory power, established the State of Greater Lebanon, giving the country her present frontiers. Lebanon since then became a republic (1926) and achieved independence (1943), joining the League of Arab States and the United Nations as a founding member (1945). Before 1920, however, the situation of the country was entirely different.

Between 1516 and 1918 the territory of the modern Lebanese Republic fell under Ottoman sovereignty, and consisted officially (until 1864) of two administrative regions: a northern region forming part of the vilayet of Tripoli, and a southern region forming part of the vilayet of Sidon. The Biqāʿ, separate from these two regions, formed part of the vilayet of Damascus – as did the southern region of Lebanon until the vilayet of Sidon was created in 1660. When the Ottomans reorganized their provincial administration in 1864, these arrangements were changed. While the Biqāʿ remained with Damascus, the vilayets of Tripoli and Sidon were abolished and replaced by the vilayet of Beirut, which absorbed their territory. Meanwhile, in 1861, an autonomous

Mutesarrifate[1] of Lebanon was created under the guarantee of the European Powers, to include that part of the present Lebanese territory which extends roughly from the watershed of the Lebanon to the sea, excluding the town of Beirut and the regions of Tripoli and Sidon. This territory, commonly called Mount Lebanon, was governed from 1861 until 1915 by a non-Lebanese Ottoman Christian mutesarrif, appointed by the Porte (with the approval of the Powers) and responsible directly to Istanbul. A locally elected administrative council assisted the mutesarrif in the government, while a Lebanese gendarmerie maintained public order.

Indeed, it was only with the establishment of the Lebanese Mutesarrifate that the term 'Lebanon' (Arabic *Lubnān*) acquired a definite official use. Before that time no political entity formally called 'Lebanon' or 'Mount Lebanon' had existed. The Maʿns, Druze emirs of southern Lebanon who established their rule over the whole of Mount Lebanon in the early seventeenth century, were usually styled 'Emirs of the Druzes'; so were their successors the Shihābs, although these emirs were not Druzes at all, but Sunnite Moslems, and later Christians. The Maʿns ruled Mount Lebanon until 1697, and the Shihābs after them until 1841. Yet until the eighteenth century there was no term, official or non-official, to denote the whole territory of the Lebanese Emirate. The term 'Mount Lebanon' (Jabal Lubnān) was used at the time in a restricted sense, to mean the northernmost districts of Bsharrī, Batrūn, and Jubayl, which were inhabited by Maronites. Further south, the region of Jabal Kisrawān, also inhabited by Maronites, was sometimes included under 'Mount Lebanon', but more often considered separately. South of the Kisrawān, and separated from it by the Beirut–Damascus road, was the region of Jabal al-Shūf, also known as the Druze Mountain (*Jabal al-Durūz*). This region, with its Druze population, had scarcely any connexion with the Maronite regions of the north, and certainly until the seventeenth century was never referred to as 'Mount Lebanon'. It was only in the late eighteenth century, after many Maronites had settled in the Druze districts, that the name 'Mount Lebanon' came commonly to apply to the whole Shihāb domain. The Maronites, deeply attached to their original homeland in the north, seem to have carried its name with them as they migrated southwards in the seventeenth and eighteenth centuries, until 'Mount Lebanon' came to include the whole territory in which they settled.

The territory of the Maʿns and the Shihābs, which can be conveniently called the Lebanese Emirate, was never a clearly defined unit. Its core consisted of the Maronite and Druze districts which the Lebanese emirs controlled as feudal overlords, and which later came to form the Mutesarrifate of Lebanon. The Maʿn and Shihāb emirs, however, usually controlled additional territories, either as tax-farmers for the Ottoman government, or simply by the military imposition of their authority. Sidon and Beirut, never strictly part of the Emirate, were often under the rule of the Maʿn emirs, and served them as capitals. Tripoli for a time was under Maʿnid dominion. Beirut, in the eighteenth century, was frequently ruled by the Shihābs. Although the Biqāʿ was formally a part of Damascus, its central region was almost continually under the control of the Lebanese emirs, who would frequently extend their sway also over the plain of ʿAkkār, to the north-east of Tripoli. In the northern Biqāʿ, the shiʿites of the Baalbek region were so involved in the affairs of the Lebanese Emirate that their history cannot be considered apart from that of Mount Lebanon, although they were never directly ruled by the Maʿns and the Shihābs. In the southern Biqāʿ, the region of Wādī al-Taym (at the foot of Mount Hermon) was the home district of the Shihāb family, and consequently became part of the Lebanese territory when the Shihābs succeeded to the Emirate. Considering these facts, the Lebanon of Ottoman times can be historically defined as the whole territory, from the crest of the Anti-Lebanon to the sea, which normally felt the impact of Maʿn and Shihāb government – a territory which, in extent, did not differ much from present-day Lebanon.

Within the limits of this territory, an evolving form of political authority has continued without interruption from the early seventeenth century to our own time, giving Lebanon a separate and distinct identity. Yet the political unity of Lebanon, developed and maintained by successive dynasties and governments, has often been belied by deep divisions among the country's inhabitants. Indeed, it would be difficult for a historian to speak of a Lebanese people without reserve. At the level of feudal leadership, common political considerations frequently brought the chieftains of the various Lebanese communities together and unified their ranks. Among the emirs and sheikhs (as these chieftains were called), difference in religion was no barrier to close co-operation between the Maronite, the Melchite, and the Druze, the Shiʿite and the Sunnite Moslem. All belonged to the same political system, and feudal chieftains of different religions and sects would formally address one another as brothers, or as cousins. Differences and rivalries between the leading emirs and sheikhs would sometimes lead to the formation of feudal parties, cutting across religious divisions and permeating all classes of the population. Feudal chieftains would often come together in times of danger, each leading his own men, to fight a common enemy; and on such occasions Druze, Christian, and Moslem peasant warriors would fight side by side in defence of some common feudal cause, or perhaps of a common homeland. Under the leadership of the Maʿn and Shihāb emirs the Lebanese sects came to form what was in fact a confederacy. But actual contact between the various sects was almost entirely restricted to political and military co-operation. Socially, each religious community remained ignorant as well as independent of the others, and relations within the same village between neighbours of different sects rarely transcended casual or business acquaintance.

Relationships between the various religious groups in Lebanon have developed considerably since the time of the Emirate. Nevertheless, religious divisions remain important. Today, as in the past, the Maronites continue to be the leading sect among the Christians of the country, followed in traditional importance by the Greek Orthodox and the Greek Catholics. According to the last official population figures published in 1956, the Maronites in Lebanon number 423,500, the Greek Orthodox 149,000, and the Greek Catholics 91,000. The remaining Christian sects (Armenian Orthodox, Armenian Catholics, Protestants, and others), taken together, number 122,000 – a figure which includes the 6,500 Lebanese Jews. Among the major non-Christian groups the Lebanese Moslems, divided almost equally between the Sunnite and Shiʿite sects, dwarf the small but traditionally important community of the Druzes. According to the official figures, the Sunnites number 286,000, the Shiʿites 250,500, and the Druzes 88,000.[2] To appreciate the historical and political peculiarities of Lebanon, it is important to understand the circumstances in which each of these various sects became established in Lebanon, and the manner in which they developed.

Among the sects of Lebanon today, the Shiʿites and Sunnites have lived for the most part outside Mount Lebanon proper. These two Moslem groups originally differed over the question of the Prophet's succession, the Shiʿites (literally 'partisans') supporting the claims to the Caliphate of Muḥammad's cousin and son-in-law ʿAlī, while the group later called Sunnites (literally 'orthodox') insisted that the faithful should choose the Caliphs by acclamation. In Lebanon, Shiʿites of the moderate variety known as the Twelvers[3] (locally called Mitwālīs) are at present predominant in the region of Baalbek, and in Jabal ʿĀmil, east of Tyre. There was a time, however, long before the Ottoman period, when Shiʿites of one variety or another dominated nearly the whole country – all except the northern districts of Bsharrī, Batrūn, and Jubayl which were under Maronite control. The Kisrawān, today predominantly Maronite, was until the fourteenth century a distinctly Shiʿite region. Jabal al-Ḍanniyya, north of Bsharrī, carries until this day the name of the esoteric Shiʿite (probably Ismaʿilite) community which was established there on the eve of the Crusades.[4] The Biqāʿ was Shiʿite territory from an early time, and parts of it (notably the Baalbek region) remain so today. At the time of the First Crusade a Shiʿite dynasty (Banū ʿAmmār) ruled in Tripoli and its environs; their subjects were probably also Shiʿites. Earlier on, Ismaʿilite Shiʿism had flourished in Wādī al-Taym, and probably also in the Shūf, until the inhabitants of these two regions became converts to Druzism some time in the early eleventh century. Towards the end of that century, when the first Crusaders arrived in Syria, the regions of the Shūf and Wādī al-Taym in Lebanon were already Druze territory; otherwise, Shiʿite predominance in the country was undiminished.

This situation was to change after the twelfth and thirteenth centuries. Until the time of the Crusades, the Shiʿites in Lebanon (and elsewhere in Syria[5]) enjoyed the patronage of the Fatimids of Egypt: Shiʿite caliphs who had established Ismaʿilite Shiʿism as the state religion in Cairo, and who challenged the authority of the Sunnite Caliphate of the Abbasids at Baghdad. During the tenth and eleventh centuries, while the empire of the Abbasid caliphs was disintegrating, the Fatimids were at the height of their power in Egypt, and more than once succeeded in extending their rule over Syria. Under their protection, Syrian Shiʿism enjoyed its golden age. On the eve of the Crusades, however, Fatimid power in Syria and Egypt began to decline. The caliphs of Cairo were entirely discredited in the wars against the Christian invaders, and failed to provide effective leadership for a Moslem counter-Crusade. In the absence of a Shiʿite leadership, a succession of Sunnite dynasties appeared who took the initiative against the Crusaders, and who ultimately succeeded in uniting an important portion of the Moslem world under their leadership. The success of these Sunnite dynasties spelt the end of Shiʿite predominance in the region. Upon the final expulsion of the Crusaders from Syria in the late thirteenth century, the Mamlūk sultans who now replaced the Fatimid caliphs in Cairo turned against the Shiʿites and tried to suppress them everywhere. Mamlūk expeditions were fitted out against the leading Shiʿite regions in Lebanon starting in 1292, one year after the Mamlūk capture of Acre. Jabal ʿAkkār and the Ḍanniyya were easily reduced, and their inhabitants were either forcibly converted to Sunnism, or else scattered and replaced in the two regions by Sunnite Moslems. The Shiʿites of the Kisrawān put up a stronger resistance, holding out against the Mamlūks for thirteen years; but they were finally defeated and dispersed in 1305. As the years went by, Maronite settlers from the north replaced them in the region. Meanwhile, pressure and persecution caused the Shiʿite community in Lebanon to shrink even further. Soon Shiʿism began gradually to disappear from most of the coastal towns, Tyre alone remaining predominantly Shiʿite until this day. In the Druze mountain only two Shiʿite villages survive today in the Gharb, south-east of Beirut, along with a few coastal settlements outside Beirut, and some villages in the southern Shūf, in the district of Jazzīn. After the sixteenth century, Shiʿites from the Baalbek region crossed the Lebanon heights to settle in the districts of Jubayl and Bsharrī as well as in the Kisrawān. By the end of the eighteenth century, however, most of these settlers had been expelled from these Maronite regions by the Shihābs, leaving only the few shiʿite communities which still survive today in the district of Jubayl.

The Sunnite Moslems in Lebanon, compared to the Shiʿites,

are a community of more recent development, whose growth belongs mainly to the Mamlūk and Ottoman periods. It was indeed during the Mamlūk period, as a result of insistent persecution, that many Christians and Shi'ite Moslems throughout Syria became converts to Sunnite Islam, giving Sunnism the ascendancy which it maintains in the region until this day. Until the late thirteenth century, a vast proportion of the Syrian population was still Christian, and among the Moslems the Shi'ites were still predominant in many parts of Syria. During the Crusader period the manner in which these Christians and Shi'ites behaved was to arouse the rancour of the Sunnite state against them: the Christians, naturally suspected of favouring Crusader rule, would often openly assist the Crusaders against the Moslems; the Shi'ites, in their wariness of Sunnite Islam, would sometimes waver in their loyalty to the point of treason. Consequently, once the Crusader period ended, the Sunnite state promptly fell on both communities, subjecting them to years of systematic persecution.

It was probably at this time that the first important Sunnite Moslem communities developed in Tripoli, Beirut, and Sidon – coastal towns which strongly felt the impact of Mamlūk rule. In later times the Sunnite population of these towns in Lebanon was to grow even further, as Sunnite merchants and traders from the Syrian interior, Egypt, North Africa, and elsewhere came to settle in the well-placed and often prosperous business centres. Today Sidon and Tripoli are predominantly Sunnite towns, and Beirut likewise has a substantial Sunnite population. This has been so since certainly the seventeenth century, and in each case the Sunnites live side by side with large communities of Melchite Christians, divided since the late seventeenth century into Greek Orthodox and Greek Catholic communions.

Tripoli, Beirut and Sidon were not the only Lebanese centres of Sunnite Islam. To escape persecution, or perhaps to find favour with the ruling Mamlūks, the Druzes and Shi'ites of the Biqā', Wādī al-Taym, and the Shūf appear to have frequently practised Sunnite Islam by *taqiyya* – a practice common among the Shi'ite sects, which permits an adherent under duress to deny his true faith and pretend the religion of the dominant group. As the years went by, some communities which practised Sunnism by *taqiyya* over several generations apparently forgot their original dissent and began genuinely to identify themselves as Sunnite Moslem. This, in all probability, explains the origin of the old Sunnite communities which are found today in the villages of the central Biqāʿ, in Wādī al-Taym, and in some villages of the Kharrūb district in the Shūf. It may also, in part, explain the present Sunnism of the ʿAkkār and Ḍanniyya regions. For these two regions, however, another factor came into play. In the early fourteenth century, as the Mamlūks established their dominion in Syria, Turkoman and Kurdish clans were brought over to settle in the various coastal regions of Syria, where they acted as Mamlūk agents and watched over the turbulent hinterland. Among others, there was an important settlement of Turkomans in the Kisrawān, and of Kurds in the Tripoli region (the ʿAkkār and Ḍanniyya regions). There were also, apparently, some Sunnite settlements further inland, in the region of Baalbek, quite apart from other minor ones which were possibly established in the country. Whatever their racial origin, these new settlers were all Sunnite Moslem, and their presence in Lebanon contributed to the development of the Sunnite community in the country. Today there are no Sunnite Moslems in Kisrawān; but large Sunnite communities continue to thrive in the Tripoli region, and also among the Shiʿites in the region of Baalbek.

The Shūf and Wādī al-Taym, in present-day Lebanon, continue to be home regions of the Druzes – followers of the Fatimid Caliph al-Ḥākim (996–1021) who proclaimed his own divinity in the early eleventh century, deviating from traditional Ismaʿilite Shiʿism. The Druzes were so-called after Muḥammad ibn Ismāʿīl (*alias* Nushtigīn) al-Darazī, one of the sect's founders, who was primarily responsible for preaching the cult of al-Ḥākim among the Ismaʿilites of Syria. Following the Ismaʿilite manner, Darazī and his associates organized their followers as a secret sect, with a select class of initiates (*ʿuqqāl* or *ajāwīd*) leading the mass of the non-initiates (*juhhāl*). The faithful were taught the use of secret formulas for recognizing one another wherever they met. In hostile surroundings they were enjoined to conceal their religion, if it exposed them to danger, and to conform by *taqiyya* to the manner of the dominant group. On the other hand, they were urged always to maintain their solidarity, and to follow the considered counsel of their *ʿuqqāl*. These *ʿuqqāl* alone performed religious duties, meeting in homes or special retreats (*khalwāt*, sing. *khalwa*) where they would pray and discuss the general affairs of the community. The *juhhāl* were neither expected to pray nor to interest themselves in religious matters, although they were encouraged to desire initiation. Because the Druzes faced severe persecution at the start, they abandoned proselytism at an early date and declared their sect 'closed' to new converts.

Circumstances of their early history caused the Druzes to develop in a special way as a community of mountain peasants organized for war. The sect had scarcely been in existence for one century when the first Crusader invasion of Syria took place, forcing the Druzes to take the side of the Sunnite state of Damascus against the invaders. During the two centuries that followed the Druzes were almost continuously at war with the Crusaders in their surroundings, raiding Crusader positions in the Biqā', northern Palestine, and the Lebanese coastal regions from the mountain fastnesses of the southern Lebanon and Anti-Lebanon. Impressed by the courage of the Druze mountaineers, the successive Sunnite dynasties which controlled the Syrian interior frequently sought their services as local auxiliaries, attracting them with subsidies of various kinds. Their feudal chieftains were recognized as regional commanders, and received titles which indicated their exalted ranks. This association between the Druze feudal chieftains and the Moslem central government was strongly to influence the Druze social structure, concentrating power in the hands of the feudal aristocracy who now superseded the religious *'uqqāl* in the leadership of their community. The *'uqqāl* had henceforth to content themselves with a subordinate position and became the agents of the feudal aristocracy, using their influence among the commoners to maintain their discipline under feudal control.

During the seventeenth century the Druzes in Mount Lebanon became politically associated with the Maronites – an originally Monothelete Christian sect which, starting from the twelfth century, had become united with Rome as a Uniate church with its own priesthood and liturgy. Originally established in the northern districts of Bsharrī, Batrūn, and Jubayl, the Maronites began to migrate southwards into the Kisrawān after the dispersal of the Shi'ites of the region by the Mamlūks. Later, under the protection of the Ma'n and Shihāb emirs, Maronites from the north came in large numbers to settle in the Druze districts of the south, and in other parts of present Lebanese territory which fell at the time under the control of the emirs. Indeed, a veritable Maronite colonization of Lebanon took place in the seventeenth and eighteenth centuries, with the result that the Maronites became the most widespread community in the country. By the late seventeenth century the northern districts of the Kisrawān (the Futūḥ, Inner Kisrawān, and Outer Kisrawān) were already predominantly Maronite regions, and large numbers of Maronites were also established among the Druzes of the Matn (south Kisrawān). Meanwhile the Maronite migration to other parts of Lebanon had already begun. So many Maronites came to settle in the various districts of the Shūf (the Gharb, the Jurd, and the Shūf proper) that by the late eighteenth century they already formed a clear majority there. In the north, some Maronite villages had always existed in the predominantly Melchite district of the Kūra, near Tripoli; but in time Maronites began to settle in Tripoli itself. There were also Maronite settlements further down the coast in Beirut, Sidon, and Tyre. Outside Mount Lebanon and the coastal towns, large Maronite communities were established among the Shi'ites of the Baalbek region and of Jabal 'Āmil, the Sunnites of 'Akkār and the Biqā', and the Sunnites and Druzes of Wādī al-Taym. In almost every region where Maronites settled, they were followed by substantial numbers of Melchite settlers, mostly from the Syrian interior, who further added to the growing Christian predominance in the country.

The spread of the Christians, and particularly of the Maronites, in Lebanon was to become a prime factor in the country's social development. Wherever the industrious Christian peasantry settled, they brought with them their way of life which was to some extent imitated and adopted by their Moslem and Druze neighbours. The Maronite and Greek Catholic monasteries established in the Druze and Shi'ite districts, usually with the help and encouragement of the local chieftains, strongly affected their surroundings both economically and socially. In the same way, the influence of the Roman Catholic missions among the Maronites and other Uniate Christians in Lebanon was not confined to these groups, but also affected the other Christian and non-Christian communities among whom they lived.

The Maronites, like the Druzes, were warlike mountain peasantry whose history testified to their military prowess. In the early centuries of Arab dominion in Syria they had put up a determined resistance to Moslem encroachments on their territory. Forced to retreat from many parts, they nevertheless managed to hold out in the more rugged regions of northern Lebanon which became their home. During the twelfth and thirteenth centuries the Maronites were the friends and allies of the Crusaders, and Maronite chieftains led their men to fight the Moslems as Crusader auxiliaries. Later, after the departure of the Franks from Syria, Maronite guerrillas desperately tried to repel Mamlūk invasions of their territory, and apparently co-operated more than once with their Shi'ite neighbours to the south in defending the Kisrawān. Yet, while the Maronites resembled the Druzes in being warlike mountaineers, they strongly differed from them in social organization. Maronite feudalism did not develop beyond the system of unco-ordinated village chieftainships, unlike the feudalism of the Druzes which was highly co-ordinated and organized from an early time. Besides, there was never systematic co-operation between the Maronite clergy and feudal aristocracy, as there was between the Druze *'uqqāl* and feudal chiefs. Before the time of the Ma'ns, the villages of the Maronite districts in the north were controlled by village headsmen called 'muqaddams', who generally managed the affairs of their villagers in times of peace and led them against the enemy in times of war. Until the early fourteenth century these muqaddams appear to have enjoyed great popularity, and to have co-operated with the Maronite clergy in the leadership of their community. But scarcely had the first century of Mamlūk rule gone by than these warlike village chieftains degenerated into fiscal agents subservient to the Mamlūk provincial government in Tripoli. As tax-farmers, the muqaddams became identified with the oppressive foreign rule and grew unpopular with peasants and clergy alike. Neglecting the interests of their people, they concentrated mainly on currying favour with their Mamlūk (and later Ottoman) masters, obsequiously imitating their manner to the extent of adopting Moslem names and pious titles. This left the Maronite patriarch and his clergy as the only true leaders of their community, and dealt an early blow to Maronite feudal power. The Maronite clergy, coming mostly from peasant origin, were close to their flock, and naturally took up the cause of the peasants against the often cruel and rapacious muqaddams. A traditional opposition between the Maronite clergy and feudal aristocracy consequently developed, which was to continue as an important factor in Maronite social life until the last years of feudalism in Lebanon.

The Greek Orthodox and Greek Catholics of Lebanon today are to be found, like the Maronites, in nearly all parts of the country. The Maronites, however, vastly outnumber them. Furthermore, while the Maronites are mostly mountain peasantry, the Greek Orthodox and Greek Catholics tend to concentrate in the coastal towns and larger mountain villages, where they are established mostly as traders and artisans. Maronite families, descended from generations of peasants attached to their land, commonly carry the name of their village or district of origin – a testimony to the deep-rooted provincialism of their community. The comparative urbanism of the Greek Orthodox and Greek Catholics, on the other hand, is reflected by the frequent occurrence among them of family names indicating a trade or occupation, such as Ḥaddād (Smith), Laḥḥām (Butcher), Ṣāyigh (Goldsmith), Ṣabbāgh (Dyer), Najjār (Carpenter), Khayyāṭ (Taylor), or Ḥāyik (Weaver).

The Greek Orthodox and Greek Catholics in Syria and Egypt are so called because they follow the Byzantine rite and use the Greek language in their liturgy. Originally the two communities formed the Melchite church, which included all Syrian and Egyptian Christians who accepted the decrees of the Council of Chalcedon (AD 451) against the Nestorians and Monophysites. In 1054, when the schism took place between the Churches of Rome and Constantinople, the Melchites followed Constantinople and were consequently classed by Rome as schismatics. It was only in the late seventeenth century that a group of Syrian Melchites, influenced by Jesuit missionaries, separated from the main body of their church and entered into communion with Rome. The separation took place in 1683 under the leadership of Euthymius Ṣayfī, Bishop of Tyre and Sidon (1683–1723); but the Uniate Melchites did not become organized as a church on their own until 1701. Later, when the Melchite see of Antioch fell vacant in 1724, the Uniate and non-Uniate Melchites elected each their own patriarch to succeed, and the separation between the two churches became complete. The Uniate Melchites since then became known as Greek Catholics, and the non-Uniates as Greek Orthodox.

Of the Greek Catholics and Greek Orthodox in Lebanon, a large proportion were late-comers who settled in the country during the Ottoman period, especially after the two sects had separated. Melchites, however, were to be found in Lebanon at a much earlier date. An old community of Melchite peasantry has apparently been flourishing in northern Lebanon, in the Kūra district (south-east of Tripoli), since the early eighth century, when Melchites of this district are said to have clashed with the neighbouring Maronites. During the seventeenth and eighteenth centuries many of these Melchites followed the Maronites as they migrated southwards to the Druze districts, so that a number of Greek Orthodox and Greek Catholic families in different parts of Lebanon today trace their origin from the Kūra. Being peasants, the Kūra Melchites settled mostly in the rural parts of Lebanon, establishing themselves among the Maronite and Druze peasantry whose way of life they shared. But of the present Melchite population of Lebanon those originally from the Kūra form only a small proportion. The larger proportion came from the outside: from the Ḥawrān region (east of Mount Hermon), northern Palestine, or the towns of the Syrian interior (Damascus, Homs, Hama, and Aleppo). Some of these Melchites, like other Syrian Christians, immigrated into Lebanon during the Mamlūk period to escape the anti-Christian persecutions which followed the destruction of the Crusader states. Many more followed in Ottoman times, attracted by the tolerant and relatively beneficent rule of the Maʿns and the Shihābs. The Greek Catholics, in particular, sought refuge in Lebanon during the eighteenth century from their persecution by the Greek Orthodox in Aleppo and other Syrian towns. Unlike the peasant Melchites of Kūra, most of the Melchites coming from Palestine and the Syrian interior were townsmen and were not attracted to agricultural life in the mountains. Accordingly, only a small proportion among them ultimately became peasantry, the rest settling in the coastal towns and larger mountain centres where they followed their original trades.

Coming from diverse origins and established in the country under different circumstances, the various religious communities of Lebanon grew as distinct groups, each with its special social character. The Shi'ites, Druzes, and Maronites developed as rebel mountaineers, hardy and clannish, with a staunch particularism and a strong spirit of independence. For the most part, the three groups are alike industrious peasantry, conventionally generous and hospitable, naïvely cunning in their political and social dealings, and passionately fond of heroics. Here, however, the similarities end. Among the Shi'ites, a prolonged history of persecution and repression has reflected itself in the community's characteristic political timidity, and its seemingly haphazard organization. Politically more successful, the Maronites and Druzes exhibit a tight social organization, and the self-confidence of communities long used to self-rule. The two sects, for a long time major partners in the Lebanese Emirate and Mutesarrifate, nevertheless differ in some important respects. The Druzes have traditionally excelled the Maronites in their sense of solidarity, their social discipline, their strict obedience to their leaders, and their general resilience and adaptability. Despite flashes of vindictiveness, they have normally been the more tolerant group, happy to compromise and co-operate with others when not offended. As a rule, they tend to be reticent, secretive, and urbane, masters of the ruse in politics and of the stratagem in war. The Maronites, on the other hand, are notoriously forward and outspoken, their habitual indiscretion contrasting sharply with the Druze reserve. Headstrong individualists, the Maronites have generally been the more adventurous and enterprising people, greatly excelling the Druzes in economic and cultural achievement. But Maronite individualism has also had an adverse effect. It has weakened the solidarity of the community, encouraged a tendency to pettiness, and too often subordinated common benefit to personal interest. Maronites, in times of crisis, have frequently divided on trivial issues and lost the advantage of their numbers and undoubted military valour in useless personal and factional quarrels.

The Sunnite and Melchite communities of Lebanon differ from the Shi'ites, Druzes, and Maronites in being essentially townsmen, with none of the ruggedness and particularism of the mountaineers. Rural Sunnites, it is true, are superficially much like the

Shiʿites in their manner and way of life, while Greek Orthodox and Greek Catholic peasants often differ from their Maronite neighbours only in their greater submissiveness and looser organization. It is, however, the Sunnites and Melchites of Tripoli, Beirut, and Sidon, rather than those of Mount Lebanon, the Biqāʿ, and ʿAkkār, who are more clearly typical of their respective groups. Historically, the Sunnites and Melchites in Lebanon represent Moslem and Eastern Christian orthodoxy, unlike the Maronites, Shiʿites, and Druzes who first established themselves in the country as dissenters and rebels against central authority. Consequently, while the Maronites, Shiʿites, and Druzes remained isolated communites, secluded in their mountain fastnesses, their Sunnite and Melchite countrymen, especially those of the coastal towns, maintained important connexions with the world around them. The Sunnites, even when they lived in the mountains, continued to feel a community of interest with co-religionists elsewhere, particularly in the immediate Syrian neighbourhood. The Melchites, likewise, remained conscious of a solidarity with fellow-Melchites throughout Syria and Egypt, and also with other Christians who followed the Byzantine rite in Greece and the Slavic countries.

The Sunnite and Melchite communities were indeed alike in their essential urbanism and breadth of social horizons; but they were dissimilar in other respects. Throughout the Ottoman period, not to mention earlier times, the Sunnites among the Lebanese sects enjoyed the special security of privileged membership in a universal Moslem State. They were among the most loyal and submissive of the sultan's subjects, took no sustained interest in the internal politics of Lebanon, and were for the most part content to enjoy the advantages of professing the State religion. Because of their customary dependence on government favour, they never developed the self-reliance of other Lebanese sects, like the Maronites or Druzes. Following the collapse of the Ottoman Empire, when the State of Greater Lebanon was organized as a completely separate political entity under French mandate, the Lebanese Sunnites suddenly found themselves at a loss; without the prerogatives they had enjoyed as Ottoman subjects, they knew no way of adapting themselves to their changed situation. Consequently, they became a major element of instability in the

Lebanese Republic during the mandatory period, and to some extent remained so even after Lebanon became fully independent.

The case of the Melchites was different. As Christians, the Melchites enjoyed no special privileges under Ottoman rule. Unlike the Maronites, however, they lived for the most part not in mountainous isolation, but among the Sunnites in the major Syrian and Egyptian towns. Hence they developed habits of behaviour which made it possible for them to thrive in predominantly Sunnite surroundings as an affable, enterprising, but politically self-effacing minority. So well did the Melchites adapt themselves to their special circumstances that the community on the whole came to enjoy a general prosperity unknown among the other sects. At the present time, the Greek Orthodox and Greek Catholics of Lebanon continue to exhibit the traditional complaisance and resourcefulness of their Melchite predecessors. Politically shy, they still excel in those fields where there is least government interference, and are economically and culturally the most active communities in the country.

The Maronites and Druzes, along with the Sunnites, Shiʿites, Greek Orthodox, and Greek Catholics have been politically associated in Lebanon since the days of the Emirate. Other sects joined them in time. A small Protestant community, converted mostly from Greek Orthodoxy by British and American missionaries, became active in Lebanon in the nineteenth century. In the eighteenth century, dissensions within the Armenian church in Cilicia (1737–40) had already led to the establishment in Lebanon of a considerable community of Armenian Catholics, then newly organized as a separate church in communion with Rome. From the late nineteenth century, systematic persecution by the Turks drove a large number of other Armenians, mostly of the Gregorian church, to seek refuge in Lebanon, so that the Gregorians (or Armenian Orthodox, as they are often called) rank today as the seventh largest sect in the country, next to the Druzes.[6] At one time or another, Jews, Jacobites, Latins, Nestorians, Syrian Catholics and others also established themselves in Lebanon in small numbers, making up what are today called the Lebanese 'minorities'. Under the rule of the Shihābs, the various Lebanese communities lived peacefully side by side, bound together by a common allegiance to the ruling emir. Each sect managed its own internal affairs independently of the others, took a fierce pride in its separate identity, and jealously guarded its rights. Yet immemorial custom regulated polite relationships between the different groups and prescribed a friendly manner in which ordinary differences could be settled. It is true that the Lebanese people did not then constitute a nation, united in purpose and consciousness of identity; nevertheless, they did stand out as a distinct community of sects, organized according to what has been perhaps the nearest known approximation to a 'social contract'. The history of Lebanon since the eighteenth century primarily involves the development of this 'social contract' and its reflection in the political organization of the country. At various times, internal and external factors have seriously affected the political and social relationships of the country's major sects and precipitated fundamental changes in them. The following chapters will briefly trace the development of the Lebanese Emirate from the early seventeenth to the late eighteenth century, and proceed to deal in greater detail with the changes which have taken place from the accession of Emir Bashīr II in 1788 until the present day.

Part I

MOUNT LEBANON

Ce petit pays qui est si important . . .

CLEMENS METTERNICH

CHAPTER I

THE SHIHĀB EMIRATE

IN THE early seventeenth century Fakhr al-Dīn II, Maʿnid Emir of the Shūf, brought the whole of Lebanon under his rule. Hereditary master of the Druze districts of the south, he made use of favourable circumstances to extend his dominion over the Maronite districts of the north, establishing a tradition of Maronite–Druze union which became the mainstay of Lebanon's autonomy as an Ottoman province. The career of Fakhr al-Dīn II in its time attracted attention in Europe. The Medici of Tuscany, who had plans to establish their own empire in Syria, took a keen interest in the Emir's activities and encouraged him to rebel against his Ottoman suzerains. Assured of Tuscan backing, the Emir successfully challenged Ottoman authority, fought the neighbouring pashas, and extended his sway over most of Syria. But when the Porte retaliated, the Tuscans failed to send in their support. Fakhr al-Dīn II, left on his own, was defeated and taken prisoner by the Ottomans in 1633, then sent in chains to Istanbul where he was put to death by strangling in 1635. Of the Emir's five sons one had died fighting the Turks, three were executed with their father, and only the youngest, Ḥusayn, survived as a page in the Ottoman court, later rising to distinction as chamberlain and ambassador to India. It was Fakhr al-Dīn's nephew Mulḥim who succeeded him in Lebanon, followed in 1657 by his son Aḥmad. In 1697, when the Maʿnid male line became extinct with Emir Aḥmad's death, the Ottomans permitted the Lebanese notables to meet and elect as his successor his nephew Bashīr Shihāb of Wādī al-Taym. Once Bashīr was elected, the Ottoman Government insisted that the succession should properly go to young Ḥaydar Shihāb, a grandson of Aḥmad Maʿn and distant cousin of Bashīr Shihāb. After some negotiation, a compromise was finally arranged whereby Bashīr I would rule as regent until his cousin Ḥaydar came of age. Thus it was that the Shihābs, kinsmen of the Maʿns and paramount chiefs of Wādī al-Taym, became emirs of Lebanon.

In religion the new emirs of Lebanon were Sunnites, but the Emirate to which they succeeded was controlled largely by Druze feudal interests. Christians, it is true, were numerically predominant in the country, the Maronites alone forming an absolute majority in the mountain districts. But in spite of their numbers, the Christians were politically weak. Since the mid-seventeenth century the Maronite districts of Bsharrī, Bartūn, and Jubayl, and the Melchite district of the Kūra, had fallen under the control of the Ḥamada sheikhs – Shiʿites from the Baalbek region who held these Christian districts from the Ottoman Pashas of Tripoli. The Ḥamādas did not recognize the overlordship of the Lebanese emirs, and their rule in north Lebanon was violent and oppressive. Meanwhile in the Kisrawān, Maronite sheikhs of the Khazin family, backed by the Maʿns, had succeeded in recovering considerable lands from the Shiʿites who had resettled there since late Mamlūk times. But it was only in the Kisrawān that the Christians enjoyed a strong position. In the Shūf and its surroundings, heart of the Maʿn and Shihāb domain, the Maronites and Melchites were still politically unimportant. The Maʿns had indeed encouraged the settlement of Christians in these Druze districts, and by the time the Shihābs succeeded large numbers of Christians were already established there. These Christians, however, had come to the Shūf mostly as peasants, settling on the estates of Druze feudal chiefs. It was their Druze feudal masters, the powerful lords of the Shūf, the Gharb, and the Jurd, who stood out as the strongest political force in the land. No wonder that the Shihāb emirs, certainly until the mid-eighteenth century, tried to pass for Druzes.

From the time they were first established in Lebanon, the Druzes had managed their internal affairs as a virtually autonomous community and developed a peculiar feudal system. Ordinary Islamic feudalism was based on the non-hereditary *iqṭāʿ* – the revocable right to the revenue of a village or district, granted by a sovereign to a civil or military officer as part of his pay. Under such a system it was difficult for local feudal aristocracies to develop, for the *iqṭāʿ* frequently changed hands, and remained throughout under the direct control of the central government. In the Druze mountains, however, as in northern Lebanon, Transjordan, and other rugged parts of Syria, the *iqṭā'* system did not regularly apply. Even during the Mamlūk period, when Islamic feudalism was most strictly organized and centralized, the Druzes, along with other isolated Syrian communities, maintained their peculiar feudal traditions with the tacit recognition of the Mamlūk government. The central government, indeed, invested the leading Druze chief of his day with some formal authority, technically as an officer of the sultan's provincial cavalry. But this modest position was far exceeded by the local power and prestige which such a chief enjoyed. As supreme emir, the paramount Druze chief headed a feudal system based on hereditary land tenure, and was the overlord of a number of feudal families who controlled the various Druze districts. During the Mamlūk period the leading Druze emirs were the Buḥturs, also called the Tanūkhs, who were hereditary lords of the Gharb. When the Ottomans conquered Syria in 1516, the Buḥturs lost their supremacy and were replaced in the paramount Druze chieftainship by their kinsmen the Ma'ns, lords of the Shūf.

The Ottomans did not attempt to change the Druze political status. Like their Mamlūk predecessors, they permitted the Druzes to maintain their special feudal traditions and to manage their internal affairs as they pleased. Under the Ottomans, however, the Ma'ns came to enjoy a power and prestige which the Buḥturs, under the Mamlūks, had never known. Fakhr al-Dīn II, third emir of the Ma'nid line, whose foreign relations have been traced above, was able to extend the hegemony of his dynasty over the whole of Mount Lebanon, establishing his rule most firmly in the Kisrawān. Under him and his successors, the Druze feudal system was introduced into the northern Lebanese districts, and Druze political ascendancy was established throughout the country. In the Kisrawān and elsewhere, new Maronite families like the Khāzins were raised to feudal dignity as associates of the Druze feudal sheikhs. Such Maronite families held and administered their districts in the Druze manner, recognized the overlordship of the Druze emir, and imitated their Druze associates even in their social behaviour.

The Druze hegemony in Lebanon, established in the early seventeenth century, remained unchallenged for a long time.

Although Maronite notables frequently rose to positions of influence as the assistants and advisers of the emirs, it was the Druze feudal chiefs who remained the mainstay of the Lebanese Emirate. In time, however, Druze power began to decline. By the mid-eighteenth century the growth of the Maronite community in numbers and social importance had become a matter of political consequence. The Druze ranks, on the other hand, had been steadily weakened by internal divisions which reflected power rivalries among the Druze feudal families, and which the Shihāb emirs hastened to exploit.

The Druzes, like other communities in Syria, were for a long time divided into Qaysites and Yemenites. This division had its origins in the rivalry between the north-Arab (Qaysite) and south-Arab (Yemenite) tribes which settled in Syria and elsewhere at the time of the Arab conquest. But the Qaysite-Yemenite partisanship in many cases outlived accurate genealogy and was used to express all manner of political conflict; this was particularly the case in Lebanon. Here families of non-Arab origin – Turkomans, Kurds, and Maronites – eagerly gave their allegiance to one or the other of the two factions, while others of allegedly Arab origin changed sides with little regard to actual descent. The main issue which separated the two factions was the competition between the leading Druze families, notably the Buḥturs, Maʿns, and ʿAlam al-Dīns. Under the Mamlūks, the ʿAlam al-Dīns led the Yemenites in opposition to the ruling Buḥturs who were politically Qaysites, although they were presumably cousins of the Yemenite ʿAlam al-Dīns. When the Maʿns succeeded the Buḥturs in 1516, the ʿAlam al-Dīns and the Yemenites remained in bitter opposition, while the Buḥturs and the Qaysites gave their full support to the new dynasty. It was indeed during the first two centuries of the Ottoman period that the Qaysite-Yemenite rivalry in the Druze mountain became most intense, leading more than once to virtual civil war.

The career of the great Emir Fakhr al-Dīn II had established a firm basis for the Qaysite supremacy in Lebanon. Before his time the position of the Maʿnid emirs was often precarious, and this had encouraged the Yemenite Druze leaders to conspire with neighbouring chieftains against them. In 1585, a Yemenite conspiracy against Emir Korkmaz, Fakhr al-Dīn's father, had brought about the invasion of the Shūf by Ottoman troops and the death of Emir Korkmaz in flight. But the Yemenites had not been able to reap the advantage of this Maʿnid defeat. Within a few years Fakhr al-Dīn II had managed effectively to succeed his father, and the Qaysite supremacy was reasserted. The downfall of Fakhr al-Dīn II in 1633, described at the beginning of the chapter, gave the Yemenites a second chance. To replace the defeated emir, the Ottomans chose as his successor his enemy ʿAlī ʿAlam al-Dīn, leader of the Yemenite party. But again the Yemenite success was short-lived. The ʿAlam al-Dīns inaugurated their brief tenure of power by a general massacre of the Buḥturs; and this started a civil war among the Druzes which seems to have continued for two years. A semblance of peace was restored when Fakhr al-Dīn's nephew Mulḥim finally succeeded in recovering the Emirate for his family. But for a long time the situation remained confused. Under Mulḥim (1635–57), indeed, and his son Aḥmad (1657–97) the Qaysite supremacy in Mount Lebanon was re-established. The Yemenites nevertheless remained powerful. When the Shihābs succeeded the Maʿns in 1697, the Yemenite Druzes were still a force to reckon with in Lebanon, and the ʿAlam al-Dīns still considered themselves candidates for the Emirate.

Throughout the seventeenth century, while the Maʿns ruled Lebanon, the Ottomans were able to keep the country under control by discreetly encouraging the rift between the rival Druze factions. This the Ottomans continued to do after the succession of the Shihābs. But the new emirs of Lebanon, more capable on the whole than their predecessors, were better able to deal with the Yemenite opposition. Under Bashīr I (1697–1707), the internal situation in the country was relatively peaceful, and the Emir was able to extend his influence southwards over Jabal ʿĀmil and northern Palestine. This extension of Shihāb power disturbed the Ottoman Pasha of Sidon. But when Ḥaydar Shihāb (1707–32), cousin and successor of Bashīr I, stressed his authority over Jabal ʿĀmil in 1708 by removing the local governor appointed from Sidon and replacing him by one of his own men, the Pasha was infuriated. In retaliation, he nominated Yūsuf ʿAlam al-Dīn, the head of the Yemenite party, as Emir of Lebanon, and sent him with Ottoman troops from Sidon to expel Ḥaydar from Dayr al-Qamar. The town was occupied in 1709, and Ḥaydar was forced to escape. But the triumph of Yūsuf 'Alam al-Dīn was short-lived. Smarting at their defeat, the Qaysite Druzes soon rose to strike back, rallying their forces around the young Shihāb Emir. The Yemenites reacted by attacking the Qaysite forces assembled at the village of 'Ayn Dārā in 1711. But the Yemenite attack was a complete failure. The Yemenite forces were utterly routed in a fierce battle, their leaders the 'Alam al-Dīns were slaughtered to a man, and Yemenite power in Lebanon was completely crushed. The Yemenite Druzes who survived the battle were expelled from Lebanon and forced to seek refuge in the Ḥawrān, beyond the Anti-Lebanon, where a large Druze community thrives to this day.

The defeat of the Yemenites at 'Ayn Dārā was an event of great importance in Lebanese history. It firmly established the power of the Shihābs, and temporarily ended the dissensions among the Druzes. The expulsion of Yemenites from the country was to be of serious consequence in the long run, for it reduced the size of the Druze community and increased the relative numerical strength of the Maronites. But for the moment the balance of sectarian power remained unchanged. In fact, the immediate effect of the resounding Qaysite victory was to bolster up the Druze political ascendancy, as the Qaysite Druzes rallied around Ḥaydar Shihāb to divide the spoils of battle. The Emir himself, determined to prevent any further challenge to Shihāb rule, took advantage of his victory to reorganize the Lebanese feudal system. The various districts in the country, including those formerly held by Yemenites, were taken over and redistributed among the leading Qaysite feudal families. Each family was to hold the district assigned to it in collective feudal tenure, and to be directly responsible to the supreme emir through its recognized head. Old Qaysite feudal families were raised in rank, and the newly created ones were given titles to indicate their position. In time, a strict protocol came to determine precedence among these feudal families, and the manner in which they dealt with one another and with the ruling emir.

The Shihābs ranked first among the Lebanese feudal families, and were called emirs. Custom permitted every member of the family to use the princely title, which was shared by two other families: the Abū'l-Lam's and the Arslāns. But the ruling Shihāb emir was distinguished from the others by being called the Great

Emir (*al-amīr al-kabīr*), or Governor (*wālī*). The original district held by the Shihāb family was Wādī al-Taym, outside Mount Lebanon. But in 1711 Ḥaydar Shihāb extended his direct control to a number of other subject districts (Bsharrī, Batrūn, Jubayl, the Biqā', and Jabal al-Rīḥān in the southern Shūf), along with the larger towns like Dayr al-Qamar; and these were later divided among his descendants. So well did Emir Ḥaydar establish the political position of his family in Lebanon that their overthrow remained for a long time unthinkable. Revolts against the ruling Shihāb emir were indeed frequent in later years, but they were always organized in the name of some Shihāb pretender, who could be a mere child.

Next to the Shihābs came the Abū'l-Lam's, originally the Druze muqaddams of the Matn. Because of their bravery at the battle of 'Ayn Dārā, Emir Ḥaydar raised the Qaysite Abū'l-Lam's to the rank of emirs, extended their feudal domain, and married into their family. Ḥaydar also gave his sister, and later his daughter, in marriage to Abū'l-Lam' emirs, and so established a tradition of exclusive intermarriage between the Shihāb and Abū'l-Lam' families which continues to some extent until this day.

The third family of emirs were the Druze Arslāns, masters of the Gharb since the 'Alam al-Dīns exterminated the Buḥturs in 1633. Mild Yemenites, the Arslāns in 1711 managed to survive the plight of their party, and were allowed to retain the lower Gharb – a part of their original fief. But because of their previous political record, the Arslāns remained an unfavoured and relatively unimportant family throughout the Shihāb period. In spite of their distinguished title, they were surpassed in power by families of lesser rank like the Janbalāṭs and the 'Imāds. It was only after the fall of the Shihābs in 1841 that the Arslāns rose again to political prominence.

When the Abū'l-Lam' muqaddams were created emirs in 1711, there remained only one family of muqaddams in Lebanon: the Druze Muzhirs. These ranked next to the Arslān emirs in titular prestige, but their actual power was limited to the tenure of one village: that of Ḥammānā, in the Matn. The families of sheikhs were more numerous, and vastly more powerful. Among the Druzes, the old sheikhly families were the Janbalāṭs, the 'Imāds (also called the Yazbaks), and the Abū Nakads. To these Ḥaydar

Shihāb added two new families: the Talḥūqs and the ʿAbd al-Maliks. These five families formed the special Druze class of 'great sheikhs' (*al-mashāyikh al-kibār*), and were bound together by a convention of exclusive intermarriage. Ranking with the Druze 'great sheikhs' were the three Maronite families of the Khāzins, Ḥubayshes, and Daḥdāḥs. Because each of these eight families received in 1711 the feudal tenure of at least one district, they became commonly known as the *muqāṭaʿajiyya*, or fief-holders. The Janbalāṭs, most powerful among these families, held most of the Shūf region, leaving the Manāṣif district (around Dayr al-Qamar) to the Abū Nakads, and the ʿUrqūb district to the ʿImāds. In the Gharb, the Abū Nakads held the district of the Shaḥḥār, while the Talḥūqs held the upper Gharb which had previously belonged to the Arslāns. The Jurd, smallest of the Druze regions, was held by the ʿAbd al-Maliks. Among the Maronite *muqāṭaʿajiyya* the Khāzins controlled most of the Kisrawān, leaving the Ghazīr district to the Ḥubayshes, and the Futūḥ district to the Daḥdāḥs. Other families which later held fiefs in the northern Lebanon were the Maronite Ḍahirs who held the extreme northern district of the Zāwiya, the Melchite ʿĀzārs who held the Kūra, and the Shiʿite Ḥamādas who held the Munayṭra (north of the Kisrawān). But these families were not 'great sheikhs' of the regular variety.

Among the 'great sheikhs' invested by Ḥaydar Shihāb, the Janbalāṭs enjoyed by far the highest prestige. The ancestor of this family, a Kurdish chieftain called ʿAlī Jānbūlād (mispronounced Janbalāṭ), had usurped the vilayet of Aleppo in the early seventeenth century, and rebelled against the Ottomans with the help of Fakhr al-Dīn II of Lebanon. The rebellion failed, ʿAlī was defeated and executed, and his family were forced to seek refuge with Fakhr al-Dīn II, who allowed them to settle in the Shūf under his protection. Here the Janbalāṭs soon rose to prominence and were accepted as Druzes, taking over the chieftainship of the region after the Maʿnid family became extinct in 1697. When Ḥaydar Shihāb reorganized the Lebanese feudal system, the Janbalāṭs were formally recognized as sheikhs of the Shūf. Later they extended their feudal control southwards over Jazzin and the neighbouring districts of Tuffāḥ and Jabal al-Rīḥān, so that they became the rivals of the Shihābs in wealth and power. The success of the Janbalāṭs, however, was to arouse the jealousy of the other

Druze sheikhly families, particularly the ʿImāds (or Yazbaks) who considered themselves their equals. By themselves the ʿImāds were no match for the Janbalāṭs; but they could certainly stand their ground against them as the leaders of a sheikhly coalition. Thus, hardly had the Qaysite-Yemenite rift ceased to exist, when the Druzes began to divide along new lines, some supporting the Janbalāṭs and others their opponents.

The origins of the new Druze rift are uncertain; but its development was clearly connected with Shihāb dynastic quarrels. Emir Mulḥim, who succeeded his father Ḥaydar in 1732, retired in 1754 in favour of his brother Manṣūr, leaving his other brother Aḥmad bitterly disappointed. Manṣūr enjoyed the backing of the Janbalāṭs, who commanded a strong Druze following and had the powerful Khāzins among their Maronite allies. Aḥmad, on the other hand, found his support among the discontented sheikhly families: the Druze ʿImāds, Talḥūqs, and ʿAbd al-Maliks, and the Maronite Ḥubayshes and Daḥdāḥs, grouped together as the Yazbakī party. After Mulḥim's death in 1761, Aḥmad contested the Emirate with Manṣūr, and the Yazbakī-Janbalāṭī rift became complete. Henceforth, only the Abū Nakads among the Druze sheikhs remained aloof from the party contest, taking sides only when critical issues were to be decided. The Abū'l-Lamʿs, who were emirs, refused to become involved in sheikhly affairs, and formed a party on their own. The Arslāns remained completely neutral. As for the ruling Shihābs, they stood in principle above the parties; in practice they were always involved in the Yazbakī-Janbalāṭī struggle, as they backed one side or the other to their own advantage.

By the late eighteenth century the Yazbakī-Janbalāṭī partisanship, starting among the Druzes, had come to involve the whole Lebanese Emirate. But the fact that the Druzes could still impose their party divisions on the rest of the country was poor compensation for their steady, and now evident, loss of power. When Emir Mulḥim retired, the Druzes were already a minority in their own districts. The Maronites, on the other hand, were becoming noticeably stronger. Impressed by the unmistakable shift in the sectarian balance, Mulḥim, who was himself a devout Moslem, permitted and possibly encouraged his children to embrace Christianity after his retirement. Meanwhile, the struggle between the

Yazbakīs and Janbalāṭīs further weakened the Druze position; and as the years went by other Shihāb and Abu'l-Lam' emirs followed the example of Mulḥim's sons and became Christians. In 1770, when Emir Manṣūr relinquished the Emirate, the Maronite Emir Yūsuf, eldest son of Mulḥim, succeeded him, and the rule of the Christian Shihābs began.

The growth of Maronite power in Lebanon, which culminated in the succession of the Shihābs, was certainly a result of the general Maronite expansion. But other causes were also significant. Important was the association of the Maronites with Lebanese silk production, which prospered as the trade between Europe and the Near East revived. As the foremost Lebanese producers, the Maronites grew rich on the silk trade, and their economic ascendancy in the country became established. The arrival in Lebanon of rich Greek Catholic families from Syria further enhanced the importance of the Maronites, for the Greek Catholics, who were Uniates, identified themselves with the Maronites politically. The Maronites had, moreover, yet another political asset. Their church, united with Rome in about 1180, had for centuries been developing relations with Europe. Maronite clerics had studied in Italy since the late fifteenth century, and more regularly since the establishment of the Maronite College in Rome in 1584. In Lebanon, Roman Catholic missionaries (Franciscans, Jesuits, and others) were the advisers of the Maronite patriarchs, and assisted in the supervision and administration of their church. In 1596 and 1736, the synods of Qannūbīn and Luwayza, held in Lebanon and attended by Papal delegates, finally sealed the union of the Maronite church with Rome. Similar developments had already taken place at a different level. In 1535 a treaty between Francis I and Suleiman the Magnificent gave France the first capitulatory privileges in the Ottoman Empire, and the French began to develop interests in Syria. As the foremost Catholic Power in Europe, France considered herself the protector of the Maronites, who were then the only Uniates in the region; and as the centuries went by, a strong friendship developed between the Maronites and France. In 1655 a Maronite sheikh of the Khāzin family was appointed French deputy consul in Beirut, then consul; and his descendants continued to hold this position after him until 1758. Other Maronites were later appointed to the same office, like

Ghandūr al-Sa'd of 'Ayn Trāz, who was secretary to Emir Yūsuf. Such Maronites were highly influential with the Shihābs, and under their influence the emirs of Lebanon learnt to look upon Catholic Europe, and especially France, as a friend.

The Roman Catholic connexions of the Maronites were useful in providing them with outside political support. But the cultural aspect of these connexions was also important. Graduates of the Maronite College in Rome, returning to Lebanon as priests, founded village schools which spread literacy in their community. Some of these schools, placed under the administration of Jesuit or other missionaries, became important educational centres, and their graduates were employed as secretaries and agents by the Shihāb emirs (*see* p. 125). Indeed, a class of educated Maronites soon developed which assumed a position of authority in public affairs, and often determined the policy of the Emirate. Not only the Shihābs but all other feudal families, including the Druzes, employed Maronites as clerks and household managers. The French traveller Volney, who visited Syria in 1782–85, remarks:

> The most solid advantage which resulted from these missionary works, was that the art of writing became more common among the Maronites, and that for this reason they came to be in these districts what the Copts are in Egypt, namely that they took over all positions of clerks, intendants, and kiayas[1] to the Turks, and especially to the Druzes, their neighbours.[2]

Finally, the direct political influence of the Roman Catholic missionaries was important. These missionaries had grown numerous in Lebanon since Fakhr al-Dīn II first extended to them princely protection; and already in his time they had exercised considerable authority in Lebanese affairs. By the eighteenth century several missionary orders were active in Lebanon: Franciscans (Friars Minor and Capuchins), Lazarists, Carmelites and Jesuits, all enjoying favour with the emirs and having direct access to them. These orders were determined to advance the Maronite interest in Lebanon; and their influence with the emirs no doubt helped them to achieve this end.

Whatever the case, it is certain that the Maronite-Druze balance of power in the eighteenth century underwent a serious change, as the Maronites replaced the Druzes in political predominance.

The conversion of Emir Mulḥim's sons to Christianity in 1756, and the succession of the Maronite Yūsuf Shihāb in 1770 finally set the seal to the Druze decline. But although the Maronites were now recognizably the dominant group, the Druzes remained a powerful force with which the Shihābs had to reckon. The Maronite Shihābs, in fact, were so concerned about keeping Druze goodwill that they refrained from publicly admitting their Christianity, and for a long time continued to profess Druzism.[3]

It is difficult to estimate how soon the Druzes became aware of their own loss of power. For a long time they continued to regard the Maronites as allies, and apparently remained without suspicion of Christian political ambitions. Maronites were allowed to settle freely in the Druze villages; so were the Greek Orthodox and Greek Catholic immigrants from inner Syria, who arrived in Lebanon to swell the country's Christian population. But Druze hospitality was not always received with good grace by the Christians. Visiting Lebanon during the reign of Emir Yūsuf (1770–88), Volney was struck by the Druze religious tolerance 'which contrasts sharply with the zeal of the Moslems and Christians'. Druzes and Christians live together at peace, he says; 'but the Christians often display an indiscreet and annoying zeal which might cause this peace to be disturbed.'[4]

As it was, the peace between the Druzes and the Christians in Lebanon remained undisturbed for many years. Throughout this time, the prevailing issues in the internal politics of the country were the unceasing struggle for power among rival Shihābs and the conflict between the Yazbakī and Janbalāṭī Druzes. Meanwhile, the general situation in the Near East had begun to change. The weakness of the Ottoman central administration, increasing steadily as the eighteenth century went by, permitted a number of adventurers to assume power in such provinces as Syria and Egypt, to the serious embarrassment of the Porte. At the same time, the steady decline in Ottoman power awakened the keen interest of Europe in Ottoman affairs; Russia in particular took advantage of the Ottoman decline to extend her dominion southwards. In 1768, Russia was at war with Turkey for the third time in a century; and as the war went on, the Russians found it possible to divert Turkish attention from the war front by fomenting trouble in Syria. It was under these circumstances that the affairs of Ottoman Syria became involved for the first time in a serious international conflict.

The Russian intervention in Syria did not immediately involve the Lebanese Emirate, but rather concerned neighbouring Palestine. Here, a local chieftain called Ḍāhir al-'Umar had earlier made himself master of the whole Galilee region, taking Acre in 1750. The Ottomans at first allowed him to do as he pleased, for he behaved as an ideal vassal. But as his power grew, the Porte became wary of him, while the pashas of Damascus, Sidon, and Tripoli fanned its growing suspicions. Relations between Ḍāhir and the Syrian pashas became tense; and Ḍāhir, feeling himself threatened, began to consider measures of precaution. Russia was by then at war with Turkey, and the opportunity in Palestine was too good to miss. A Russian naval squadron was accordingly sent to cruise in the eastern Mediterranean and give Ḍāhir encouragement against the Turks. The moment was indeed suitable for action, for while the Ottomans were seriously engaged on the Russian war front Ḍāhir could easily find allies among his neighbours. In Egypt the Mamlūk 'Alī Bey, who had seized power in 1763 and declared himself independent of the Porte in 1768, was interested in extending his control over Syria. Now Ḍāhir proposed common action between them against the Pasha of Damascus; there was Russian backing for the project, and the occasion was ripe.

Operations began in 1770. 'Alī Bey sent his general Muḥammad Abū Dhahab to advance with Ḍāhir against Damascus. The Ottoman Pasha of Damascus fled, the city surrendered after a brief resistance, and the triumphant Abū Dhahab became for the moment the virtual master of Syria. Powerless to stop his further advance, the Ottomans approached him with the subtle suggestion that he should turn against his master 'Alī Bey, and receive in return the Pashalik of Egypt.

Now an ally of the Ottomans, Abū Dhahab left Ḍāhir al-'Umar and withdrew from Syria, then advanced against 'Alī Bey and expelled him from Egypt in 1772. Still enjoying Russian support, Ḍāhir tried to stand his ground against the Ottomans, assisted until 1773 by 'Ali Bey.[5] But in 1774 the Treaty of Küchük Kaynardja ended the war between Turkey and Russia. The Porte could now turn all its energies to the reduction of its rebellious vassal, and the Russian ships sailed back home, leaving Ḍāhir to his fate. In 1775, the Ottomans attacked and took Sidon from him, then advanced by sea to bombard Acre. Ḍāhir was advised to capitulate; but he was shot dead by one of his own men as he prepared to leave the town.

The Ḍāhir al-ʿUmar episode, from the internal aspect, was normal in the politics of Ottoman Syria. It was not unusual for Lebanese or Palestinian chieftains to gain power, extend their territory, and challenge the Ottomans when they found them at a disadvantage. What was new in the situation was the part played by Russia – a European Power taking sides in a local issue and using it for her own ends. From 1770 onwards, there was scarcely an event in Syria or any other part of the Ottoman Empire which remained the purely internal concern of local chieftains and Ottoman officials. As the rivalry between the European Powers in the Near East developed, such local events acquired an international importance and attracted attention abroad. Russia, Britain, France and Austria intervened everywhere. But in the nineteenth century nowhere did conditions invite intervention more than in Lebanon, where feudal quarrels and sectarian tension provided ample material for crisis.

Until the end of the eighteenth century, however, Lebanon remained in the background, as the rulers of Acre dominated the Syrian scene. In 1775, following the defeat of Ḍāhir al-ʿUmar, the Ottomans appointed to the Pashalik of Sidon the Bosnian adventurer Jazzār Aḥmad Pasha, who established his seat in Acre and became the dominant figure in Syria until his death in 1804. Jazzār frequently held the Pashalik of Damascus in addition to Sidon, and he was determined to bring the Lebanese Emirate fully under his control. Accordingly he stripped Mount Lebanon of Beirut, and proceeded to embarrass Emir Yūsuf Shihāb by inciting against him his own brothers, Efendi and Sayyid Aḥmad, and other discontented members of the princely family. Jazzār also interfered in the quarrels between the Druze factions, supporting the Janbalāṭīs against the Yazbakīs and encouraging their intrigues against Emir Yūsuf. Consequently, in 1778, the disagreements between the Emir and his opponents in Lebanon took a serious turn; and during the next ten years one Shihāb after the other rebelled against Yūsuf and claimed the government, supported by

Jazzār and the Janbalāṭī Druzes. By 1788 the country was split by civil war, and Jazzār seized this opportunity to take direct action against Yūsuf Shihāb. The emir was defeated in battle and overthrown, and in his place Jazzār appointed Yūsuf's distant cousin and former *protégé* Bashīr Shihāb – a Christian-born prince who succeeded to the government as Bashīr II.

It was as the candidate of Jazzār and the Janbalāṭī Druzes that Bashīr II became Emir of Lebanon. External and domestic forces combined to bring him to power, and continued jointly to command his attention throughout a long reign. During this period, indeed, forces from outside the Ottoman Empire began seriously to impinge on Lebanon. Bashīr II was still at the start of his active career when Napoleon Bonaparte invaded Egypt in 1798, precipitating new and radical developments in the Eastern Question. In the decades that followed, the European contest for power in the Near East gained vastly in complexity, and the Lebanon of Bashīr II became intricately involved in the developing situation. Before the Emir's time, changes in the social and sectarian situation had already been developing under the surface of Lebanese life for nearly a century; it was under the circumstances of his own reign, however, that these changes became manifest and their full consequences developed.

CHAPTER II

THE REIGN OF BASHĪR II
1788–1840

A SMALL country is rarely involved in an international conflict to its advantage. Whatever side such a country may support, her real interest in the conflict remains of secondary importance, and is likely to be sacrificed should higher interests so dictate. Her allies will normally keep her uninformed of their ultimate motives, leaving her to drift into complex situations which she can little understand or control. Finally, as her internal affairs become entangled in the outside conflict, these affairs themselves get out of hand, leaving her at the mercy of whatever forces prevail.

It was difficult for Bashīr II, after 1798, to avoid involving Lebanon in the Eastern Question. The general situation in Syria and the Ottoman Empire, and the direct influence of Europe in Lebanon, forced the Lebanese Emirate to become involved; while the confused situation inside the country made the process hard to resist. It is possible that a ruler other than Bashīr II would not have pushed matters to a head, but rather allowed them to drift and possibly ride the wave of crisis. Bashīr II, however, was driven by ambition to play an active role in regional affairs, and to court the attention of the Powers concerned. By a clever management of internal and external forces, he successfully maintained himself in power as Emir of Lebanon for an unprecedented record of fifty-two years. But the Emir's external entanglements ultimately led to his downfall and the collapse of the Emirate, and left the country in utter turmoil.

The circumstances that brought Bashīr II to power were confused. The Emir's father, Qāsim Shihāb, was a nephew of Emir Mulḥim, designated by him as his successor in 1758. Qāsim's claims were brushed aside at the time by his uncles Manṣūr and Aḥmad; and the unsuccessful Qāsim was forced to retire to

Ghāzīr, in the Kisrawān, where he embraced Christianity in 1767. Later in the same year Qāsim died, shortly after the birth of his second son Bashīr. His widow thereupon married again; and his two sons, Ḥasan and Bashīr, were left to the care of guardians and foster-mothers.

Ḥasan and Bashīr grew up in poverty, neglected by their kinsfolk and enjoying none of the customary material advantages of princely birth. It seems, indeed, that the two brothers remained throughout obsessed by the sense of insecurity developed in their childhood, which made them suspicious of their fellow men, and especially of their family. Ḥasan, as a man, was reputed to be cruel, grim, and retiring; and it is said that he often wondered how people could feel affection for one another. As for Bashīr, he developed into a shrewd and strong-willed opportunist, of keen insight and independent judgment. Grim and cruel like his elder brother, he was yet able to conceal the hardness of his nature, when he wished, by his superior intelligence, and by his suave and pleasant manners.

On reaching manhood, Bashīr parted from his brother Ḥasan and made his way to Dayr al-Qamar to seek his fortune at the court of Emir Yūsuf, his father's first cousin. The Emir received him well and took him into his service; and the young Bashīr was soon an established figure in the Shihāb court, freely taking part in its intrigues.

It was not long before Bashīr's presence in Dayr al-Qamar attracted the attention of Emir Yūsuf's opponents. Pressed by Jazzār Pasha for larger and larger payments of tribute, Yūsuf was weighing his people down with heavy taxes; and opposition to his rule was growing, led by the Druze Janbalāṭs. It seems, indeed, that the Janbalāṭ sheikhs tried to attract Bashīr to their side soon after his arrival in Dayr al-Qamar. Bashīr was a prince of the blood. Moreover, he was a man of ambition and outstanding ability, already commanding the respect of his elders in spite of his poverty and youth. What better candidate could there be to claim the Emirate? Approached by the Janbalāṭs on the subject, Bashīr was evasive, although he left the negotiations open. The young prince, apparently, was still uncertain of his position, and he was poor.

Circumstances soon changed. In 1787 Bashīr was sent to Ḥāṣbayyā to assess the fortune left by Emir Yūsuf's maternal uncle – a Moslem Shihāb, whom the Emir had shortly before lured to his death in Dayr al-Qamar. While performing this mission, Bashīr met the princess Shams, the dead man's widow, who was herself immensely rich. Grasping the opportunity, Bashīr married Shams and returned to Dayr al-Qamar with a wife and a vast fortune.[1]

As a rich man Bashīr was in a better position to accept the Janbalāṭ proposals and claim the Emirate, especially since by this time the tyranny and rapacity of his cousin Yūsuf had become intolerable. As Jazzār's demands for tribute increased, Yūsuf strove to satisfy them by further increasing the taxes. Meanwhile, popular opposition to his rule was being encouraged by the Janbalāṭs, who were secretly supported by Jazzār. The crisis finally broke in 1788, when a rising took place among the mamlūks of Jazzār in Acre. Yūsuf Shihāb hopefully supported the rebels, encouraged by their initial successes. But when the rising failed, the Emir found himself in serious difficulty. Immediately upon restoring order in Acre, Jazzār sent his troops to Lebanon to meet and crush the forces of Yūsuf at Qab Ilyās, in the Biqā'. The blow was decisive, and Yūsuf decided in despair to abdicate. At his request, the notables of Lebanon met and elected as his successor his cousin Bashīr, the candidate of Jazzār and the Janbalāṭs, who now went to Acre to secure his appointment.

It was clearly with the help of Jazzār that Bashīr II succeeded to the Lebanese Emirate. But no sooner was the new emir established in Dayr al-Qamar than he began to feel the pressure of Acre. Upon receiving his formal appointment, Bashīr was sent back to Lebanon at the head of two thousand troops to expel Yūsuf from the country. Yūsuf was chased out of Lebanon in 1789, and forced to take refuge in the Ḥawrān. But when he finally surrendered himself to Jazzār in Acre he was well received. In the following year, Yūsuf was actually reappointed Emir of Lebanon upon promising Jazzār a huge payment of tribute. Bashīr, however, was quick to overbid his cousin and recover his position. Jazzār forthwith reconfirmed him in the Emirate and threw Yūsuf into prison, where he was shortly after hanged on suspicion of intrigue.

The death of Yūsuf in 1790 relieved Bashīr, but did not end his troubles. On three occasions, in 1793, 1794, and 1798, Jazzār recalled Bashīr from the Emirate and replaced him by the three sons of Yūsuf – Ḥusayn, Saʿd al-Dīn, and Salīm – who ruled the country jointly. On each occasion there was civil war in Lebanon, while Jazzār interfered in the country to incite Druzes against Christians and one political faction against the other. Jazzār, indeed, had just invested the sons of Emir Yūsuf with the Emirate for the third time in 1798, when news arrived that Bonaparte had landed in Alexandria. The pasha thereupon ordered the three princes to stay in Acre, while he awaited the outcome of events.

Bonaparte's conquest of Egypt and his subsequent advance into Palestine gave Bashīr a temporary respite from Jazzār's attention. When the French besieged Acre in 1799, Jazzār summoned Bashīr to his assistance; but Bashīr could easily excuse himself on the grounds that his recent recall from office was causing him embarrassment at home. When Bonaparte requested his help, Bashīr also excused himself, and wisely so, for the approach of the French expedition was causing increased tension in Lebanon between the Maronites and Druzes. The Maronites, friends of France, awaited the arrival of Bonaparte in the country with pleasant expectation, while the Druzes were gravely apprehensive. Bashīr was anxious to allay the fears of the Druzes; furthermore, he preferred not to risk the vengeance of Jazzār by helping the French, for fear that their expedition would fail.

As it was, Acre resisted Bonaparte. The French general retreated from Syria with his troops, and finally abandoned his army in Egypt and returned to France alone. Bashīr had all this time offered no help to the French, but neither had he helped Jazzār; and the triumphant Pasha was not willing to forgive him his negligence. During the four years that followed, the intervention of Jazzār in Lebanon reached its climax and caused untold confusion, as five different Shihāb princes received from Acre the title to the Emirate. Meanwhile Bashīr, strongly opposed by Jazzār, left Lebanon on a British ship with the help of Sir Sidney Smith, who commanded the British fleet in the eastern Mediterranean. Smith took Bashīr to Cyprus, then to al-ʿArīsh, on the Egyptian frontier, where it was arranged for him to meet the Ottoman Grand Vizier Sulaymān Pasha (1801). Bashīr had earlier won the gratitude of the Ottomans by offering provisions to the Turkish army as it advanced in Syria against Bonaparte; and Sulaymān Pasha, who now headed a Turko-British expedition against the remaining French forces in Egypt, agreed to intercede for him with Jazzār. Bashīr accordingly returned to Lebanon and tried in the following years to regain favour with the master of Acre. But it was only the death of Jazzār in 1804 that brought him final relief.

After 1804, the first concern of Bashīr II was to consolidate his position in Lebanon. Three decades of intervention by the Pasha of Acre had greatly reduced the traditional prestige of the Emirate, as Jazzār backed one feudal faction after another against the governing Emir. Even the Janbalāṭs, who had helped bring Bashīr II to power in 1788, were encouraged after 1799 to oppose him and support the claims of rival Shihābs. With Jazzār out of the way, it was now possible for Bashīr II to curb the power of the feudal families, especially the Druze *muqāṭaʿajiyya* (*see* p. 10), and to restore the undisputed supremacy of the Emirate. Already in 1797, following his third appointment by Jazzār, the Emir had taken the opportunity of his return to office to incite the Janbalāṭs and the ʿImāds against their rivals the Abū Nakads, who supported the sons of Emir Yūsuf. The leading Abū Nakad sheikhs, five brothers in all, were killed, their homes in Dayr al-Qamar were destroyed, and their property in the town confiscated. The surviving members of the family fled, first to Damascus, then to Acre, where they stayed for some years as the clients of Jazzār before they finally returned to Lebanon. The Abū Nakads, however, were only the first of Bashīr's enemies to be cut down. Once Jazzār was dead, the Emir turned to deal with his remaining opponents, beginning with the sons of Emir Yūsuf and their supporters. The princes themselves were cruelly persecuted, and finally blinded and left destitute, while their supporters were hunted down or lured to their deaths. The Emir next turned against the Druze emirs and feudal sheikhs, robbing them of their wealth and prestige. The Arslāns, Talḥūqs, ʿImāds, and ʿAbd al-Maliks, one family after the other, were opposed and reduced to subservience, and only the Janbalāṭs were left to enjoy their feudal privileges undisturbed. In the end Sheikh Bashīr Janbalāṭ, the head of his family, remained as the only Druze chief rich and powerful enough to compete politically with the governing Emir. It was not surprising that the Druze opposition to Bashīr II, when it finally appeared, came to rally around Bashīr Janbalāṭ.

Meanwhile Bashīr II, having clipped the wings of his foes, proceeded to promote his own prestige by magnificence. In *circa* 1806 he ordered the building of a splendid palace on the hill of Bayt al-Dīn (or Btaddīn), not far from Dayr al-Qamar, and shortly afterwards moved the seat of his government there. The palace of Bayt al-Dīn, and the canal constructed in 1812–15 to supply it with water from the springs of Nahr al-Ṣafā, some ten miles away, remain until this day the most impressive of the Emir's public works. Bashīr II also built bridges which are still standing, and ordered the construction of paved mule-tracks to replace the old dust tracks. The Emir, however, did not only advance his prestige by public works; he also added to the splendour of his reign by taking an interest in the good of his subjects, and by substituting his own strict justice for the caprice and tyranny of the feudal emirs and sheikhs, whose influence he had curbed. His name, indeed, is still remembered in Lebanon as a symbol of stern benevolence and justice.

Between 1804 and 1819, circumstances permitted Bashīr II to be complete master of Lebanon, and to pose as the champion of the Ottomans in Syria. When Jazzār died in 1804, the Porte appointed as his successor a certain Ibrāhīm Pasha; but in Acre a former courtier of Jazzār, Ismā'īl, was proclaimed Pasha by his followers and prepared to resist Ibrāhīm. Ismā'īl held the eldest son of Bashīr II as a hostage, and the Emir was forced to remain openly his friend. Nevertheless, when Ibrāhīm advanced through Lebanon to claim his Pashalik, Bashīr II discreetly assisted him with men and provisions. Ismā'īl was defeated and killed in battle; and Ibrāhīm entered Acre, where he was replaced before the end of the year by a certain Sulaymān Pasha. Bashīr II, now in Ottoman favour, became the firm friend and ally of Sulaymān, and enjoyed the Pasha's steady support throughout the fifteen years that followed. During this period, indeed, Bashīr II reached the height of his power, and his influence was felt throughout Syria. Certain of his position at home, he could send his troops to assist the Ottomans in other regions; in 1810 he marched fifteen thousand men to Damascus to help defend the city against the Wahhābīs of Arabia.

These Wahhābīs were Sunnite puritans, the followers of Muḥammad ibn 'Abd al-Wahhāb (*d.* 1792) who was active in central Arabia in the second half of the eighteenth century. In his time 'Abd al-Wahhāb secured for his movement the backing of the Sa'ūdī family, powerful chiefs of the Najd; later, under the leadership of this family, his followers raided their neighbours in Arabia and expanded his power. By the early nineteenth century the pressure of the Wahhābīs was already felt beyond the Arabian borders, especially after they sacked the Shi'ite holy city of Kerbela in Iraq (1801), and captured Mecca (1803) and Medina (1804) in the Hejaz. In 1805 they invaded Iraq and Syria; and in 1810 they appeared before Damascus. Here, however, the Wahhābī attack was successfully repelled by the Ottomans, with the help of Bashīr II of Lebanon. Later the Wahhābīs were forced to retreat to Arabia, where they were finally reduced by Muḥammad 'Alī Pasha of Egypt in 1818. Meanwhile, their appearance in Syria had seriously embarrassed the position of the Christians and dissident Moslems of the region, especially in the vilayets of Damascus and Aleppo. Here the Ottoman governors tried to allay the fury of the fanatically puritan Wahhābīs by a stricter enforcement of the *Sharī'a*, or Moslem holy law, especially in the treatment of non-Moslems. Old restrictions against the Christians and Jews were revived, including humiliating distinctions in dress and public behaviour. In the face of such pressure, large numbers of Christians from the Syrian interior flocked to Lebanon, and especially to Beirut which now revived as a commercial centre. Bashīr II, for his part, encouraged this Christian immigration and opened the country to the fugitives. Moreover, he invited the persecuted Druzes of the Aleppo region to settle in the villages of the Shūf and the Matn, and shared with Sheikh Bashīr Janbalāṭ the expenses of their transfer to Lebanon in 1811. At the peak of his glory, Bashīr Shihāb could stand out as the champion of persecuted Christians and Druzes in all parts of Syria.

In 1819, however, Sulaymān Pasha of Acre died and was replaced by 'Abdallāh Pasha, the son of an important Ottoman official and an ambitious and active youth of twenty-one. Like Jazzār, 'Abdallāh had no wish to see a strong emir in Lebanon, and was determined to bring Bəshīr II to his knees. Consequently, no sooner was he appointed to Acre than he demanded from Bashīr II an exorbitant tribute. When the Emir remonstrated, 'Abdallāh applied pressure by ordering the arrest of all the Emir's

Lebanese subjects who happened to be in Sidon and Beirut at the time, some one hundred and seventy in all. Bashīr II was forced to agree to the Pasha's demands, raised a loan for the tribute, and sent his agents to collect the amount from the country. But the tax-collectors had scarcely begun their work when the people of the Matn and the Kisrawān rose in rebellion, prompted by Ḥasan and Salmān Shihāb, distant cousins of the governing emir. Unable to control the rebellion and collect the revenue required, Bashir II abandoned the Emirate in 1820 and went into voluntary exile in the Ḥawrān, while in Lebanon his cousins Ḥasan and Salmān were appointed jointly to replace him.

It was not long before 'Abdallāh Pasha discovered his mistake. With Bashīr II out of the country, the situation in Lebanon quickly degenerated into complete disorder, the two Shihāb princes who replaced him proving utterly incompetent as rulers. To control Lebanon, 'Abdallāh needed Bashīr II. Consequently, when the Emirs Ḥasan and Salmān abdicated in 1821, the Lebanese notables met and re-elected Bashīr II to the Emirate, with the Pasha's full approval. The re-established Emir forthwith advanced against the rebels in the various districts, crushed them, and re-established order in the country.

As an ally of 'Abdallāh Pasha, Bashīr II soon became involved in external problems. 'Abdallāh wished to secure for himself the Pashalik of Damascus, as Jazzār had often done before him; but Damascus at the time was in the hands of the ambitious Muḥammad Darwīsh Pasha, a man whom Bashīr II had special reason to dislike. Coveting the fertile Biqā', which Bashir II controlled, Darwīsh had sent troops there in 1820 to assert his claims; but his troops had been beaten and driven back by Bashīr's men. When Darwīsh and 'Abdallāh came to blows the following year, Bashīr II hastened to side with 'Abdallāh, trusting that the Porte would also support him. So eager was he to prove his loyalty that he personally led his men to attack Damascus upon his ally's request, beating the troops of Darwīsh at the battle of Mazza on 26 May 1821. The Emir, however, had miscalculated. No sooner had Darwīsh been defeated at Mazza than the Porte intervened to condemn 'Abdallāh Pasha and decree his removal from Acre, whose Pashalik was now added to Darwish. Unwilling to make peace with Darwīsh on his terms, Bashīr II chose exile again, this time in Egypt, leaving the Emirate in Lebanon to another distant cousin, ʿAbbās Shihāb.

In Acre ʿAbdallāh Pasha refused to surrender, even when the pashas of Damascus, Aleppo, and Adana advanced with their troops to overthrow him. Besieged in Acre in August 1822, he turned for help to Muḥammad ʿAlī of Egypt, begging for his intercession with the Porte. Meanwhile Bashīr II of Lebanon had been well received in Cairo, where he personally appealed to Muḥammad ʿAlī in favour of his ally ʿAbdallāh. Partly under his influence, the Egyptian Pasha agreed to intercede for ʿAbdallāh and secured his pardon from Istanbul. Shortly after, Bashīr II left Egypt carrying a decree of reappointment which he delivered to ʿAbdallāh in Acre; from there he triumphantly returned to Lebanon.

By 1821, when Bashīr II went into exile, the ruler of Egypt, Muḥammad ʿAlī Pasha (1805–49), was already recognized as the strongest vassal of the Sultan. He had a well-trained army and a navy at his disposal and had only recently rendered the sultan a service by subduing the Wahhābīs of Arabia. Now, like other rulers of Egypt, he coveted Syria, and hence began to develop his relations with the two most powerful figures in the region: Bashīr II of Lebanon and ʿAbdallāh Pasha of Acre. The Ottomans, meanwhile, had begun to suspect his intentions towards Syria; it was probably for this reason that they willingly accepted his intercession for ʿAbdallāh in 1822. A strong pasha in Acre, it was thought, would secure southern Syria against the Egyptians. Whatever the case, Muḥammad ʿAlī had as yet no plans for the immediate annexation of Syria. The Greeks had just risen in revolt against the Ottomans in the Morea, and the Egyptian Pasha at the moment was preparing to answer the summons of his suzerain Maḥmūd II, the Ottoman Sultan, by organizing an expedition against the insurgent Greeks. While Bashīr II was in Egypt, he negotiated an alliance with his host, promising, among other things, to supply Muḥammad ʿAlī with ten thousand Lebanese troops to assist in the projected Greek campaign, should such additional troops be needed.

Back in Lebanon as the friend and ally of Muḥammad ʿAlī, Bashīr II felt strong enough to turn against his remaining rivals in the country, particularly his former ally Bashīr Janbalāṭ. While the Emir was away in Egypt, Bashīr Janbalāṭ had sought to prevent his return to the Emirate, plotting against him with 'Abbās Shihāb, who had temporarily replaced the Emir in the government. Bashīr II was well informed of these plots – a fact which caused Bashīr Janbalāṭ grave concern when the Emir returned to Lebanon. Consequently, no sooner had Bashīr II arrived in his palace at Bayt al-Dīn than Bashīr Janbalāṭ hastened there to assure him of his continued friendship and submission. Janbalāṭ, however, was not received as a friend. His greetings and compliments were answered with rebukes and excessive demands for money. Unwilling to agree to the Emir's terms, Janbalāṭ fled to the Ḥawrān. Meanwhile Bashīr II advanced against Mukhtāra, the seat of the Janbalāṭ family, destroyed the great sheikh's palace there, and proceeded to confiscate his property in the Shūf. This was enough provocation for Bashīr Janbalāṭ, who now returned to Lebanon determined on rebellion. Rallying around him various other feudal sheikhs and emirs, he proclaimed revolt against Bashīr II in early January 1825. The revolt, however, failed. The rebels advanced from Mukhtāra to Bayt al-Dīn, only to be beaten back by the Emir's men. Bashīr Janbalāṭ, deserted by many of his allies, was forced to escape with the rest to Damascus; but upon reaching the city he was placed under arrest and sent to prison in Acre. Here, at the orders of 'Abdallāh Pasha, he was shortly afterwards strangled at the urgent request of Bashīr II.

The fall of Bashīr Janbalāṭ was an event of great consequence. By crushing his rich and powerful rival, Bashīr II had finally established his position as undisputed master of Lebanon; but he had also destroyed the only effective Druze leadership that remained. The Emir, in effect, had dealt a last blow to Druze political dominance in the country; the Druzes never forgave him for it. Weakened and leaderless, they henceforth ceased to cooperate wholeheartedly in the affairs of the Emirate and awaited the opportunity for revenge. The Christian Shihāb, it is true, had crushed the Druze Janbalāṭ not because he was a Druze, but because he was a powerful political rival. The Druzes, however, were to remember the incident differently; and Bashīr's subsequent policy was to make them look upon him more and more as a Christian enemy to their community.

Meanwhile the War of Greek Independence was attracting the attention of the world. Unable to deal with the Greeks single-handed, the Ottoman Sultan Mahmūd II summoned his vassal Muḥammad ʿAli of Egypt to his assistance. The Greeks, helped by the Powers, nevertheless succeeded in breaking away from the Ottoman Empire and achieving independence. In return for his services, Muḥammad ʿAlī received only Crete from the Sultan. The Morea, the governorship of which had been promised to his son Ibrāhīm, had been lost to the Ottomans, and Mahmūd II was not willing to give other territory in compensation. Muḥammad ʿAli was insistent, and asked for Syria as a reward; and when the Sultan refused his request, the Pasha decided to take the country by force. Picking a quarrel with ʿAbdallāh Pasha of Acre as an excuse, Muḥammad ʿAlī sent his son Ibrāhīm to conquer Syria in the autumn of 1831. Ibrāhīm forthwith advanced into Palestine and on 23 November besieged Acre.

The advance of the Egyptian army in Palestine had immediate repercussions in Lebanon, where the excellent relations between Bashīr II and Muḥammad ʿAli were already well known. Trouble apparently broke out between the Maronites and Druzes in the country even before Ibrāhīm Pasha arrived at Acre; there was fighting in Dayr al-Qamar, the Matn, and the Biqāʿ, while the Druzes tried to organize a rebellion against Bashīr II to embarrass Ibrāhīm Pasha in his advance. The Druzes had no special reason to fear the advance of Ibrāhīm Pasha; their attitude towards him, it seems, was determined purely by their hostility to Bashīr II. Since it was expected that the emir, sooner or later, would openly ally himself with Ibrāhīm, his Druze opponents decided to pose as the champions of the Porte, whom they expected to win in the end. A number of leading Druze sheikhs – Janbalāṭs, ʿImāds, and Abū Nakads – accordingly left Lebanon and went over to join the Ottoman army which advanced against the Egyptians. As for the Maronites, they looked upon the Egyptian conqueror as a friend, as did other Christians in Syria. In every town he occupied Ibrāhīm removed the traditional restrictions imposed on Christians and Jews, and placed these communities on an equal footing with the Moslems. Hence he appeared as a liberator to all the Christians of Syria, and especially to those of Lebanon who recognized him as the friend of their Emir.

Upon his arrival at Acre, Ibrāhīm Pasha summoned Bashīr II to come to his assistance. The Emir hesitated and tried to offer excuses, for he was fearful of taking sides openly against the Porte, and pleaded that the threat of civil war in Lebanon commanded his full attention there. Ibrāhīm was willing to allow Bashīr II time to make up his mind; but his father Muḥammad ʻAlī was less patient. In a curt note, he bluntly reminded Bashīr II of his promises, threatening to invade Lebanon should he waver in keeping them. The effect of this note was decisive. No sooner did Bashīr II receive it than he hastened to comply with the summons of Ibrāhīm Pasha, placing his men and resources wholly at Ibrāhīm's disposal. During the nine years that followed he remained the faithful and obedient agent of his Egyptian overlords, carrying out their instructions even when they contradicted his own better judgment.

Ibrāhīm Pasha was not immediately successful in his siege of Acre. While the town resisted, he provided Bashīr II and his sons with Egyptian troops and asked them to occupy the other coastal towns of Syria. Tyre, Sidon, and Beirut were easily taken and occupied; Tripoli, which offered some resistance, was finally taken when Ibrāhīm himself stepped in to assist his Lebanese allies. Meanwhile, Egyptian troops occupied Bayt al-Dīn and Dayr al-Qamar to maintain order in the Druze mountain. When at last Acre fell on 27 May 1832, and ʻAbdallāh Pasha surrendered, Ibrāhīm could proceed with his Syrian conquests, and he advanced with Bashīr II on Damascus. The Ottoman Pasha fled the city, but was pursued by the Egyptian and Lebanese forces to Homs, where he was defeated in battle on 9 July. For the time being, the issue was settled, and Syria fell completely under Egyptian rule.

The new régime which Ibrāhīm established in Syria was, at least at the beginning, an improvement on what had existed before. An efficient administration was established, an effective system of police and of justice was put in force, and special representative councils were established in the towns and larger villages to assist in the management of municipal affairs. Ibrāhīm also made an effort to fight the bribery and corruption to which, as he said, 'the people of Arabistan are much inclined',[2] and tried his best to improve the general condition of the people. In particular, he insisted on promoting a political and social equality between Christians and Moslems, much to the distress of the latter. Indeed, the conquest of Syria by Ibrāhīm Pasha brought about the virtual emancipation of the Christians there. Not only did these Christians begin to dress and ride as they pleased, but they also started competing with the Moslems in fields of trade which had previously been their preserve, such as the trade in grain and in livestock. While Ibrāhīm's policy was quick to win him popularity among the Christians, it also won him the hostility of the Moslems of Syria, who were not willing to share their traditional privileges with non-Moslems. This hostility became even more intense when actions by Christians which were provocative to Moslems went unpunished.

It was not long before the good effects of the Egyptian conquest of Syria began to wear off. The cost of the Egyptian army of occupation was high, and the construction of fortresses along the Anatolian frontier added considerably to Ibrāhīm's expenses. Impoverished by centuries of misrule and neglect, Syria was proving to be an economic liability to her new masters, and her due of tribute to the Porte had often to be paid by Egypt. Consequently, Ibrāhīm was forced to increase the Syrian revenue by imposing a heavy taxation; and, being short of money and men, he resorted to such unpopular measures as forced labour and military conscription. Reduced to a mere instrument of Egyptian policy, Bashīr II of Lebanon simply executed Ibrāhīm's orders there, and consequently shared in the Pasha's growing unpopularity. The Lebanese found the new taxation unbearable; they reacted even more strongly to the forced labour which had hitherto been unknown in their country, and to the hated conscription which Ibrāhīm soon introduced. The Druzes and the Maronites, who were excellent soldiers, would fight for their emirs with enthusiasm whenever the occasion called, but they had a strong dislike of regular military service, especially in a foreign army. The Maronites felt that it was their privilege as Christians not to serve in the armies of the Moslem State,[3] be that State Ottoman or Egyptian; as for the Druze *ʿuqqāl* (*see* pp. xviii-xix), they would not agree to have young men serve with Moslem soldiers in the same army, for fear that their Druzism might become corrupt. Moreover, conscription meant ruin to the Lebanese peasantry, for it took its best elements away from the fields to distant lands, to fight wars in which they had no interest.

The first revolts against Egyptian rule in Syria broke out in 1834 in Palestine, Tripoli, and the region of Lattakia. Ibrāhīm succeeded in putting down the three risings, and in each case he received considerable help from the Lebanese Emir. Bashīr II led his troops in person to assist in crushing the rebellion in Palestine; his son Khalīl helped reduce the risings in Tripoli, and afterwards in Lattakia. In every case the beaten insurgents were forced to surrender their arms, then were immediately conscripted into the Egyptian army.

Ibrāhīm next turned to Lebanon, asking Bashīr II to conscript one thousand six hundred young Druzes to serve in the Egyptian army for the regular term of fifteen years. Bashīr II pleaded that the number was too large, whereupon it was reduced to eight hundred. But even then the Emir faced great difficulty in carrying out the Pasha's orders. When the Druzes were summoned to send eight hundred of their young men for the conscription, they were greatly disturbed and refused to comply with the Emir's request. At about the same time, there were rumours that Ibrāhīm intended to conscript one thousand five hundred Lebanese Christians, and these rumours provoked a violent reaction. The Maronite Patriarch immediately declared his firm determination to resist the conscription of his people, and threatened to call upon France to intervene should that be made necessary; meanwhile the European consuls in Syria applied pressure on Ibrāhīm to leave the Lebanese Christians unmolested. None, however, took up the cause of the Druzes, whose case was anyhow different. Apart from their special worth as soldiers, the Druzes were known to be keenly opposed to Egyptian rule, and always prone to rebel. Muḥammad ʿAlī was determined to crush their power and use them in his army, and he insisted that Ibrāhīm should conscript them at all costs. Bashīr II was not himself inclined to favour such a treatment of the Druzes, well knowing the outcome to be expected. But the will of Muḥammad ʿAlī prevailed, and before the summer of that year the Lebanese Emir managed to provide Ibrāhīm Pasha with one thousand Druze conscripts. As a special concession to Druze opinion, Ibrāhīm had these conscripts organized into special regiments and kept apart from the rest of his army.

No sooner had the Druze conscripts been enrolled than Muḥammad ʿAlī urged the general disarmament of the Druzes, ostensibly because they had resisted conscription. Ibrāhīm was not at first happy with his father's decision; the Druzes had been a great help to him in dealing with the risings in Palestine and Lattakia in the previous year, and he was anxious to keep their goodwill. On the other hand, their general attitude did not encourage him to trust them, and he had suspicions that they were secretly in league with the Ottomans against him. Accordingly, when Muḥammad ʿAlī insisted on their disarmament, Ibrāhīm finally agreed. An Egyptian force, led by Ibrāhīm Pasha in person, arrived in the Shūf for the purpose in the early autumn of 1835, and Bashīr was summoned to co-operate. Bowing again to the determination of his Egyptian masters, the Emir sent word around urging the Druzes and Christians of the region to surrender their arms without resistance.

Meanwhile, the Egyptian conquest of Syria had caused important changes to take place in the international situation, giving the Eastern Question a new turn. In May 1832, when Acre fell to the Egyptians, the Porte declared Muḥammad ʿAlī an outlaw and sent an army to drive his son Ibrāhīm out of Syria. Ibrāhīm met the Ottoman army at the Beilan Pass, in the Taurus Mountains, and there dealt it a crushing defeat on 29 July. The Turkish troops fell back in utter confusion, and Ibrāhīm advanced into Anatolia. A second Turkish force sent to meet him was crushed on 21 December at Konia. Ibrāhīm thereupon advanced to Kütahya, and was on the point of taking an even more threatening position at Brusa. It appeared that Istanbul itself would soon be at his mercy. But at this moment Russia suddenly intervened. Shortly following the first Ottoman defeat Maḥmūd II, the Sultan, had appealed to the Powers for help against his formidable vassal; but of all the Powers only Russia seemed ready to offer assistance. Britain was for the moment preoccupied with internal and European affairs; France, on the other hand, was clearly enthusiastic about the success of Muḥammad ʿAlī whom many Frenchmen had come to regard as the spiritual successor of Bonaparte in Egypt. Consequently, Russia alone came to the rescue of the Sultan in his hour of need, sending a powerful naval squadron to Istanbul in February 1833.

Britain and France were alarmed by the appearance of the Russian warships at Istanbul, and immediately urged the Sultan to join them in demanding their withdrawal. The Russians, however, refused to withdraw until the Egyptian forces were out of Anatolia; while Muḥammad ʿAlī, finding himself in a good position to bargain, asked for the cession of the whole of Syria and some adjoining territory before he would consent to retire. Britain and France, anxious to secure the quickest Russian withdrawal, applied pressure to the Sultan to accept his vassal's terms. Consequently, on 8 April 1833, a Convention was signed at Kütahya whereby it was agreed that Ibrāhīm Pasha would withdraw from Anatolia against the cession of Syria to Muḥammad ʿAlī. It remained for Russia to withdraw her naval squadron from Istanbul; but Russia was not willing to do so before dictating special terms. After three months of tiresome negotiations, Turkey was forced to pay for the Russian assistance received by signing with Russia the Treaty of Hünkâr Iskelesi, on 8 July 1833. The Treaty marked the zenith of Russian influence in the Ottoman Empire; in a secret article, the Porte promised to assist Russia when necessary by closing the Dardanelles against the ships of any other Power, thus securing for Russia a pre-eminent position at Istanbul.

Britain and France were greatly upset at the conclusion of this Treaty, but they were not in agreement on what policy to follow. It was clear to both that, by the terms of the Treaty of Hünkâr Iskelesi, any further clash between the Porte and Muḥammad ʿAlī was likely to bring the Russians back to Istanbul. But while Britain sought to forestall the possibility of such a clash by curbing the ambitions of Muḥammad ʿAlī, France was determined to uphold the Pasha's claims and refused to accept any settlement of affairs at his expense. This divergence in Near Eastern policy between Britain and France was to determine the development of events in Syria in the years that followed.

British political activity in Syria started in earnest early in 1835 when Richard Wood, an official of the British Embassy at Istanbul, arrived in Beirut on a special mission. The first aim of Wood was to attract Bashīr II away from Muhammad ʿAlī. The

Lebanese Emir was known to be the dominant figure in the internal politics of Syria, and it was his rallying to the side of Muḥammad ʿAlī in 1831 which had so easily brought the whole of Syria under Egyptian control. A wedge in the relations between the Emir and the Pasha was certain to cause serious embarrassment to the Egyptian position in Syria. However, when Wood approached Bashīr II and presented his proposals, the Emir's response was evasive. Wood next took the British proposals to another Bashīr Shihāb, a nephew of Bashīr II's predecessor Yūsuf, and a second cousin to the governing emir. This Bashīr showed every willingness to co-operate with the British, in return for adequate support. Having found his man, Wood remained in Lebanon for another year to encourage the Druzes in their opposition to Bashīr II and Ibrāhīm Pasha, and to attempt, as a British Catholic, the difficult task of attracting the Maronites away from France.

It was not long before fresh internal troubles started in Syria, to foreshadow a renewal of crisis. The Convention of Kütahya had ended the first round in the struggle between the Ottoman Sultan and his Egyptian vassal, and it had been a victory for the latter. But neither of the two sides considered the settlement as permanent. Muḥammad ʿAlī was now anxious to make himself completely independent from the Porte, while the Sultan, Maḥmūd II, was bent on revenge. Aware of the military superiority of his vassal, the Sultan soon began to prepare for the second round by completely reorganizing his army. As for Muḥammad ʿAlī, he proceeded to strengthen his frontiers in northern Syria, and to increase his armed forces by further conscription. Thus, towards the end of 1837, his son Ibrāhīm Pasha received orders to reinforce the Egyptian army in Syria by fresh drafts of Druzes from the Ḥawrān, and of Moslem clansmen from the Syrian desert border.

The reaction to the new conscription orders in Syria was almost instantaneous, and Ibrāhīm Pasha was soon faced with a major Druze insurrection in the Ḥawrān. The governor of Damascus immediately sent an Egyptian force against the rebels; but the Egyptian troops were repelled and forced to retreat. The Druzes then left their homes in the Ḥawrān and retired with their families and provisions to the nearby Lajā – a rugged area of volcanic rock extending over some three hundred square miles, ideal for guerrilla tactics. Here the rebels were soon joined by other Druzes from the Shūf and Wādī al-Taym, and by Moslems from the Nāblus region in central Palestine. Two expeditions sent against them in the early months of 1838 were lured into the worst parts of the Lajā desert, then attacked and decimated in their retreat; after this the Druzes, encouraged by their success, began to threaten Damascus and incite the villages around the city to revolt. Responding to an appeal from their co-religionists in the Ḥawrān, the Druzes of Wādī al-Taym rose in rebellion in the early spring of that year, supported by other Druzes from Mount Lebanon. The revolt in Wādī al-Taym was led by a local chieftain, Shiblī al-ʿAryān of Rāshayyā, who had been away earlier in the year fighting the Egyptians in the Lajā. ʿAryān was assisted by Nāṣir al-Dīn al-ʿImād, Ḥasan Janbalāṭ, and a number of other Druze sheikhs who left the Shūf with their followers and proceeded to Wādī al-Taym, apparently with the blessing of Bashīr II. The Lebanese Emir, indeed, was not allowed by custom to prevent his Druze subjects from taking up arms in a cause of honour, or from supporting fellow Druzes in distress. It is possible that he also saw an advantage in the temporary departure of a large number of armed Druzes from the Shūf, where they had recently been giving him trouble. Whatever the case, Bashīr II did not remain for long uninvolved. The governor of Damascus, who was in charge of dealing with the spreading insurrection, soon found himself unable to control the situation single-handed; his Egyptian and Albanian troops were no match for the Druzes in mountain warfare. At his suggestion, Ibrāhīm Pasha requested the Lebanese Emir to send his own son Khalīl, with four thousand Christian mountaineers from Lebanon, to take part in the operations in the Ḥawrān and Wādī al-Taym and assist in subduing the Druze rebels.

This request by Ibrāhīm Pasha was completely opposed to Lebanese political tradition, and it seriously embarrassed Bashīr II. Lebanese internal policy had until then carefully avoided direct clashes between the sects, particularly between Druzes and Maronites. To abandon this policy risked serious consequences, especially since Bashīr II was already identified by his Druze subjects as a Christian and, at least to some extent, an enemy. For the Emir to send his own son to fight the Druzes with Christian troops meant the final alienation of the Druzes; and whatever sequels that entailed. Bashīr II, however, was no longer his own master, and had no choice but to obey Ibrāhīm's request. To reduce the risks to a minimum, he instructed his son Khalīl to use his utmost discretion in the fighting. Jirjis al-Dibs, a Christian well acquainted with Wādī al-Taym, was chosen by the Emir to serve Ibrāhīm Pasha as a guide on the campaign; this Jirjis kept the Druzes, informed whenever possible, of Ibrāhīm's movements, and frequently gave the Egyptian army wrong directions.

It was in the early summer of 1838 that the joint forces of Ibrāhīm and Bashīr II advanced on Wādī al-Taym. Led by Nāṣir al-Dīn al-ʿImād, Ḥasan Janbalāṭ, and Shiblī al-ʿAryān, the Druzes there put up a fierce resistance, and the first enemy attacks were repelled with heavy losses. But the Druzes were no match for their assailants in numbers and equipment. Attacked from three sides by the Egyptians, the Christian auxiliaries under Khalīl Shihāb, and other Moslem auxiliaries from Palestine, they were forced gradually to retreat up the slopes of Mount Hermon until they were finally surrounded at the village of Shabʿa – the last inhabitable spot up the mountain. Here the rebels were beaten and forced to surrender on generous terms; Jirjis al-Dibs was then sent with the same terms to negotiate the surrender of the rebels in the Ḥawrān.

The discontent of the Syrians with Egyptian rule, which expressed itself in the Druze insurrection of 1838, encouraged Maḥmūd II of Turkey to speed up his plans for revenge. Heedless of the advice of the Powers, he opened hostilities against Muḥammad ʿAlī in the spring of 1839, and sent a large Turkish force across the Euphrates to attack the Egyptians in Syria. The outcome of the attack was disastrous. Hardly had the Turks crossed into Syria, on 24 June, than their forces were completely routed by Ibrāhīm Pasha at Nizib, not far from the frontier; the Egyptians took nearly fifteen thousand prisoners, along with almost the whole of the Turkish artillery and stores. The battle of Nizib was scarcely over when the Turkish fleet was treacherously surrendered to Muḥammad ʿAlī at Alexandria. Maḥmūd II died before hearing the news of the defeat and treachery; his sixteen-year-old son and successor ʿAbd al-Majīd opened direct negotiations with

Muḥammad 'Alī, who now asked for no less than the hereditary government of both Egypt and Syria as his price for peace.

Young 'Abdal-Mejīd had almost agreed to the Pasha's terms when, on 27 July 1839, he received a collective note from the Powers demanding the immediate suspension of the negotiations with Muḥammad 'Alī. The Powers had decided to intervene; but they were hardly in agreement on what course to follow. Britain, Russia, Austria, and Prussia were firmly determined to prevent the break-up of the Ottoman Empire and the replacement of the feeble Turkish Sultanate by an extension of Muḥammad 'Alī's rule in the Near East. France, however, took a different view of the situation and continued to encourage Muḥammad 'Alī, hoping that his success would guarantee her pre-eminence in the region. Long negotiations followed; and when it became clear that France would not give up her support of the Egyptian Pasha, the other Powers decided to act alone. On 15 July 1840, they concluded with the Porte the Convention of London, offering Muḥammad 'Alī the hereditary Pashalik of Egypt and an enlarged Pashalik of Acre (to include the whole of southern Syria) for life, provided these terms were accepted within ten days. Failing that, the offer of the Pashalik of Acre would be withdrawn. Should the Pasha give no answer within twenty days, the whole offer would be withdrawn, and the Sultan would be free to take any action he pleased. The terms of the Convention of London caused profound indignation in France; but, as the British Foreign Minister Lord Palmerston had guessed, the French were not ready to risk a European war by pressing their support of Muḥammad 'Alī. Meanwhile the other Powers began to take precautionary measures: the British Mediterranean squadron was ordered to cut off all communication by sea between Egypt and Syria; on 11 August, British and Austrian warships appeared outside Beirut.

In pressing Muḥammad 'Alī to accept the terms of the Convention of London, the Allies could use the strong opposition to Egyptian rule which had grown in the different parts of Syria, often at the instigation of British and Ottoman agents. In Lebanon the Porte and Britain could certainly count on the support of the Druzes, bitter opponents of Egyptian rule from the start. They could also expect help from the Shi'ites of Jabal 'Āmil who had revolted against the Egyptians in November 1839, and whose revolt had been put down with the help of Bashīr II. By 1840 even the Lebanese Christians had ceased to approve of Ibrāhīm Pasha's rule. In 1838, as has been mentioned, Ibrāhīm had armed four thousand Christians to fight the Druzes in the Ḥawrān and Wādī al-Taym; two years later, following the battle of Nizib, Muḥammad ʿAlī had sent orders to have all the Christians in Lebanon disarmed. The Egyptian Pasha was afraid that Christians, if they remained armed, might easily join the Druzes and Moslems in a general revolt against Egyptian rule, as Britain hoped they would. While on his mission in Lebanon in 1836, the British agent Richard Wood had won over to the Ottoman side a number of Christian leaders including the Maronite Patriarch Yūsuf Ḥubaysh, and had promised on behalf of the Porte to maintain a Maronite Emirate in Lebanon, with a large measure of autonomy and a reduced tribute. Early in 1840, while the second Egyptian crisis was at its height, a number of other European agents appeared in Lebanon and in Syria to foment trouble against the Egyptians, and there were rumours that the Powers were going to intervene. Muḥammad ʿAlī began to prepare for resistance, increasing his forces and organizing fresh regiments. For this purpose he drafted, among others, some Lebanese students enrolled at the medical school in Cairo (*see* p. 133). The news of the conscription of these students caused great alarm in Lebanon, where rumours spread that Muḥamad ʿAlī intended this time to conscript both Moslems and Christians. The alarm became even more serious when fresh batches of Egyptian troops arrived in Baalbek and in Tripoli, and when a cargo of Egyptian army uniforms was unloaded in the harbour of Beirut. Then Muḥammad ʿAlī sent orders to have the Lebanese Christians disarmed. This, normally, was the first step towards conscription; the Christians of Lebanon decided to resist it at all costs, even if that meant joining the Druzes, Shiʿites, and Moslems in opposition to their Emir.

Towards the end of May 1840 Bashīr II, in obedience to Muḥammad ʿAlī's orders, summoned the Christians and Druzes of Dayr al-Qamar to surrender their arms. The men of this town were the best armed in the Shūf, and their early disarmament was found to facilitate the operation in other parts of the country. As it happened, however, the people of Dayr al-Qamar were in no mood to obey the Emir without resistance. On 27 May, representatives of the Druzes, Maronites, and Greek Catholics of the town met in the local Druze *khalwa*[4] and took a solemn oath to oppose their disarmament by force. Bashīr II did not take this event seriously at first, considering it to be a local matter which could easily be settled by negotiation. But the Emir was soon forced to realize that the issue at hand was by no means local, and that it could not be settled by kind words and promises. The armed resistance, starting in Dayr al-Qamar, was quick to spread to other towns and districts in Lebanon; and before Bashīr II or Ibrāhīm Pasha knew it, the whole country was in revolt.

CHAPTER III

THE END OF THE EMIRATE 1840–42

OUTSIDE POLITICAL forces played an important part in bringing about the Lebanese insurrection of 1840, yet it is wrong to think of the movement as a mere response to external events. Apart from its connexions with the Eastern Question, the insurrection reflected an internal social crisis which had been in the making for some years, drawing together the peasants and feudal sheikhs of Lebanon in the face of a common danger. Each of these two groups had a special interest in the movement. The Maronite and Druze peasants rebelled against oppression, injustice, and an odious foreign domination; their feudal sheikhs rose to reclaim lost privileges and rights and a prestige which had been heavily trespassed upon. The efforts of both groups, however, were directed against one target: the hated administration of Bashīr II and of Ibrāhīm Pasha; and it was this union of efforts, added to the outside encouragement received, which gave their movement its force and made possible its success.

The establishment of orderly government and the advancement of his own prestige had made it necessary for Bashīr II to crush the power of his feudal subordinates, either directly by force, or indirectly by inciting one feudal faction against the other. Backed by the pashas of Acre, and later by Muḥammad ʿAlī of Egypt, the Emire had succeeded in subduing the Lebanese feudal aristocracy and in establishing the supremacy of the Emirate. But the policy of ruthless repression which he followed made it impossible for him to count on the support of the feudal families when he finally needed it. In fact, it was these feudal families who, attracted by offers of outside help, volunteered to organize the armed resistance against Bashīr II in 1840; and it was the Abū Nakads, worst treated of the Druze feudal sheikhs (*see* p. 22), who led the first rising of that year in Dayr al-Qamar. As for the peasants, they had at one time been enthusiastic supporters of the emir, whose suppression of the feudal sheikhs had rid them of oppressive masters. But the excessive taxation which ruined Lebanon during the period of Egyptian rule, and the forced labour and conscription which Bashīr II introduced upon Ibrāhīm Pasha's insistence, finally alienated the peasantry from the emir and compelled them to join forces with their feudal lords against him. The opposition was already well developed, and its leaders in contact with British and other European agents, when Ibrāhīm Pasha sent his orders to Bashīr II to have the Christians disarmed, thereby provoking the crisis.

With the Maronites and Druzes, peasants and feudal lords, all set against him, Bashīr II could only keep power by relying exclusively on Egyptian support. France took up his cause at the international level, by virtue of her support of Egypt; but inside Lebanon the French were traditionally the friends and protectors of the Maronites and Druzes, and were in no position openly to assist the Emir against them. All they could do in the circumstances was to mediate between the two sides, trying on the one hand to prevent the insurrection from spreading, and on the other to procure concessions from Ibrāhīm Pasha to end the conflict. Meanwhile, the Porte and Britain were giving the Lebanese insurgents steady encouragement. The Ottomans, actively supported by the British, were determined to expel Ibrāhīm Pasha from Syria, and hoped also to use the opportunity to undermine the Lebanese Emirate. From early Ottoman times, the privileged status of Lebanon had been guaranteed by the popularity of her emirs, and the armed backing they could get from the peasants and feudal magnates in times of danger. In 1840, however, the Lebanese Emir stood alone, with all his subjects ranged against him. Circumstances were particularly favourable for the Ottomans to end the special Lebanese status, as the Porte could now use against the emir those very forces which had once supported his predecessors. Thus, no sooner had the risings in Lebanon begun than Turkey and her ally Britain intervened to back the insurgents and supply them with arms and other necessities. Russia and Austria also stepped in to encourage the rebels, particularly the Christians among them, Russia seeking to re-enforce her position as the protector of the Greek Orthodox of Syria, while Austria took advantage of the embarrassments of France to try and replace her as the protector of the Lebanese Catholics.

From the very start of the insurrection the position of Bashīr II and Ibrāhīm Pasha seemed hopeless. Hardly had the rebels of Dayr al-Qamar met to resist their disarmament (27 May) when the whole country rose to support them. On 4 June, rebel leaders of all sects – Christians, Druzes, and Moslems – assembled in Antilyās, immediately north of Beirut, to discuss their grievances and make plans for resistance; and similar gatherings followed in other parts of the country. The rebels everywhere demanded that the disarmament and conscription orders be revoked, and that the forced labour and oppressive taxation introduced since the Egyptian conquest be abolished. When Ibrāhīm Pasha refused to make any concessions to these demands, the rebel leaders gave the word, and by the middle of June there was armed revolt in every part of the country. The Convention of London, signed less than a month afterwards, gave heart to the rebels, who could now look forward to direct intervention by the Powers. Meanwhile, the first efforts of Bashīr II to control the insurrection, or to sow discord among its leaders, proved completely unsuccessful.

The insurgents in the beginning were mostly Christians and Druzes of the Shūf and Kisrawān regions, and the main centres of the revolt were Beirut, Dayr al-Qamar, and Jazzīn. It was not long, however, before the Shi'ites of the northern Biqā' joined the rebellion, followed by the Sunnites of the Tripoli region and the Christians of north Lebanon. Armed with old rifles, scimitars, daggers, or simply with axes and sticks, the rebels organized themselves in guerrilla bands and blocked the mountain roads, stopping normal communication between Beirut, Sidon, and Damascus. Egyptian convoys were successfully waylaid and attacked; Bashīr II, meanwhile, could do nothing to stop the rebel mischief. On several occasions the rebels tried to cut the water supply of Beirut, while bands of insurgents occupied the water mills around the town in an attempt to reduce its Egyptian garrison to starvation. Despairing of Bashīr's ability to deal with the rebellion, Ibrāhīm Pasha finally declared Mount Lebanon to be in a state of blockade, and took strict measures to stop all arms and provisions from reaching the insurgents. So firmly were these measures applied that the rebel bands, threatened by hunger and defeat, soon lost hope and began to disperse. Before long Bashīr II was able to crush what remained of the insurrection, and its principal leaders were arrested and sent into exile in upper Egypt.

Bashīr's success, however, was short-lived. The terms of the Convention of London were not yet formally presented to Muḥammad ʿAlī when British and Austrian warships began to arrive outside Beirut in early August to threaten intervention. by then Richard Wood (*see* pp. 33–4) and other Allied agents had resumed their political activity in Lebanon, where they tried to re-establish contact with the Lebanese rebel leaders and urge them not to yield. When Muḥammad ʿAlī did not accept the terms of the Convention of London in time, events took a more radical turn. On 11 September the commanding officer of the Allied forces outside Beirut, Commodore Sir Charles Napier, summoned the commander of the Egyptian forces in Lebanon to surrender Beirut without delay. The latter refused, and Beirut was subjected to a heavy bombardment. Meanwhile Turkish, British, and Austrian troops, eight thousand five hundred in all, were landed a short distance to the north, at the Bay of Junieh, where they were soon joined by the Lebanese rebel guerrillas who now emerged from hiding.

Upon the bombardment of Beirut and the landing of Allied troops at Junieh, the Egyptians withdrew from the coastal towns to the hills and established their headquarters in al-Hadath, south-east of Beirut. Within two weeks the Allies were easily able to occupy the main towns of the coast. Meanwhile the Egyptian army in Syria, demoralized by its retreat and weakened by malaria and dysentery, began quickly to fall apart. By early October the total of Ibrāhīm's forces had fallen from thirty thousand to a mere ten thousand, and his position in Syria had become hopeless. Acre, the last important coastal position he held, fell to the Allies on 3 November. After this Ibrāhīm began to withdraw his forces from Syria, leaving it to his father to arrange for a final settlement by diplomacy.

The breakdown of Ibrāhīm Pasha's rule in Syria meant the end of Bashīr II as Emir of Lebanon. In the weeks that followed the Allied landings at Junieh the Emir became convinced that the Egyptian cause in Syria was lost. Nevertheless, he continued to support Ibrāhīm Pasha and refused to consider British and Ottoman offers to change sides. Finally, on 10 October, Ibrāhīm's forces in Lebanon were completely defeated at the battle of Bharsāf, in the Matn. Two days later Bashīr II left Bayt al-Dīn and went to Sidon, where he boarded a British ship which took him to exile in Malta. So ended the reign of Bashīr II. To replace him, the Allies now brought to the Emirate the incompetent and unimpressive Bashīr III (*see* p. 34) – the Shihāb prince whom Richard Wood had discovered in 1835, and whom the Porte had already appointed Emir of Lebanon by a special firman on 3 September.

With the fall of Bashīr II and the accession of Bashīr III, a new period in the history of Lebanon began. Until the last few months of his reign Bashīr II had remained master of the internal politics of his country, able to keep under control the sectarian and partisan divisions which his own policy often helped to create. But with his disappearance from the scene the last control was gone. During the months of the insurrection a common hostility to the Emir brought together the Druzes and the Christians, the feudal lords and the peasants. But once the insurrection had succeeded, and Bashīr II was out of the way, no force was left to keep the various Lebanese groups and factions together; on the contrary, there were outside forces interested in keeping them apart. Under Bashir III, dormant feuds were revived and social and sectarian tensions brought to the point of crisis; and there followed two decades of civil unrest and strife which brought the country to almost complete ruin.

The internal developments in Lebanon during this period were influenced by a number of external factors, not least among them the policy of centralization followed by the Ottomans after their reoccupation of Syria in 1840. In the previous year, when the young Sultan ʻAbd al-Majīd succeeded to the throne, he issued a special reform decree called the Hatt-i Sherif of Gülhane, stressing among other things the necessity of making the various provinces of the Ottoman Empire more dependent on Istanbul. This Hatt-i Sherif was only the first of a series of Ottoman reforms, known collectively as the *Tanzimat* (1839–76), all of which emphasized the importance of centralization. Accordingly, when the Ottomans regained control of Syria in 1840, they were determined to increase the direct power of the central government in the region by reducing the prerogatives of the Syrian pashas. All vestiges of local autonomy were to be destroyed, particularly in the case of Lebanon; and here the presence of the cowardly and weak-willed Bashīr III offered a golden opportunity for Ottoman intervention. All the Turks had to heed in Lebanon was the policy of the other Powers, especially Britain and Austria, who had helped expel the Egyptians from Syria, and hence became strongly influential in the region.

Internally, the situation in Lebanon after the downfall of Bashīr II was highly unstable. Scarcely had Bashīr III succeeded to the Emirate when the Druze and other feudal chiefs who had been forced to leave Lebanon in the last years of Egyptian rule began to return home, to lay fresh claim to the rights, privileges, and feudal estates they had lost in the previous reign. The leaders of the returning exiles were Naʿmān and Saʿīd Janbalāṭ – sons of the renowned Bashīr Janbalāṭ who had been killed at the instigation of Bashīr II in 1825. But in Lebanon Naʿmān and Saʿīd were joined by other prominent Druze chiefs, like Ḥusayn Talḥūk and Amīn Arslān, who had also suffered considerable losses in property and prestige under Bashīr II, although they had not been compelled to leave the country. These chiefs jointly presented their demands to Bashīr III, asking for the complete reinstatement of the Druze feudal families as masters of their respective districts. The new Emir, however, was not willing to concede such claims. Confident of British backing, he refused the demands of the Druze chiefs and even took further measures to reduce their authority. A number of Druze emirs and sheikhs were arrested, others were robbed of more feudal prerogatives, and those who procured firmans from Istanbul to have their confiscated properties restored found the Emir unwilling to execute the imperial orders. Within a short time relations between the Emir and the Druze chiefs had become highly strained, as the Emir tried to crush what remained of Druze feudal power.

By the early spring of 1841 tension was acute between Bashīr III and the Druze feudal aristocracy. The Emir, without having the ability of his predecessor, had tried to follow his policy in opposing the Druze chiefs and reducing their influence. He had also followed the same policy with the Christian feudal families, notably the Khāzins and Ḥubayshes of the Kisrawān, forcing these families to make common cause with the Druze chiefs against him.

The French in Lebanon discreetly backed the joint feudal opposition; so did the Ottomans who, like the French, were growing suspicious of the British influence at Bʿabdā. As for the Druze and Christian chiefs, they tried to embarrass the Emir by pursuing a policy of complete non-co-operation, as a result of which the country quickly fell into anarchy. The Emir proved utterly incapable of controlling the governmental collapse or of enforcing his will, while his personal unpopularity and his complete lack of princely demeanour only contributed further to the general political breakdown.

Taking advantage of the confused situation, the feudal party in Lebanon, backed by the French Consul in Beirut, suggested that the crisis in the country be resolved by removing Bashīr III from the Emirate and replacing him by Salmān Shihāb – a Sunnite prince whose children had all been raised as Christians, and who was himself known for his Christian sympathies. Salmān had already governed Lebanon once before in 1820–21, while Bashīr II was in exile in the Hawrān[2] (*see* p. 25), and he was certainly more popular than Bashīr III and better equipped to rule. The Maronite Patriarch Yūsuf Ḥubaysh, however, insisted that only a Maronite was acceptable as Emir of Lebanon, and he refused to consider a Sunnite as candidate for the position. When it became clear that Salmān would not be accepted as Emir, the French Consul in Beirut tried to find someone else to replace Bashīr III, and finally suggested Ḥaydar Abū'l-Lamʿ – a devout Maronite and close friend of the Patriarch, who belonged to the second princely family in Lebanon. Of this suggestion the British agents in Lebanon heartily approved, as they were beginning to realize that their support of Bashīr III was only bringing them discredit. But, to the surprise of both the British and the French, the Patriarch again refused to consider the proposed candidate, and urged that Bashīr III be kept as Emir. The Patriarch, indeed, was fully aware of the incompetence of the governing emir; but he hoped that if the Emir continued to mismanage affairs long enough, a large proportion of the Lebanese would forget their grudges against his predecessor, and the administrative breakdown in the country would force the Ottomans to restore Bashīr II – the man whom the Patriarch wished to see back. Hence the Patriarch insisted that Ḥaydar Abū'l-Lamʿ

was unsuited for the Emirate, first because he took no decisive stand during the insurrection of 1840, and second because he was not a Shihāb, and hence unlikely to command the respect of all the feudal families in the country. Although the Abū'l-Lamʿs were emirs, the leading sheikhly families refused to think of them as superiors; the Maronite patriarch, as a Ḥubaysh, had no wish to see an Abū'l-Lamʿ emir raised in political dignity high above his sheikhly colleagues.

With the Maronite Patriarch's support of Bashīr III and his intrigues to restore the exiled Bashīr II, alienation between Maronites and Druzes was complete. By 1841, the causes of discord between the two communities were already numerous. Fresh in the minds of the Druzes was the collaboration of their Christian compatriots against them in the Egyptian campaigns against Wādī al-Taym and the Ḥawrān; the reign of Bashīr II, moreover, had left behind it other causes of Christian-Druze misunderstanding where material interests were involved. By confiscations and forced sales, Bashīr II had robbed the Druze feudal class of vast lands, and these lands had come in time to be redistributed among the rising class of well-to-do Christian villagers and townsmen. When the Druze feudal families, after 1840, began to reclaim their former estates, a major difficulty arose from the fact that large sections of these estates were now in Christian hands. As Prosper Bourée, the French Consul in Beirut, remarked at the time: 'There is scarcely any piece of property about which a Christian and a Druze cannot have a case.'[3]

Property disputes were not the only cause of the Druze-Christian tension after 1840. The eight years of Egyptian rule in Lebanon had left behind them a legacy of ill-feeling between the two groups which could not easily be forgotten. Under Ibrāhīm Pasha, the Druzes in Lebanon had enjoyed none of the favoured treatment which had made the Christian communities prosper. Moreover, they had been forcibly disarmed and robbed of their choice youth, who were taken away from their homes and fields to fight in distant wars. When their grievances against Egyptian rule finally drove them to revolt, Ibrāhīm Pasha had suppressed their rising and sent the foremost Druze leaders into exile. No wonder that many Druze families at the time were broken up and dispersed, and that the community on the whole became weak and impoverished. When the Druze exiles returned home after 1840, they found their families and friends destitute, while the Christians flaunted their new prosperity. This alone was enough cause for Druze resentment, especially when many rich Christians held lands which had formerly belonged to Druzes. There was added, moreover, the provocative political attitude which the Christians now assumed. Among the Druzes the feudal chiefs were the natural leaders, and the whole community backed their claims to their lost privileges and estates. At one time these chiefs had enjoyed certain traditional prerogatives in their districts: they collected taxes for the government at a profit, maintained peace and order and, most important, exercised judicial authority of the first instance over all civil and criminal cases involving penalties short of death.[4] Under Bashīr II the Emirate had, for the most part, absorbed these functions, which the feudal chiefs now claimed back along with their estates. But the Christians living in the Druze districts, having grown rich and influential, were unwilling to permit the restoration of the feudal prerogatives, particularly those pertaining to the exercise of judicial authority by the feudal chief. Bashīr III, at the suggestion of Richard Wood and the Ottoman authorities, tried to compromise on this issue by arranging for a council of twelve men representing the major religious sects to assist him in the administration of justice. The Maronites, Druzes, Greek Orthodox, Greek Catholics, Shīʿites, and Sunnites were all to be represented in the council. But the Druzes refused to co-operate in this arrangement, seeing in it an attempt on the part of the Emir to legalize what was in fact a usurpation of feudal power. When the Druze refusal became known, the Maronite Patriarch sent out a circular, signed by him and by other leading Maronites, calling upon the Christians of the Druze districts to renounce the judicial authority still held by the feudal chiefs, and assume this authority themselves. To the Druzes, this was extreme provocation, for by sending out the circular the Maronite Patriarch appeared to be asserting his power to withdraw authority from their own emirs and sheikhs, thus challenging them in their own districts. Smarting under the challenge, and with the original claims of their leaders still unanswered, they could only use force to reassert what they considered their usurped rights.

An incident which seems to have taken place early in 1841 was apparently the starting point of the first Maronite-Druze clashes in Lebanon. One day, it is said, a Maronite from Dayr al-Qamar shot a partridge on a Druze property just outside the neighbouring Druze town of Bʿaqlīn. This led to a quarrel which quickly took on a sectarian colour; and before the end of the day armed Christians from Dayr al-Qamar had attacked Bʿaqlīn, killing seventeen Druzes there, and returning home in triumph. The Maronite Patriarch, when he heard of the incident, immediately expressed his regrets, and sent a special delegation of Khāzin and Ḥubaysh sheikhs to the Shūf to negotiate a settlement of the issue. A formal reconciliation, as a result, was soon effected; the Janbalāṭ and Abū Nakad sheikhs professed their sincere intention to forget the incident. But at heart the Druzes were not to consider this reconciliation as final. The Christian triumph at Bʿaqlīn had been a hard blow to Druze prestige, especially since the Christians of Dayr al-Qamar had not of late been showing much respect to their Druze sheikhs, the Abū Nakads. Consequently, while they openly accepted the Christian apologies, they secretly prepared for revenge.

Later in the year, Bashīr III summoned the Druze chiefs to a meeting in Dayr al-Qamar to consider the distribution of taxes and other questions of general interest. The chiefs answered the summons and arrived outside the town on 13 October, each accompanied by a large party of his own men and of other Druze horsemen from Wādī al-Taym and the Ḥawrān. In the preceding weeks, armed Druzes from many parts of the Shūf had been quietly infiltrating into the Druze quarter of Dayr al-Qamar, where they waited for a sign from their leaders to attack. When the Druze chiefs arrived outside Dayr al-Qamar, Bashīr III was alarmed by the size of their escort and sent a party of one hundred and fifty Christians to forbid them entry into the town. At this moment, while all attention was directed outside, the armed Druzes inside Dayr al-Qamar suddenly came out of hiding and fell on the main square and the thoroughfares, taking the Christians of the town by complete surprise. Led by the Abū Nakad sheikhs, Druzes on horseback rode noisily through the town, shooting at the shops and killing any Christians they could find, while others went around pillaging Christian homes or setting them on fire. There were losses in life on both sides: some forty Christians and several Druzes, including an Abū Nakad sheikh, were killed. By the evening, however, the Druzes were still masters of the situation. Bashīr III, forced to take refuge in the old princely palace of Dayr al-Qamar, now appealed for help to the Ottoman authorities in Beirut, and to his own Christian supporters in Bʿabdā and elsewhere.

The event of 13 October 1841 in Dayr al-Qamar was only the beginning of the troubles. In Dayr al-Qamar itself, the fighting between Christians and Druzes went on for two more days, raising the total of dead reportedly to one hundred and eighteen Druzes and one hundred Christians,[5] and it was only stopped in the end by the intervention of Salīm Pasha of Beirut,[6] and of the British Consul, Colonel Hugh Rose. Even then the Druzes kept the town in a state of siege and stopped men and provisions from reaching the Christians inside. Meanwhile, fighting broke out in other parts of the country, as parties of Christians from Ihdin, Zahleh, Bʿabdā, and Jazzīn[7] advanced to the relief of Dayr al-Qamar and clashed with Druzes and Ottoman irregulars on the way. Indeed, once the conflict between the Christians and Druzes spread, Salīm Pasha in Beirut appeared to be clearly on the Druze side. The Ottomans, anxious as ever to discredit Lebanese autonomy, saw advantage in supporting a sectarian movement that promised to disrupt the Lebanese Emirate. Ottoman arms were accordingly sent to the Druzes from Damascus, and Ottoman troops frequently helped the Druzes in the fighting. It was even suspected at the time that the Ottomans had been involved in the initial Druze plot against the Christians. Whatever the case, it was not long before the Druzes managed to gain the upper hand in the Shūf and the surrounding districts; and as the troubles there began to subside, serious clashes started elsewhere in the country.

The town of Zahleh, on the eastern flank of Mount Lebanon, was the leading Christian centre in the Biqāʿ, and after Dayr al-Qamar the second Christian town in Lebanon. On the opposite side of the Biqāʿ valley lay the town of Rāshayyā – the principal Druze centre in Wādī al-Taym. When the Christians of Zahleh, who were mainly Greek Catholics, answered the appeals of the Maronites in Dayr al-Qamar and sent armed parties to help them, the Druzes of Rāshayyā took it upon themselves to attack Zahleh and teach its people a lesson. Led by Shiblī al-ʿAryān (*see* pp. 35, 36), and joined by other Druzes from Wādī al-Taym, the Shūf, and the Ḥawrān, the Rāshayyā Druzes advanced against Zahleh in the early autumn. The Christians of that town, assisted by Shiʿite tribesmen from the Baalbek region, set out to meet them at the nearby village of Shṭūrā. Here the Druzes were badly beaten in a first encounter on 25 October, then pursued and defeated in a second encounter at Qab Ilyās. Before the end of October the Druzes were retreating in complete disorder, the Christians and Shiʿites harassing them as they fled across the Biqāʿ.

The Druze defeat in the Biqāʿ was an encouragement to the Christians throughout Lebanon, but it made little material difference to the situation in the Shūf. Here the Druzes continued to meet with success and present a solid front, while their Christian opponents steadily lost ground, and were moreover hopelessly divided. The Greek Orthodox, suspicious of the Maronites and resentful of their numerical superiority, were reluctant to take up their cause, and occasionally helped the Druzes against them. This was not the case with the Greek Catholics, who remained throughout the firm allies of the Maronites. But the Maronites themselves were not united in purpose, and adequate leadership among them was entirely lacking. The very cause for which the Maronites and Greek Catholics were fighting was, in fact, unclear. While the Druzes were determined to overthrow Bashīr III, not many Christians were enthusiastic about maintaining the incompetent Emir in power. Many Christian leaders coveted the Emirate for themselves; and when Bashīr III remained under siege in the palace of Dayr al-Qamar for over three weeks, none among them showed the least eagerness to relieve him. Divining the Christian position, the Druzes finally attacked the palace in Dayr al-Qamar in early November. Bashīr III was seized and treated with the utmost disrespect, and not a finger was raised to help him. Meanwhile, on 5 November, the seven thousand armed Christians gathered in Bʿabdā attacked the neighbouring town of Shwayfāt, whose mixed population of Greek Orthodox and Druzes had until then maintained strict neutrality. The unprovoked attack ended in complete failure, the assailants taking flight before a single shot had been fired. Taking heart, the Druzes now proceeded to plunder and burn Christian villages, while the Christians offered little resistance.

It was only after Bashīr III was safely in Druze hands that the Ottomans, under pressure from the Powers, finally decided to intervene, presumably to settle the issue between the warring sects in Lebanon. Muṣṭafā Pasha, a leading officer of the Ottoman army, was specially sent to Beirut for the purpose, arriving there towards mid-November. But it soon became clear that Muṣṭafā Pasha's mission was not purely one of mediation. Still determined to end Lebanon's self-rule, the Ottomans were anxious to demonstrate the impossibility of an effective reconciliation between the Maronites and the Druzes. Accordingly, while Muṣṭafā Pasha pretended to mediate between the two sects, he secretly tried to convince Christian leaders of the advantages of direct Ottoman rule, and at the same time encouraged the Druzes to continue ravaging Christian villages. Hardly any measures were taken to stop the plunder and bloodshed in the mountain districts; meanwhile, fugitives from the ravaged villages, as they passed near Beirut, were attacked and robbed by the Ottoman troops stationed there to restore order.

Once complete anarchy had come to prevail, the Ottomans dealt their final blow. On 13 January 1842, three months after the start of the troubles, Bashīr III was summoned by Salīm Pasha and Muṣṭafā Pasha to Beirut, where a ship lay waiting to take him to Constantinople. The Emir insisted on leaving Dayr al-Qamar in full princely dignity, accompanied by an armed bodyguard. As he left the town, however, a party of Druzes attacked his escort and stripped them of their arms, then proceeded to manhandle the Emir. So ended the rule of the Shihābs in Lebanon.

CHAPTER IV

THE DOUBLE KAYMAKAMATE 1842–58

BASHĪR III had no sooner left Lebanon when Muṣṭafā Pasha summoned the Lebanese notables to Beirut, on 16 January 1842, and announced to them the fall of the Shihābs. The Christian Emirate in the country was declared at an end, and the Croat 'Umar Pasha, a member of Muṣṭafā Pasha's staff, was appointed Governor of Mount Lebanon.[1] This was a distinct triumph of Ottoman policy; the Ottomans, moreover, had chosen the right moment to act. By 1842, the Maronite-Druze solidarity on which Lebanon's autonomy had long rested was already a thing of the past, and scarcely a possibility remained for common action against the new dispositions. The Druzes hailed the announcements of Muṣṭafā Pasha with unreserved enthusiasm and exulted in the blow dealt to the Christian prestige in the country, little realizing that the establishment of direct Ottoman rule in Lebanon would ultimately affect their own community. The Christians, meanwhile, refused to recognize the new arrangements as permanent, and insisted on a restoration of the Emirate which could only be achieved with Druze co-operation.

As Governor of Mount Lebanon, 'Umar Pasha's main concern was to put an end to all thought of a Shihāb restoration. Immediately upon establishing himself in the palace of Bayt al-Dīn, he began to rally around him all those elements in the country who were already opposed to the Shihābs, winning their support by showing them special favour. The Druze feudal chiefs who had been dispossessed by Bashīr II and Bashīr III were given back their old estates and reconfirmed in their traditional prerogatives, as were the more important among the Maronite emirs and sheikhs. A number of chiefs of both sects – such as Manṣūr Daḥdāḥ, Khaṭṭār al-'Imād, and the brothers Aḥmad and Amīn Arslān –

were appointed by the new governor as his advisers and agents, and hence became staunch supporters of the new régime. Among the Christian emirs, the well-regarded Ḥaydar Abū'l-Lamʿ, who had only recently been proposed as a candidate to replace Bashīr III in the Emirate, refused to co-operate with a government of which the Maronite church and most of his fellow Christians strongly disapproved. When offered the post of deputy governor, he courteously declined the appointment. Thereupon ʿUmar Pasha and Muṣṭafā Pasha turned to his kinsman Bashīr Aḥmad Abū'l-Lamʿ, a recent convert from Druzism who enjoyed little popularity with Christians, and won him over to their cause 'by a large grant of land and a round sum of money'.[2] Henceforth Bashīr Aḥmad became the principal agent of the Ottomans among the Christians of Lebanon, and a man on whom ʿUmar Pasha strongly depended.

Having gained the support of the Lebanese feudal aristocracy, ʿUmar Pasha next tried to secure the loyalty of the Christian and Druze commoners, among whom the Christians, for the most part, were still staunch supporters of the Shihābs. The Ottomans were anxious to show the Powers that their direct rule in Lebanon enjoyed general Lebanese backing, while ʿUmar Pasha was personally eager to demonstrate the efficiency and popularity of his government. Consequently, agents were hired to draw petitions and circulate them for signature throughout the country, praising the direct Ottoman rule in Lebanon and begging the Porte to prevent the return of the Shihābs. The Druzes, in general, did not object to these petitions and were willing to sign them. The Christians, however, refused to do so; and the Maronites in particular were encouraged to persist in their refusal by their strongly pro-Shihāb clergy. To procure enough Christian signatures for their petitions, the Ottomans and their Lebanese agents were forced to resort to corrupt methods ranging from bribery and false promises to intimidation and blackmail. Bashīr Aḥmad Abū'l-Lamʿ, taking his cue from ʿUmar Pasha, went around the Matn district campaigning for signatures among his peasants, and his example was closely followed by other feudal chiefs, mainly the Khāzins, Ḥubayshes, and Daḥdāḥs of the Kisrawān. Among the Christian leaders, only the Maronite Patriarch had the courage to denounce the petitions and urge his followers not to sign them.

Meanwhile, as the extortion of Christian signatures went on by 'bribery... threats and blows, and every species of personal indignity',[3] the European consuls in Beirut joined together in protesting against the use of such methods, and declared the petitions to be completely unrepresentative of true Lebanese opinion.

Muṣṭafā Pasha, who had not yet left Beirut, regarded the protests of the consuls as undue interference in the internal affairs of Lebanon, which indeed they were. By 1842, however, consular intervention had become a common feature of Lebanese political life. During the long and troubled centuries of Ottoman rule the various Lebanese communities, always suspicious of the Ottomans, had learnt to look to the European consuls in the coastal towns for help and protection; and such consular protection had considerably gained in importance during the decade of Egyptian rule. By the time of 'Umar Pasha the French and Austrian consuls in Beirut were already competing for recognition as the protectors of the Maronites and other Uniate Catholics in Lebanon, while the Russian consuls openly championed the Greek Orthodox. The Druzes, until 1841, had not enjoyed a regular consular protection; in that year, however, their cause was enthusiastically taken up by the British Consul, Colonel Hugh Rose, and the British consuls in Beirut hence became the recognized champions of the Druzes.

In fact, it was only with the events which led to the fall of the Shihābs that the pattern of consular protection in Lebanon became clear. True, the special relations between the Maronites and France dated back to early Ottoman times; but it was only in 1841 that the Maronites began to seek advice and support exclusively from the French consuls, and that the Druzes began to look upon the French consulate in Beirut with feelings of hostility. Earlier, the French consuls and political agents, who had acted as guardians of the Maronite interests, had also done their best to maintain an influence with the Druzes; and even as late as 1840 and 1841 the efforts of the French were directed mainly towards keeping both the Druzes and the Maronites away from the influence of the British, Austrian, and Russian representatives. The French agents at the time had mediated between the Maronites and the Druzes, thinking that the best way to preserve the autonomy and integrity of Lebanon was by getting the two major Lebanese communities reconciled. The French Consul Prosper Bourée clearly summed up this policy: 'The presence of the Christians,' he said, 'is necessary for the Druzes, and that of the Druzes indispensable for the security of the Christians.'[4] Such a policy, however, was not one which the common run of Maronites could readily appreciate, and to many of them it seemed like a betrayal of their cause. What the Maronites in general expected was out and out French support, and this the French were only willing to give in the last resort. Consequently, misunderstandings between the Maronites and the French consuls were not infrequent, and the Austrian consuls invariably took advantage of such misunderstandings to promote their own position as champions of the Lebanese Catholics. The political activity of the Austrian Consulate in Beirut was certainly embarrassing to the French in Lebanon; but even more embarrassing to them was the activity of some Catholic missionaries who, like the Lithuanian Jesuit Father Ryllo,[5] went around the country inciting the Lebanese Christians to rise against the Druzes and vindicate their political claims by force. It was perhaps these missionaries who were primarily responsible for the irreparable breach which came to exist between the Maronites and the Druzes in Lebanon, and which first became manifest in the events of 1841.

It would indeed be difficult to appreciate the situation in Lebanon during the years that followed the fall of the Shihābs without taking into account the important role played by the European missionaries. Among these missionaries, the Catholics had been established in the country for a long time, and had come over the centuries to wield an influence over all classes of the population (*see* pp. xx-xxi, 13). Compared with them the Protestant missionaries were certainly newcomers. American Protestant missionaries began to arrive in Lebanon in 1820, and shortly after established their headquarters in Beirut; but it was only after the expulsion of Ibrāhīm Pasha in 1840 that British Protestants began to establish themselves in the rural parts of the country. From the very beginning, the Protestant missionary movement provoked a strong reaction from the Maronite church. A young Maronite converted to Protestantism in 1825, As'ad al-Shidyāq, was seized by his brother and handed over to the Maronite Patriarch who had him imprisoned and tortured to death in 1829. Later, the appearance of British missionaries in the rural districts caused the Maronite church so much concern that the Patriarch forbade his followers to send their children to the Protestant schools, and ordered them to refuse the missionaries provisions. A number of incidents occurred in which Protestant missionaries were attacked and driven out of Christian villages. In the summer of 1841 Protestant Bibles which had been distributed among the villagers of the Shūf were collected and publicly burnt in Dayr al-Qamar. No less opposed to Protestantism than the Maronites, the Greek Orthodox clergy, encouraged by the Russian Consulate in Beirut, also strove to protect their flock from British and American missionaries and their Protestant teaching.

This opposition to the Protestant missionaries, nourished by the local Christian clergy and the Roman Catholic religious orders, was to have a decisive effect on the relations between the Christians of Lebanon, especially the Maronites, and the British. During the period of Egyptian occupation, the British official Richard Wood had managed, as a Roman Catholic, to attract a number of Maronite leaders to the side of Britain, making use of the special circumstances that prevailed at the time (*see* pp. 33–4). But to attract the whole Maronite community away from France was an end which no British agent could hope to achieve. To the Maronite clergy and their followers, the British remained heretics, freemasons, and enemies of the true Church. A certain degree of co-operation with them was possible while the struggle against Ibrāhīm Pasha was in progress. But no sooner had the Egyptians left Syria than the alliance between the Maronites and Britain, on which so much effort had been wasted, collapsed; and the appearance of the British missionaries in Mount Lebanon dealt the final blow.

Unsuccessful in winning the support of the Maronites, the British turned their attention to the Druzes whose relations with France, until then, had remained friendly. Even when the Maronite-Druze tension in 1841 was at its height, the French Consulate in Beirut had maintained contact with a number of Druze chiefs, principally those of the Yazbakī party. Now the Ottomans, anxious to limit the French influence in Lebanon, joined the British in their efforts to arouse Druze suspicions against France by depicting her as the avenger of the Maronites. Rumours accordingly spread that the French were arming the Christians of Lebanon against the Druzes, and that a considerable

French force stood ready to intervene on behalf of the Christians in case of trouble. To the Druzes such rumours did not appear improbable. A number of Maronite monasteries had recently been raising the French flag, seemingly in defiance of the Druzes; furthermore, the appearance of a French naval squadron outside Beirut in January 1842 appeared to support the rumours of an intended French intervention. By that time, however, a first Anglo-Druze alliance had already been established. On 24 September 1841, five prominent Druze chiefs of the Janbalāṭī party had gone on board a British frigate anchored outside Sidon, and there vowed full Druze adherence to Britain. In return, Britain promised to protect the Druzes and uphold their interests. As an additional gesture of friendship, the British supplied the Druzes with a quantity of arms, and offered to educate a number of young Druze sheikhs in Britain. This Anglo-Druze alliance ended all hope of a reunion between the Maronites and the Druzes. Henceforth the Maronites, feeling insecure, threw themselves completely on the side of France, while the Druzes tried to demonstrate their friendship for Britain by welcoming to their districts the Protestant missionaries rejected by the Maronites.

The shift of British interest from the Maronites to the Druzes was reflected by the swift change of British policy in 1841. Until the autumn of that year Colonel Rose and his staff continued to support Bashīr III, whom the British had actually brought to power in the previous year. Britain, at the time, still hoped to gain the friendship of the Maronites; hence her backing of the Emir against strong Druze opposition. Once Bashīr III was in trouble, however, his British friends did surprisingly little to help him. In fact, no sooner had the emir been overthrown and replaced by an Ottoman governor than the British, in agreement with the Druzes, came out openly in support of the new arrangements. So cordially did Colonel Rose back the Ottoman policy in Lebanon in the early months of 1842, that he was suspected at one time of actually encouraging a plan by Muṣṭafā Pasha to abduct the Maronite Patriarch because of his opposition to ʿUmar Pasha's government.[6]

The Anglo-Druze support of ʿUmar Pasha, however, did not last long. The pasha's main interest was to establish his own authority in Lebanon and make the direct Ottoman rule of the country practicable. Meanwhile the Druze sheikhs, elated with their conquests, affected an air of independence, asserted their feudal superiority over the Christians, and denied the right of any to intervene between them. In many instances they proceeded to ill-treat and abuse such of the Christians as were peculiarly obnoxious to them; and when the former presented petitions to the pasha, asking for protection and redress, they resented it as an insult.[7]

The Druze leaders felt that it was by their own efforts that the Shihābs had been overthrown and the régime of direct Ottoman administration established, and they were therefore unwilling to receive dictation from the Turks. In the face of such Druze pretensions, ʿUmar Pasha turned for support to the Maronites, employing a number of them in his service as troops under their own leaders. This only alienated the Druzes still further, especially as some of the Maronite leaders now serving the Pasha had played prominent roles in the events of the previous year. By the time the petitions in praise of ʿUmar Pasha's administration were being circulated in Lebanon for signature, the relations between the Pasha and the Druzes had already begun to deteriorate. The British, no longer bound to support the Pasha's position, were now able to join the other European Powers in protesting against the validity of the petitions; and Colonel Rose in Beirut added his voice to that of the other consuls in denouncing the methods by which the signatures for the petitions were being procured.

The protests of the consuls in Beirut were strong and eloquent, but they made little impression on Muṣṭafā Pasha; nor did they have much effect on the special envoy, Salīm Bey, who was sent by the Porte in April 1842 to report on the situation in Lebanon. When, by early August, a sufficient number of petitions in favour of ʿUmar Pasha's government had been procured, Muṣṭafā Pasha summoned the European consuls to a special meeting to hear Salīm Bey report on his findings. Salīm Bey's report, however, completely ignored the protests of the consuls, while it extolled the 'sympathy and attachment which the Lebanese of all classes show towards the wise government of ʿUmar Pasha'.[8] The consuls left the meeting in utter disappointment; meanwhile the report and the petitions were turned over to Istanbul, where they became the concern of the Ottoman Foreign Minister Ṣārim Efendi and the ambassadors of the Powers.

The Porte, until this time, was still counting on the support of

Britain in the settlement of the affairs of Lebanon, and Ṣārim Efendi was confident of the diplomatic backing of the British Ambassador, Sir Stratford Canning, in this matter. The Ottomans were, however, to be disappointed. Instead of upholding the Turkish position, Canning openly condemned the 'intimidation and corruption' by which 'Umar Pasha had procured his petitions, and joined the other ambassadors in a unanimous denunciation of Salīm Bey's report. The proposal of the Porte to maintain direct Ottoman rule in Lebanon was completely rejected; the ambassadors insisted on the establishment of a new form of government for the country which would suit its needs and be acceptable to the Porte and Powers.

Meanwhile, the situation inside Lebanon had seriously deteriorated. In his attempts to use Christian help against the Druzes, 'Umar Pasha had only succeeded in prejudicing his own position. The Christians, loyal as always to the Shihābs, remained strongly suspicious of him and refused him their full co-operation. As for the Druzes, they were completely alienated by his policy and became his bitter enemies. By the early spring of 1842, the Druze opposition to 'Umar Pasha had become so intense that the Pasha was forced to take strong action against it. Accordingly, on 6 April, as five leading Druze chiefs arrived in Bayt al-Dīn upon the Pasha's invitation to dinner, they were summarily arrested and sent to prison in Beirut. A few days later two other Druze chiefs were placed under arrest, raising the total number of prisoners to seven: Nu'mān and Sa'īd Janbalāṭ, Aḥmad and Amīn Arslān, Nāṣīf Abū Nakad, Ḥusayn Talḥūq, and Dāwūd 'Abd al-Malik. These important chiefs represented nearly all the Druze feudal families, and their arbitrary arrest and imprisonment provoked an immediate reaction.

Thus, while the Powers in Istanbul brought pressure on the Porte to settle the Lebanese question, the Druzes in Lebanon, led by Yūsuf 'Abd al-Malik of the Jurd, prepared for rebellion and began to block the roads to Bayt al-Dīn. Knowing the Christians to be equally opposed to 'Umar Pasha, the Druzes appealed to them to forget past quarrels and agree to a renewal of the Maronite-Druze union 'which alone could stop their common ruin'. In a special appeal to the Maronite Patriarch, the Druzes proposed for their part a new Maronite-Druze alliance, promising to agree to the return of the Shihābs and the compensation of Christians for losses suffered in 1841. Such terms were indeed attractive, and the French Consul urged the Maronites to accept them and join the Druzes in their revolt against ʿUmar Pasha. But the enmity between the two communities had already gone too far for a union of efforts between them to be still possible.

Had the most ordinary principle of patriotism presided over these attempts at reconciliation, the better to overwhelm a common foe, the power of the Turks might have been seriously compromised. But mutual jealousy and distrust rendered all the endeavours of both parties abortive. The Druzes promised to declare in favour of the Shehabs, but on condition that the Maronites should first begin the insurrectionary movement. The Christians stipulated that the Druzes should strike the first blow, and give a written document signed with the seals of all their leading sheikhs, demanding a Shehab, as a guarantee for their good faith . . . Hence arose a sort of dispute which could never be settled, both sides suspecting each other's intentions. The Turks, in the meantime, were fully alive to the necessity of thwarting this ominous alliance, and lost no time in bringing all their allurements to bear upon the well-known and often experienced venality of the Maronites. A visierial order – giving protection to the Maronite patriarch, the liberation of such of their chiefs as had been thrown into prison on account of their refusing to petition for a Turkish governor, the promise of restoration of the property plundered by the Druzes, a sword to one, a shawl to another, a watch and a few hundred piasters to a third – sufficed to soothe the Maronite disaffection, and to break up the threatened coalition.[9]

When all attempts at a reconciliation had failed, the Druzes decided to act alone. Towards the end of October Shiblī al-ʿAryān, veteran leader of the 1838 rising against Ibrāhīm Pasha, led the Druzes of the Ḥawrān and Wādī al-Taym across the Biqāʿ, advanced into the Shūf, and proceeded to block the road from Beirut to Damascus. The Christians were once more invited to join in the revolt; meanwhile, as their leaders tried to make up their minds on the matter, Shiblī's men occupied all the heights around Bayt al-Dīn and cut the water supply of the palace. By the end of November ʿUmar Pasha and the Turkish garrison in Bayt al-Dīn were surrounded, and an attempt on their part to break through the siege was successfully repelled. Asʿad Pasha, who now replaced Muṣṭafā Pasha in Beirut, was alarmed by the

Druze success and sent emissaries to negotiate the withdrawal of Shiblī al-ʿAryān from the Shūf. The Druze leader, however, refused to withdraw before certain specific conditions were met: the Druze chiefs under arrest were to be set free; Mount Lebanon was to be made immune from conscription and disarmament, and to be exempted from taxation for a period of three years; ʿUmar Pasha was to be immediately dismissed. Asʿad Pasha was in no mood to accept conditions from the Druzes; the audacity of Shiblī al-ʿAryān, moreover, aroused his fury. In a final attempt to vindicate Ottoman authority, he sent a body of Turkish and Albanian troops with some pieces of artillery to Dayr al-Qamar to take the Druze forces from the rear; ʿUmar Pasha, meanwhile, was instructed to make a second sortie and attack them from the front.

The Druzes were unable to resist the double attack single-handed. Shiblī al-ʿAryān, until this moment, was still expecting to receive help from the Christians, whose leaders had just met in Anṭilyās to consider openly joining the Druze insurgents. But Asʿad Pasha, by various promises and concessions, had secured Christian neutrality. Within a few hours of the Turkish attack, the Druze resistance in the Shūf gave way. The leading sheikhs fled to the Ḥawrān, their men dispersed in various directions, and Shiblī al-ʿAryān himself was forced to surrender.[10] Asʿad Pasha followed his victory on 7 December by removing ʿUmar Pasha from Bayt al-Dīn and replacing him there by a certain Muḥammad Pasha. On the same day the Powers and the Porte agreed on a new plan for the government of Lebanon, which was to be put into effect at the start of the new year.

The new plan, suggested by the Austrian Chancellor Prince Metternich, was a compromise between the French and the Ottoman points of view. To France the only proper solution for the Lebanese question was to restore the Emirate to the country, preferably with a Shihāb as emir. This was the point of view of the Lebanese Christians, and it was also supported on the international plane by Austria. But the Porte was completely opposed to the restoration of the Emirate, which would have meant the full reinstatement of Lebanese autonomy; and Britain was unwilling to accept the return of the Shihābs. In the face of the French proposal, the Ottomans insisted on the complete integration of Lebanon in the Ottoman Empire, whereby Mount Lebanon and the adjacent lands would be administered directly by the Pasha of Sidon, now residing in Beirut. The Ottoman plan was backed by Russia, but it was opposed by both France and Britain. As a way out, Prince Metternich proposed his own solution: Mount Lebanon would be divided into two administrative districts, a northern district administered by a Maronite district governor, or *kaymakam*, and a southern district administered by a Druze, while the last word on matters of importance would rest with the Pasha of Sidon. This proposal was immediately accepted by Britain and France, and the Porte finally agreed to implement it.[11] Accordingly, on 1 January 1843, As'ad Pasha appointed Ḥaydar Abū'l-Lam' as kaymakam of the Christian district, while Aḥmad Arslān was released from jail[12] (*see* p. 60) and appointed kaymakam of the Druze district.

From the very beginning the double Kaymakamate presented serious difficulties. It had been instituted on the false assumption that the Beirut–Damascus road divided Mount Lebanon into two distinct parts: a northern part inhabited entirely by Christians, and a southern part inhabited entirely by Druzes. In reality, many Druzes lived among the Christians in the Matn, the southernmost district of the Christian Kaymakamate, while the number of Christians living in the Druze Kaymakamate was more than double that of the Druzes. Of all the Druze districts, the Shūf alone had a Druze majority. Even there, however, the Christians were numerous; and Dayr al-Qamar, in the heart of the Shūf, was the leading Christian town in Lebanon

In the original scheme presented by Metternich, the Christian and Druze kaymakams were to be each responsible for his own co-religionists. This, in practice, meant that no strict boundary between the two administrative districts would be possible, and that in the Druze Kaymakamate, in particular, the authority of the Christian kaymakam would conflict with that of the Druze feudal chiefs. To overcome this difficulty the Porte decided to limit the jurisdiction of each kaymakam to his own territory, thus depriving the Christians in the Druze districts from the right of appeal to a Christian authority in judicial and fiscal matters. France, as the defender of the Christians, opposed the Porte's decision; Britain, however, approved of the Ottoman arrangement, as she was anxious to safeguard the rights of the Druze aristocracy. Meanwhile Russia demanded the establishment of a third Kaymakamate for the Lebanese Greek Orthodox, who felt that their number was large enough to justify their recognition as a separate entity.

The establishment of the double Kaymakamate in Lebanon was in itself a source of difficulty; in the words of a contemporary observer, it was the formal organization of civil war in the country. Other difficulties, however, arose from the manner in which the new system was applied. There was indeed no problem in choosing the Christian kaymakam, as Ḥaydar Abū'l-Lamʿ was obviously the man best suited for that position: he came from the second princely family in Lebanon, and he was known to be a moderate man uninterested in partisan politics. It was not easy, on the other hand, to choose the Druze kaymakam. The British suggested for the position their own protégé Saʿīd Janbalāṭ, who was, in fact, the most powerful Druze chief. But the choice of a Janbalāṭ as kaymakam meant first that free rein would be given to British influence in the Druze districts, and second that the Yazbakī Druzes would be so alienated as to make common cause with the Christians against the kaymakam; the Ottomans looked with alarm on either contingency. Asʿad Pasha, therefore, decided to let the Druzes settle the matter on their own, and he called upon the Druze chiefs who were still under arrest in Beirut to choose a kaymakam among them. After some deliberation, the choice fell on the emir Aḥmad Arslān, whose princely family ranked highest in the Druze feudal hierarchy although it was surpassed in influence by the Janbalāts. The Arslāns, until then, had remained aloof from the Yazbakī-Janbalāṭī rivalry, and this further recommended the choice of Aḥmad as kaymakam. Before the choice was made final, however, a special agreement was reached between Aḥmad Arslān and the heads of the five Druze sheikhly families[13], whereby the latter promised the chosen kaymakam their full support, while he promised in return to guarantee the privileges and interests of the Druze feudal aristocracy.[14] True to his word, Aḥmad Arslān voluntarily returned to jail each night after his appointment to consult with his colleagues and do their bidding.

The Christian and Druze kaymakams had hardly assumed their

administrative functions when fresh difficulties began to appear. No sooner was Aḥmad Arslān in office than he began to urge the full confirmation of Druze feudal rights and the immediate release of the interned Druze chiefs. So strongly did he insist on these demands that he was removed from office and thrown back into jail three days after his appointment. On 14 January, however, he was reinstated in his position, as no other Druze would agree to replace him. Such solidarity was not to be found among the Christians. For several months after the appointment of Ḥaydar Abū'l-Lamʿ as Christian kaymakam the Maronite feudal chiefs of Kisrawān and of northern Lebanon, coveting his position, refused to acknowledge his authority. It was only upon the intercession of Asʿad Pasha and the French Consul that they finally agreed to give him grudging recognition. Meanwhile other difficulties had arisen. As a concession to the Greek Orthodox demand for a separate Kaymakamate, Asʿad Pasha changed the title of Ḥaydar Abū'l-Lamʿ from 'kaymakam of the Christians' to 'kaymakam of the Maronites'; and he dealt a further blow to Ḥaydar's prestige by detaching the large and populous district of Jubayl from his authority, on the grounds that this district had never formed an integral part of Mount Lebanon.[15] In retaliation, Ḥaydar not only protested against the reduction of his authority but also stressed the unity of the Christian cause in Lebanon and claimed full jurisdiction over all Christians in the country, including those living in the Druze districts. This claim was supported by the French Consul Prosper Bourée; it was strongly opposed, however, by Aḥmad Arslān and by Colonel Rose, both of whom maintained the principle of territorial jurisdiction. Asʿad Pasha tried his best to settle the matter by mutual concessions; when he did not succeed, he turned the question over to Istanbul and, as a temporary measure, placed the Druzes of the Christian Kaymakamate and the Christians of the Druze Kaymakamate under his own jurisdiction.

Responding to Asʿad Pasha's appeal, the Porte now sent an officer of the highest rank on a special mission to Lebanon, the Admiral of the Fleet, Khalīl Pasha; the Powers, it was hoped, would thus be impressed by the Ottoman eagerness to settle the Lebanese question. As a further show of goodwill, France and Austria were given to understand that the Shihāb Emirate in

Lebanon might be restored should Khalīl Pasha deem that advisable. This raised the expectations of the Shihāb partisans in Lebanon, among both the Christians and the Yazbakī Druzes. But when Khalīl Pasha arrived in Beirut in June 1844 he immediately made it clear that no petitions in favour of the Shihābs would be considered. Their partisans, nevertheless, continued to look forward to their restoration, placing their hopes in Amīn Shihāb, son of the exiled Bashīr II. On the international plane, France was especially active in her efforts to win support for the Shihāb cause, particularly from Britain. But the Ottomans proved insensitive to pressure, and finally the conversion of Amīn Shihāb to Islam in 1845 put an end to the last hopes of a Shihāb restoration.

Meanwhile Kahlīl Pasha settled the question of jurisdiction in Lebanon. In each of the mixed districts there were to be two agents (*wakīl*, pl. *wukalā'*), one Christian and one Druze, chosen by their respective communities with the approval of the local kaymakam, but each responsible to the kaymakam of his own sect. Each *wakīl* was to have judicial authority of the first instance over his co-religionists, and to collect taxes from them on behalf of the feudal chiefs of the district; mixed cases involving Christians and Druzes were to be heard by the two agents jointly. The town of Dayr al-Qamar was to enjoy a special status: while its district, the Manāṣif, was in the feudal domain of the Abū Nakads[16] (*see* p. 10), the town itself was to be free of feudal authority, and to have a Druze and a Christian *wakīl* of its own. Each *wakīl*, as in the mixed districts, was to be responsible to the kaymakam of his own sect; neither the Druze nor the Christian kaymakam could, however, reside in the town or have representatives there. In addition to settling the question of jurisdiction, Khalīl Pasha fixed at three thousand five hundred purses[17] the indemnity which the Druzes were to pay to the Christians for losses suffered in 1841. He finally announced his decision to the Druze and Christian leaders on 2 September 1844. The question of the Jubayl district had already been settled by reintegrating it in the Christian Kaymakamate in April 1843; in addition, the almost entirely Christian district of B'abdā, which As'ad Pasha had been administering directly, was now placed under the authority of Ḥaydar Abū'l-Lam'.

No doubt, Khalīl Pasha and As'ad Pasha were honest in their

attempts to make the system of the double Kaymakamate work. As'ad Pasha in particular tried to moderate the more extreme Druze and Maronite points of view, and to prevent serious misunderstandings from developing. But for any system to work in Lebanon it was necessary to ensure some co-operation between the leading communities in the country; and such co-operation did not, at the time, exist. The Druze chiefs, encouraged by Colonel Rose, saw in the arrangements of Khalīl Pasha an encroachment on their own authority, for the *wakīl* in the mixed districts usurped the judicial prerogative of the feudal families and shared their function as tax-collectors. Accordingly, the Druze feudal chiefs insisted that the new arrangements should be laid aside and the original decisions of 7 December 1842 be enforced; they moreover refused to pay the indemnity due to the Christians until the latter returned under their jurisdiction. The Christians, in response, 'excited by their clergy, talked loudly of the intolerable yoke of Druze oppression, and declared their determination never to submit to it again'.[18]

Khalīl Pasha was still in Lebanon when, on 2 February 1845, the Druze chiefs held a general meeting in Mukhtāra, the seat of the Janbalāṭs. The meeting was attended by the Janbalaṭī chiefs and by representatives of the leading Yazbakīs; the two Druze factions, it seemed, were uniting for some serious action. This seriously alarmed the Christians and forced them to take their precautions. 'The blow must be struck . . ., he who strikes first will have two chances to one in his favour,' the Maronite Patriarch allegedly declared.[19] There were large Christian gatherings in the district of B'abdā, outside Beirut, where members of the Shihāb family assumed the Christian leadership. In other parts of the country Christian forces were organized by veterans of the 1840–41 risings, like Abū Samra Ghānim and Yūsuf al-Shantīrī, and by Ghandūr al-Sa'd, the leading Christian sheikh of the Jurd.[20] The French and Austrian Consuls were gravely concerned about the Druze reunion in Mukhtāra and its possible consequences, although Colonel Rose assured them that the Druze sheikhs, with whom he was in close contact, were only meeting to settle some financial matters. As for Khalīl Pasha and As'ad Pasha, they rushed reinforcements to the Shūf to forestall the possibility of a clash between Maronites and Druzes, while As'ad Pasha hurried to Dayr al-Qamar in person to reassure the Christians and warn the Druzes.

To many contemporary observers it seemed that As'ad Pasha's zeal was appreciated neither by Istanbul nor by the influential Colonel Rose, who thought the Pasha was partial to the Christians. It was not long, indeed, before As'ad Pasha was recalled from his position and replaced as Pasha of Sidon by a certain Wajīhī Pasha, who arrived in Beirut on 9 April. As'ad Pasha, however, had no sooner been recalled than the situation in Lebanon began quickly to deteriorate; by the time his successor arrived clashes between Druzes and Maronites were already taking place. There were assassinations and reprisals, while 'both parties issued their proclamations, and distributed their outposts, like two opposing armies entering into a campaign'.[21] To Khalīl Pasha, who was due to leave Lebanon on 2 May, it was clear that his mission had failed; as he prepared for departure the situation in the country became steadily worse, until it finally assumed the proportions of a civil war.

This time, unlike the case in 1841, the Christians and the Druzes were equally prepared for action, and it was the Christians who on many occasions struck the first blow. As before, however, the Christians did not present a united front. The Greek Orthodox, under the influence of their clergy and the Russian Consul, refused to make a common stand with the Maronites, and even tended to support the Druzes against them; the Maronites, for their part, exhibited their usual lack of co-ordination, each of their leaders acting as he pleased. Jealous of the authority of Ḥaydar Abū'l-Lam', the Maronite sheikhs of the Kisrawān and of northern Lebanon were disinclined to join in a movement of which the kaymakam was the recognized head, and preferred to stand aside. Even Yūsuf Karam of Ihdin, whose shows of bravado were becoming a feature of Maronite politics at the time, failed to appear on the scenes of combat.[22] A further disadvantage to the Christian position was the attitude of Wajīhī Pasha, which was one of obvious encouragement to the Druzes. Once the armed conflict started in earnest Wajīhī Pasha took up a position on the Beirut–Damascus road, not far from the Druze town of 'Ālay,[23] and from there calmly watched the fighting go on. When he did interfere it was only to obstruct the movement of the Christians, while the Druzes were left to roam the country in complete freedom.

Despite all difficulties, however, the Christians managed for a time to hold their own. It was they, in fact, who started the attack in the Shūf, where the first serious clashes took place in April. Led by Abū Samra Ghānim, the Christians of the Jazzīn district advanced northwards through the Shūf to attack Mukhtāra, where large numbers of Druzes had gathered under the leadership of the Janbalāṭs. On their way they attacked and burnt no less than fourteen Druze villages. When they reached Mukhtāra the Druzes in the town offered no effective resistance; the Christian advance, however, was stopped by 'a rolling fire of musketry' from a Turkish regiment drawn up in front of the Janbalāṭ palace.[24] Meanwhile in the Gharb, the Shaḥḥār and Bʿabdā, the Christians, incompetently led by various Shihāb emirs, were totally routed in a fierce encounter at ʿAbay. The Shihāb emirs themselves were forced to surrender as prisoners, and were thereupon conducted to Beirut by none other than Colonel Rose.

All along, desultory fighting had gone on in the Matn. The Christians of the district, helped by co-religionists from Zahleh, began the attack there by burning and looting a number of Druze villages. The Druzes were quick to retaliate, surprising and defeating their assailants while the latter were distracted by the plunder. Soon, however, the Christians attacked again, forcing the Druzes to take shelter in the town of Qarnāyil where they were blockaded. A Turkish force, sent by Wajīhī Pasha, relieved the Druzes in Qarnāyil and repelled the Christian attack. But it was not long before the Druzes found themselves again on the defensive, the Christians driving their forces out of the Matn and pursuing them into the Gharb. Considering the small number of the Druzes in the Matn, their defeat by the Christians was not surprising. But here, as in Mukhtāra, Turkish troops opened fire on the Christians and stopped them from following the Druzes into ʿĀlay. By late May, the Turkish interference had completely changed the situation. Backed by the Turks, it was the Druzes who now took the offensive in the Matn, routing the Christian forces at the village of Rās al-Matn and pursuing them as they fled through the other towns and villages of the district. Wherever the Druzes passed, Christian villages and towns were looted and burned; 'then comes the old story of villages in flames, property destroyed, and Christian fugitives pursued by Druzes and Turkish irregulars, plundered, mutilated, and slain.'[25]

Under heavy pressure from the European consuls, Wajīhī Pasha finally agreed to intervene and stop the fighting, and on his summons the Druze and Christian leaders met in Beirut on 2 June. Both sides were eager to end the hostilities; but agreement between them was difficult to reach. On arriving in Beirut the Druze chiefs were warmly received by the British and the Russian Consuls. The Consuls, like Wajīhī Pasha, laid all the blame for the events on the Christians, and accused the Christian kaymakam Ḥaydar Abū'l-Lamʿ and the Shihāb emirs of the major responsibility. Colonel Rose, for his part, insisted that the leading members of the Shihāb family should be sent into exile; and he gave every assurance to the Druze chiefs that the original agreement of 7 December 1842 regarding the administration of Lebanon would be applied to the letter, and in their favour. At the same time, Rose did his best to embarrass the position of the Christian kaymakam by encouraging the other Christian leaders who had come to Beirut to oppose him; he also urged the Christians of the Jazzīn district to demand the replacement of Aḥmad Arslān by Saʿīd Janbalāṭ as Druze kaymakam. Meanwhile the French Consul, Eugène Poujade, steadily encouraged the Christians; in the interest of unity, he urged Ḥaydar Abū'l-Lamʿ to placate his rivals, the sheikhs of the Kisrawān and of northern Lebanon, by conceding them the right to administer their own districts. Well aware of Wajīhī Pasha's partiality to the Druzes, the French Consul demanded his immediate recall and the return of Asʿad Pasha to Lebanon.

The Druze and Christian leaders in Beirut were still in disagreement, and the mixed districts in the country were still ravaged by civil war, when the Ottoman Foreign Minister Shakīb Efendi, under pressure from the Powers, finally arrived in Lebanon to effect a settlement on the spot. The Porte made it clear that there would be no departure from the system of the double Kaymakamate adopted in 1842, but only minor rearrangements to make the system workable. Hence, before leaving Istanbul, Shakīb Efendi sent out a memorandum to the ambassadors of the five Powers (Britain, France, Austria, Russia and Prussia), setting out the broad lines of the settlement he had in mind and notifying them of the measures he intended to take upon his arrival in Lebanon: pending a settlement, the country would be temporarily occupied by Ottoman troops, a general disarmament would be effected, a part of the indemnity due to the Christians would be distributed among them, and the European consuls would be required not to meddle in the country's affairs.

Shakīb Efendi was true to his word, particularly in dealing with the European consuls. Shortly after his arrival in Beirut on 14 September, he summoned them to a meeting and urged them not to interfere any more in local matters. He also insisted that all Europeans resident in Mount Lebanon, Catholic and Protestant missionaries included, should be recalled to Beirut for the time being. Shakīb Efendi then proceeded to place under arrest the most important Lebanese leaders of both sects, including the Druze and Christian kaymakams, in order to forestall any resistance to the measures he intended to take. A decree followed removing Aḥmad Arslān from his position as Druze kaymakam and replacing him by his brother Amīn; Ḥaydar Abū'l-Lamʿ remained Christian kaymakam, mainly because his removal would have opened the way for the partisans of the Shihābs to press their claims. Next Shakīb Efendi supervised the disarmament of the country, effectively carried out by Wamīq Pasha who commanded the forces of occupation; two thousand purses were meanwhile distributed among the Christians as part of the indemnity due to them. Once these and other secondary matters had been attended to, Shakīb Efendi went on to settle the question of the country's administration and to publish the organic law which became known by his name. The *Règlement* of Shakīb Efendi, as it was called, was communicated to the European consuls on 29 October, and its provisions were to become immediately effective.

Lebanon was to remain divided into a Druze and a Christian Kaymakamate, each headed by a kaymakam appointed and removable by the Pasha of Sidon. To assist him each kaymakam was to have a council (*majlis*) over which he would preside, composed of a deputy kaymakam, a judge and an adviser for each of the Sunnite, Maronite, Druze, Greek Orthodox, and Greek Catholic sects, and an adviser for the Shiʿites. As the Ottomans recognized no separate Shi'ite magistracy, the Sunnite judge was empowered to act for both sects. Initially Shakīb Efendi appointed the members of both councils for life, but as positions on either council became vacant new members were to be appointed by the religious heads of the sects concerned. All appointments required the agreement of the kaymakam and the members of the council in question, and the formal approval of the Pasha of Sidon. Once appointed, a council member was to devote his time fully to the affairs of the council, and in return he was to receive a fixed monthly salary.

The council in each Kaymakamate had two main functions: it decided on the assessment, distribution, and collection of taxes, and it heard such judicial cases as the kaymakam referred to it. In principle the council voted by sects, the representatives of each religious community having reached agreement before casting their vote; scarcely any cases, however, were decided by voting. Fiscal matters required the unanimous agreement of all advisers on the council, who assessed the taxes jointly. In the absence of unanimity the Pasha of Sidon could take any decision he pleased. Cases of judicial appeal, however, were not settled by unanimous decision, but by the judge of the sect to which the contending parties belonged. When the case involved parties of different sects, it was jointly considered by the judges of the sects concerned.

By instituting the Kaymakamate councils, the *Règlement* of Shakīb Efendi dealt a severe blow to the feudal system in Lebanon. The functions it vested in these councils had previously been those of the feudal chiefs, now left in their respective districts with little more than the authority to judge cases of the first instance and carry out the fiscal decisions of the council. Even this limited authority, in the mixed districts, remained in the hands of the Druze and Christian *wakīls*, who were maintained in these districts as sectarian agents responsible to the local kaymakam[26] (*see* pp. 66–7). The *Règlement*, however, was also important in other respects. The autonomous institutions with which it endowed Lebanon were significant in two ways: externally, they implied the formal recognition by the Porte of the country's special status; domestically, they marked the first step towards modernizing the country's administration. The kaymakam and the members of his *majlis*, who in each Kaymakamate replaced in authority the governing emir and the feudal sheikhs, were in fact public officials formally appointed by the Pasha of Sidon, and received regular pay for full-time service. Such administrative improvements were in keeping with the principles of the Ottoman *tanzimat* announced in 1839 by the *Hatt-i-Sherif* of Gülhane. But also in keeping with the *tanzimat*, in their emphasis on centralization, were the wide powers reserved for the Pasha of Sidon. Indeed, while formally taking into account the special status of Lebanon, the *Règlement* of Shakīb Efendi placed the country more than ever before under the authority of the Pasha of Sidon. The Pasha was given the last word in all public appointments, apart from being made directly responsible for the government of Dayr al-Qamar. In addition to these administrative rearrangements, Shakīb Efendi partitioned the disputed district of Bʿabdā between the Christian and the Druze Kaymakamates; finally, before leaving Beirut, he replaced Wajīhī Pasha by Wamīq Pasha in the vilayet of Sidon.

The *Règlement* of Shakīb Efendi on paper seemed easy enough to apply, but it was a different matter in practice. The Christians of the Druze districts, like the Druzes of the Christian districts, found their situation in no way improved by the new arrangements and continued to complain; meanwhile the feudal families throughout Lebanon recognized the new system as a threat to their position and tried in every way to obstruct it. Immediately upon Shakīb Efendi's return to Istanbul, the Christian and Druze feudal sheikhs began to revert to the old ways and to revive old fiscal abuses, much to the distress of the peasants. To enforce the modern methods envisaged by the *Règlement*, it was necessary first to organize a cadastral survey of the country and a census; both these measures, however, proved difficult to carry out. Amīn Efendi, sent from Istanbul to organize the cadastral survey of Lebanon in 1847, abandoned the project three years later because of obstruction by the feudal sheikhs. Likewise, an attempt to organize a census ended in failure. The Christian and Druze sheikhs were determined to resist all administrative changes which threatened to reduce their power in the country, and it was strongly suspected that the British and Russian Consulates backed their determination. Indeed, with the departure of Shakīb Efendi from Lebanon, the European Consulates in Beirut resumed their activity in Lebanon with renewed vigour. France in particular was anxious to see the *Règlement* of Shakīb Efendi put into effect; and while the French Consul in Beirut encouraged all efforts in that direction, it seemed to him that his British and Russian colleagues were doing their utmost to obstruct the proper working of the new system.

The new divisions which appeared after 1845 within the Christian and Druze ranks provided further room for consular interference. Among the Christians the mutual opposition between the Maronites and the Greek Orthodox did not cease, but it gradually came to be overshadowed by a rift within the Maronite ranks. Until his death in 1845 Patriarch Yūsuf Ḥubaysh, had managed to keep the Maronites united under his leadership; his successor, Yūsuf al-Khāzin, lacking his force of character, was unable to check the growing rift between the Maronite peasants and feudal chiefs. The Maronite priests and bishops, who were mainly of peasant stock, naturally sided with the peasants against the feudal chiefs. But Yūsuf al-Khāzin himself, like his predecessor, came from a leading sheikhly family, and while he remained patriarch his clergy did not openly align themselves with the peasants. Meanwhile the conciliatory Ḥaydar Abū'l-Lamʿ, as Christian kaymakam, managed to keep the situation in the Maronite districts under control. In 1854, however, both Yūsuf al-Khāzin and Ḥaydar Abū'l-Lamʿ died. The former was succeeded as patriarch by Būlus Masʿad, a vigorous man of forty-eight and a peasant by origin, who was known for his intense religious zeal and his strong dislike of the feudal class. This meant that henceforth the Maronite clergy were finally allied with the peasants. As for Ḥaydar Abū'l-Lamʿ, his succession was to be the cause of further division among the Maronites, between the partisans of his nephew Bashīr ʿAssāf Abū'l-Lamʿ and those of his kinsman Bashīr Aḥmad Abū'l-Lamʿ. Bashīr ʿAssāf, a man 'universally allowed to be wanting in the requisite qualities', was temporarily appointed kaymakam upon his uncle's death on 11 May, and remained in the position until Wamīq Pasha and the British and French consuls agreed to replace him by Bashīr Aḥmad in August. This Bashīr Aḥmad had been born a Druze and was known to have been an Ottoman agent. The ʿAssāfīs, as the partisans of Bashīr ʿAssāf were called, refused to recognize him as kaymakam and declared him to be only nominally a Christian. The opposition between them and the Aḥmadīs, who supported Bashīr Aḥmad, added further complication to the affairs of the Christian Kaymakamate.

While divisions between peasants and feudal chiefs, Aḥmadīs and ʿAssāfīs, were rending the Christian ranks in the Kisrawān and north Lebanon, the Druzes in the southern districts were realigning themselves with the Yazbakī or the Janbalāṭī faction. Shortly after 1845 there was a rift within the Janbalāṭī party between the brothers Nuʿmān and Saʿīd Janbalāṭ. Earlier, in 1842, the elder brother, Nuʿmān, had quietly retired from the political scene, leaving the Janbalāṭī leadership to the more ambitious and capable Saʿīd; and it was not long before Saʿīd managed to establish his position as the paramount Druze chief and the leader of the Druze movement against the Christians. But Saʿīd's growing prestige soon aroused the concern of the Yazbakī chiefs, who began to regroup themselves in opposition under the leadership of Nāṣīf Abū Nakad. Even more seriously concerned were the Ottoman Pasha and the French Consul in Beirut, who saw in the increased power of Saʿīd Janbalāṭ an immoderate advantage to the influence of his British patrons in Lebanon. To counterbalance this advantage the Ottomans and the French, acting each on their own, encouraged the regrouping of the Yazbakīs; and it may be that they also went a step further and encouraged Nuʿmān Janbalāṭ to reclaim the family leadership from his brother Saʿīd. Whatever the case, it was to the French Consulate that Nuʿmān turned for assistance in 1846 when the rift between him and Saʿīd was at its worst. But it seems that by then the French already realized that the cause of the gentle and irresolute Nuʿmān Janbalāṭ was a lost one, and they offered him little more than their sympathy. Left without support, Nuʿmān finally renounced his claims to the Janbalāṭī leadership and retired to obscurity, leaving his brother Saʿīd stronger than ever.

The success of Saʿīd Janbalāṭ and the final retirement of his brother Nuʿmān was a triumph for Colonel Rose and the British influence, and in vain did the Ottomans and the French try to reduce this triumph by intriguing against the Janbalāṭī ascendancy. At the command of Saʿīd Janbalāṭ was the main body of the Druzes, who stood as a solid block, confident of their leader and of British support. The Yazbakī party, on the other hand, remained little more than a loose association of feudal chiefs bound by a common opposition to Saʿīd Janbalāṭ, and it scarcely enjoyed any popular backing. There were even some among the chiefs of the Yazbakīs, like the Talḥūqs and the ʿAbd al-Maliks, who wavered in their loyalty. To oppose the British-backed Janbalāṭīs, the Ottomans apparently resolved to have the Druze kaymakam himself lead the opposition to Saʿīd Janbalāṭ. Accordingly, in 1849, Amīn Arslān rejected the agreement which his brother Aḥmad had signed with the Druze chiefs in December 1842. By the terms of this agreement, the Druze kaymakam could take no serious action without the consent of his feudal colleagues; Amīn Arslān, however, claimed that unlike his brother Aḥmad he had been appointed to his position directly by Shakīb Efendi, not elected to it by his fellow Druze chiefs. The pretensions of the kaymakam provoked a strong reaction from Saʿīd Janbalāṭ who, as supreme Druze chief, had been guaranteed a dominant influence by the 1842 agreement. No sooner had Amīn Arslān rejected the agreement than the Janbalāṭīs spread the word that the kaymakam was not strictly a Druze – which seemed true, because he and other members of his family practised Islam by *taqiyya* (*see* p. xvii). The kaymakamate of the Druze districts, so the word was passed, should be held by a Druze; Saʿīd Janbalāṭ was obviously the man for the position.

The Ottoman opposition to Saʿīd Janbalāṭ, immediately turned the Druzes against them, and between 1849 and 1852 Druze turbulence and insubordination were to cause the Ottoman authorities in Beirut considerable annoyance. Meanwhile, the superior airs assumed by Amīn Arslān brought together the Yazbakī and Janbalāṭī chiefs in common opposition to the kaymakam; and the Druze confederacy thus formed became like a 'little independent republic'[27] allied with Britain.

> Each of the great families reigned supreme in its district. The Christians living amongst them were entirely under their control. Their kaymakam, with forces at his disposal utterly inadequate to make his authority respected, was content to receive from the sheikhs a purely nominal obedience . . . The Turkish authorities held no jurisdiction whatever. Their orders had to be conveyed through the kaymakam, and were, consequently, obeyed or not, according to the temper and

> fancy of those to whom they were transmitted . . . As every successive year seemed to assure the Druze sheikhs of increased confirmation of their power, and irresponsibility for their actions, they continued to indulge in a freedom and licence which set all restraint at defiance. Charged with collecting the imperial revenues, they appropriated them to their own uses. Houses were built, lands purchased, crown property farmed, horses gorgeously caparisoned, all surreptitiously out of the coffers of the state. Though repeatedly called to account, they always contrived to postpone, and then altogether to evade, the day of reckoning. If their kaymakam, in despair of these long arrears of taxes . . . ventured to send horsemen amongst them intreating even an instalment, be it ever so small, of their dues, they were either allowed free quarters until, tired with bootless expectation, they took their departure; or, in case of disagreeable pertinacity, unceremoniously ejected.[28]

As the abusive rule of the Druze feudal chiefs bore heavily on the Christians in their districts, the French Consulate openly urged that these districts be taken away from their Druze masters and placed, like Dayr al-Qamar, under Turkish governors appointed by the Pasha of Sidon. This suggestion was never seriously considered by the Porte; nevertheless, it increased the Druzes' wariness of Ottoman and French intervention and made them more dependent on British support.

The climax of Druze antagonism against the Turks came in 1852. The Porte in that year called for a general conscription of the Druzes, and this provoked an immediate reaction. Leaving their villages and fields in the late spring, the Druzes, as usual, came together in bands and retired to the rugged highlands of Wādī al-Taym and the Ḥawrān, where they declared rebellion. Ottoman troops were immediately sent against them; but the insurgents successfully repelled the Turkish attack and proceeded to block the roads from Beirut and the Ḥawrān to Damascus. Unable to deal with the Druzes alone, the Ottoman authorities tried, in the manner of Ibrāhīm Pasha, to incite the Lebanese Christians against them. Here the French Consul in Beirut interfered, urging the Christians in Lebanon not to get themselves involved in a sectarian struggle which could only bring them harm; accordingly, only a few minor incidents took place in which Maronites and Druzes clashed. By autumn the Ottomans changed their tactics, and the insurgents were left in peace.

Shortly afterwards, the British Consulate in Beirut arranged for a reconciliation between the Ottoman authorities and the Druze chiefs, and the Druze rebels were allowed freely to return to their homes.

After 1852, the policy which the Ottomans followed with the Druzes became different. Unsuccessful in opposing Sa'īd Janbalāṭ and the British influence, the Ottoman authorities in Beirut turned their backs on the French Consulate and began eagerly to cultivate the friendship of the Druzes, keeping Amīn Arslān in the kaymakamate while they espoused the cause of Sa'īd Janbalāṭ. A first indication of the revived Ottoman-Druze friendship came in 1853, when a Druze contingent of three thousand men was organized under the leadership of Amīn Arslān himself to take part in the Crimean War. The fact that the contingent, as a body, never left Lebanon did not seriously affect the improved relations between the two sides. Four years later, in September 1857, the appointment of Khūrshīd Pasha in Beirut was to bring the Ottomans and the Druzes even closer together, for the new Pasha from the start made every effort to attract the Druzes to the Ottoman side by a discreet show of sympathy and encouragement.

By the end of 1857 the situation in Lebanon was extremely complex. In the southern districts the tyranny of the Druze chiefs and their agents had brought the antagonism between Christians and Druzes almost to the point of crisis. Here the British supported the Druzes while the French supported the Christians. In the northern districts, however, the situation was no less tense. There the Maronite peasantry and clergy stood clearly opposed to the feudal families, the British aiding the latter while the French, and to a lesser extent the Austrians, threw their weight on the side of the former. At the same time, the French backed the kaymakam in power and his supporters the Aḥmadī party, while the British backed the 'Assāfīs. The Turks, meanwhile, encouraged the divisions in the Christian Kaymakamate and shifted their support from one side to another as the occasion required. The Lebanese question, indeed, had become so involved that scarcely an incident took place which did not have repercussions in the chanceries of Europe, particularly in London and Paris. A Lebanese chief complained:

Our affairs have become the concern of Britain and France. If one man hits another the incident becomes an Anglo-French affair, and there might even be trouble between the two countries if a cup of coffee gets spilt on the ground.[29]

CHAPTER V

LEBANON IN TURMOIL 1858–60

THE UNREST which had distracted Lebanon since the downfall of Bashīr II reached its climax in 1858–60 in a general outburst of violence which affected nearly every part of the country. In the Kisrawān, Maronite peasants revolted against Maronite feudal sheikhs, supported by an ambitious clergy jealous of feudal power. In the Shūf, the Biqā' and Wādī al-Taym, Druze villagers and townsmen, led by their feudal chiefs and encouraged by their *'uqqāl* (*see* p. xviii), attacked and massacred their Christian neighbours in a last effort to reassert a vanishing Druze ascendancy. The crisis in both cases was essentially an internal upheaval, the product of social and sectarian tensions which had long been developing in the country. Other factors, however, were also involved. Inside the country the impact of personalities was important, particularly in the case of the Maronite Patriarch Būlus Mas'ad and his leading bishops. Externally, the rivalry between British, French, and other European interests in Lebanon was perhaps equally important; so was the pro-Druze activity of Khūrshīd Pasha in Beirut, and the general atmosphere of religious fanaticism which then pervaded the whole Ottoman Empire. It was indeed by a combination of these and other related factors that the nature and course of the Lebanese disturbances were determined, from the first stirrings among the Kisrawān peasants in the autumn of 1857 until the final settlement of the crisis in 1861.

The events which led to the Kisrawān peasant revolt of 1858 had begun four years earlier, in 1854, when Bashīr Aḥmad Abū'l-Lam' succeeded his kinsman Ḥaydar Abū'l-Lam' as Christian kaymakam (*see* p. 74). The British and French Consuls had both, at the time, agreed to his appointment, their opinion being that

Bashīr Aḥmad was the only member of his family fit to replace the dead Ḥaydar in the kaymakamate. Among his own people, however, Bashīr Aḥmad was reputed to be a venal and unscrupulous intriguer and an agent of the Turks, and his appointment by Wamīq Pasha did not meet with general approval.

The new kaymakam, to be sure, proved a good administrator:

His régime was devoted to justice, and he set about restoring rights which had been trampled and abandoned. He restrained the strong from harming the weak by his bravery and great courage . . .[1]

But the kaymakam's harsh methods did not please his countrymen. Pious Maronites were suspicious of his Christianity because he was born a Druze, and the clergy were disturbed by his lack of attachment to the church. The Greek Orthodox were also dissatisfied with his rule, especially as they coveted the Kaymakamate for one of their own sect.

It was, however, the Khāzins, feudal masters of the Kisrawān, who most resented his appointment. These powerful sheikhs, despite their inferior title, did not recognize the Abū'l-Lamʿ emirs as social superiors, and they strongly objected to the distinguished status which became their lot after the fall of the Shihābs. The proposal, in 1842, to replace the Shihābs by the Abū'l-Lamʿs in the Emirate of Lebanon had met with loud remonstrance from the Khāzins; the Khāzin sheikhs, in that same year, had likewise objected to the appointment of Ḥaydar Abū'l-Lamʿ as Christian kaymakam, and they continually refused him obedience until 1845. When, following the death of Ḥaydar, another Abu'l-Lamʿ was chosen to succeed him, the anger of the Khāzins knew no bounds. The Abū'l-Lamʿs, it seemed, were being established as a new ruling dynasty and given precedence over all the other feudal families.

Relations between the Khāzins and Bashīr Aḥmad did not improve in the years that followed the latter's appointment. Soon the Khāzins and other Maronite feudal families found the new kaymakam 'invading their rights, assailing their privileges, and assuming the exercise of his own direct functions in matters which for ages had been referred to them alone.'[1] Such high-handed treatment of their feudal interests greatly added to the displeasure of the Maronite aristocracy, and caused their resentment of the kaymakam to increase. Meanwhile, as the Khāzins and their feudal colleagues became more dissatisfied with his rule, Bashīr Aḥmad turned to the Maronite clergy and commoners and tried to win their support by posing as the champion of the Roman Catholic faith. The French and Austrian consulates apparently encouraged him in this policy. Whatever the case, the kaymakam soon began to incite the Maronites against the Greek Orthodox, and permitted a number of incidents to occur in which Greek Orthodox Christians suffered harsh or unjust treatment at the hands of Maronites. When it became clear that Bashīr Aḥmad was turning for support to the Maronite clergy and the French and Austrian Consulates, the British Consulate, which had earlier agreed to his appointment, turned openly against him, throwing its weight on the side of his opponent Bashīr ʻAssāf Abū'l-Lamʻ who claimed the kaymakamate for himself (*see* p. 74). Within a short time the Khāzin and Ḥubaysh sheikhs, along with the other feudal families of the Christian Kaymakamate, had joined Bashīr ʻAssāf in common opposition to the kaymakam; and while this alliance may not have actually been the work of British agents, as it was then commonly believed to be, it certainly enjoyed British support.

The Maronite feudal sheikhs had indeed been active against Bashīr Aḥmad from the start, so much so that he was forced in 1855, and again in 1856, to take measures against them and place a number of them under arrest. It was possibly at their instigation that the Greek Catholic townsmen of Zahleh rebelled against the kaymakam in 1857, choosing a *shaykh shabāb* (chieftain of youth)[2] and a council of six elders to manage the affairs of the town in defiance of his authority. Bashīr Aḥmad had to go to Zahleh in person to restore a semblance of order there. By their rebellion, however, the townsmen of Zahleh set the example for Christian townsmen elsewhere, particularly in the Kisrawān, where popular risings were soon being organized not against the kaymakam, but against the local feudal sheikhs. It was the kaymakam, now, who was suspected of being the instigator. In Ghazīr, where the first of the Kisrawān risings took place, the townspeople declared a rebellion against their Ḥubaysh sheikhs, renounced their authority and, in the manner of the people of Zahleh, elected a *shaykh shabāb* to manage the affairs of the town. The partisans of the sheikhs rose to defend their masters and clashed with the rebels, opening the way for the kaymakam to intervene and punish both sides.

The Ghazīr incidents, however, were only a start. By the end of 1857 the Ḥubaysh and Khāzin sheikhs had made common cause with Bashīr ʿAssāf and his partisans, and the feudal party was beginning to plan a campaign of agitation against Bashīr Aḥmad. In March 1858 a general feudal rally, bringing together all the opponents of the kaymakam, was held in the village of Zūq al-Kharāb, in the Kisrawān, after which a delegation was sent to complain to the European consuls in Beirut. The delegates drew a petition against the kaymakam and presented it not only to the various European consulates, but also to Khūrshīd Pasha who now replaced Wamīq Pasha in the vilayet of Sidon. While the petition went unanswered, the opponents of Bashīr Aḥmad organized a second rally in the Matn, in the village of Bḥannis, not far from the village of Brummānā where the kaymakam resided. The feudal party this time took such a threatening attitude that Bashīr Aḥmad was forced to escape to Beirut, and only returned to Brummānā upon the orders of Khūrshīd Pasha, and with a company of Ottoman troops to protect him. By now, however, the kaymakam had lost all control over his territory. The Christian districts had fallen into complete confusion, as the feudal sheikhs challenged the authority of the kaymakam while their peasants prepared for rebellion against them. Upon pressure from the British Embassy in Istanbul, the Porte sent a special commission to investigate the situation and consider ways of restoring order,

> but like all Turkish special commissions, especially those extorted by European remonstrance, the mission proved a wilful failure. . . . [The object of the Turks] was to show that no government but their own could possibly succeed in Lebanon, and the more Lebanon plunged into disorder and confusion, the nearer they hoped they were to its attainment.[3]

As it turned out, it was the peasant movement in the Kisrawān, not the feudal rebellion against Bashīr Aḥmad, which was to dominate the events of the next two years in the northern Kaymakamate. In the spring of 1858, while the feudal sheikhs and the partisans of Bashīr ʿAssāf were busy organizing their rallies and drafting their petitions against the kaymakam, the peasants in the various villages of the Kisrawān held their own meetings to discuss their grievances against their landlords. The young men of each village assembled and organized themselves under the leadership of a *shaykh shabāb* in order to defend their community against feudal injustices and the oppression for which the Khāzin family, in particular, had become well known:

> For [the Khāzins] no longer took any account of their subjects, nor even of the leading persons among them. They would say that the peasant and his possessions belonged to them, showing not the slightest regard for him. The most insignificant of the Khāzins would insult the most reputable of the people, not to mention killing or imprisoning them and such like . . .[4]

It was, indeed, in the Khāzin districts of the Kisrawān that the excitement of the peasants against the feudal lords was greatest, and that the movement later took a violent form.

Unaware of the true motive of the peasant gatherings, the Khāzins at first encouraged them, thinking that the peasant bands which were being organized in the various villages would be useful in opposing the kaymakam. It was not long, however, before the true nature of the peasant movement became clear. Towards the end of summer the men of ʿAjaltūn, one of the larger villages on the Khāzin estates, invited their feudal sheikhs to meet with them in their village. The Khāzins accepted the invitation, and the meeting was held in September. But when the villagers of ʿAjaltūn presented the sheikhs with their grievances the latter were completely unresponsive. The villagers assured their feudal masters that they wished them no ill, that they wanted them 'to be as they had been at first, and that they had no thought of doing harm or changing anything'.[5] The Khāzins, however, were unwilling to make any concession, and the meeting finally broke up without having accomplished anything useful. On the contrary, the unfriendly attitude shown by some of the Khāzin sheikhs on that occasion, and the sweeping threats they made against the people further added to the bitterness felt against the feudal lords. Immediately the meeting was over, trouble broke out in a number of villages; led by their *shaykh shabāb*, the men of each village rose to remonstrate against their landlords. In many instances Khāzin sheikhs were attacked and beaten, and a number among them were forced to flee their homes.

Faced with such assault the Khāzins tried to organize themselves for resistance and held several meetings for this purpose, but they were divided in their opinions and could not easily reach agreement. They tried to get support from other Christian feudal families, and also sent messages to the Janbalāṭs, the Talḥūqs, and other Druze feudal sheikhs asking them for help; their efforts in this direction, however, were not successful. At last they reopened negotiations with the peasant leaders and asked them to present their terms. The peasants at first demanded that certain feudal impositions be abolished, and that feudal authority in the district be vested in only three members of the Khāzin family while the rest 'should be equal to the people'. But no sooner had the Khāzins agreed to these terms than the peasants rejected them and proceeded to make more extravagant demands. Attempts at mediation met with no success, for while the Khāzins refused to make any further concessions the demands of the peasants became more and more exorbitant. At this point Ṣāliḥ Ṣfayr, the *shaykh shabāb* of ʿAjaltūn and until then the leader of the peasant movement, became alarmed at the prospect of violence and resigned the leadership. To replace him the peasant chiefs chose Ṭāniyūs Shāhīn of Rayfūn, a half literate farrier of forty-three who, according to some contemporaries, had little to recommend him other than his tall and muscular frame and his violent temper.

Ṭāniyūs Shāhīn agreed to become *shaykh shabāb* of his village and general leader of the peasant movement on his terms.

He then began to behave in a way that had not been expected of him, addressing the Khāzin family in official speeches and arousing the countryside. He seemed to the people to be their redeemer, bringing forth all that they required of whatever sort. He gave them rest from the sheikhs as they desired; he toured from place to place and received the highest acclaim from everyone. In every village he entered, the people would prepare a grand reception for him amid joy and celebration and continuous firing of rifles, as if it were the visit of a ruler to his subjects.[6]

Indeed, the ambitious peasant leader, whom British and French observers at the time described (perhaps uncharitably) as a ruffian of despicable character, was soon assuming superior airs and being addressed by his followers as 'Sheikh' and 'Bey'.

It was shortly after the election of Ṭāniyūs Shāhīn as its leader that the Kisrawān peasant revolt, in January 1859, started in earnest. A convenient excuse for the revolt was found when the Khāzin sheikhs, having lost hope of reaching an agreement with the peasants, appealed to Khūrshid Pasha for intervention. Word was immediately passed around that the Khāzins, in league with the government, were planning the ruin of the Kisrawān; the peasants thereupon met and decided to expel the entire Khāzin family, men, women and children, from the district. This decision was promptly put into action. Led by Ṭāniyūs Shāhīn and by the other village chiefs under his command, the peasants fell on the Khāzins wherever they could be found, chasing them out of their homes and pursuing them as they fled in the direction of Beirut. There were scenes of considerable violence and a certain amount of bloodshed, while the men whom the Khāzins expected to defend them stood by without striking a blow in their defence. Soon it became apparent that Ṭāniyūs Shāhīn and his men enjoyed the moral backing of the Ottoman authorities in Beirut, quite apart from the encouragement of the French Consulate and the ineffective support of the now powerless kaymakam. As the insurrection continued through February a small company of Ottoman troops was quartered on various villages in the Kisrawān, and soon after withdrawn; beyond that Khūrshīd Pasha made no effort to restore order. Meanwhile Patriarch Būlus Masʿad and his leading clergy, who tried to appear openly as mediators, secretly backed the peasant cause, although they remained throughout suspicious of the personal ambitions of Ṭāniyūs Shāhīn.

By the early spring the Khāzins had been completely evicted from the Kisrawān:

> The people then began to strip the possessions of the shaikhs,[7] cutting the forests, breaking into their mansions, and seizing the harvest of silk, wheat, oil, and grapes, and whatever else they could lay their hands on. . . . Whenever they discovered a collaborator of the shaikhs taking anything to his master, they would lay in wait for him, seize whatever he had with him, and insult him. Then at harvest time in the year 1859 the people drew up lists of their belongings that had been taken by the shaikhs, and then proceeded to repossess some of these

properties – and far be it from us to know whether these claims were made in truth or falsehood. Ṭānyūs Shāhīn gathered some of the shaikhs' possessions from the coastal and mountain districts, including silk and wheat, and stored them in his house. . . . He opened the provisions in his house to people going and coming, provided rooms for them to sleep in, distributed arms and ammunition, and behaved as if he were the head of a great household, with the result that his name was spread far and wide. To every village that did not heed his words a crowd of people was sent from the other villages to oblige it to obey. He gave orders for the securing of rights and punishment of wrongdoers in whatever way he saw fit, without opposition, speaking with the authority of the 'republican government'. His prestige became considerable and his commands binding on all.[8]

The success of the peasant movement in the Kisrawān raised the hopes of peasants throughout Lebanon, among others those of the Druze districts. Here, however, special circumstances prevailed. The Druze feudal sheikhs in the Shūf, the Gharb, and the Jurd had among their peasants many who were Druzes, like themselves, and many more who were Christians. As the sectarian hostilities of the previous decade were still remembered in the country, the Druze peasants, distrustful of their Christian neighbours, were reluctant to join them in risings against the Druze sheikhs. In the late summer of 1859 stirrings, it seems, did take place in some Druze villages against the landlords; the latter, however, found no difficulty in keeping the movement under control. The Druze *'uqqāl*, acting on behalf of the landlords, warned the peasant Druzes of the imminence of a Christian danger, counselled them to avoid sedition, and urged them under no condition to renounce their solidarity with their chieftains. In the last days of August an armed affray accidentally took place in the Matn between the Christians and Druzes of Bayt Mirī. This was taken as a timely warning of conflicts to come, and made the Druzes in particular more anxious to maintain a united front.

Circumstances, indeed, were such that the peasant movement in the Druze districts was bound to assume a sectarian character. Anṭūn Dāhir al-'Aqīqī, a contemporary Maronite observer, clearly summarized the situation there in the latter part of 1859:

As hatred continued to grow between the shaikhs and the people [in the Kisrawān], . . . differences arose between the Christians and the

Druses in the area of al-Shūf. The reason for this was that some of the population of that region wished to rid themselves of the landholders . . . and so they embarked on a course of evil deeds. The Druse shaikhs learned of this and resorted to oppressing the people by deceitful means and promoting disturbances between the two sects. A quarrel then arose between the sects, the apparent cause being a collision between two pack-animals one of which was driven by a Christian and the other by a Druse.[9] They and their companions fought and struck each other with lethal weapons and some were injured on both sides. A cry of alarm was raised by both factions, and a battle ensued. . . . Following this discussions were held between the two sects and within each of them. A delegation of priests went to His Beatitude Patriarch Būlus Masʿad, who at that time was Patriarch of the Maronites; he forbade the repetition of this shameful affair. But at this moment His Eminence Bishop Ṭūbiya ʿAun of Beirut encouraged the Christians and protested to the Consuls. Agitation increased in the Shūf and the areas of Jazzīn and Dair al-Qamar. The Christians of these districts addressed an appeal to the people of Kisrawān through Ṭāniyūs Shāhīn, asking whether they would help them or not. Tāniyūs Shāhīn replied that he . . . could bring about 50,000 men if needed. The Christians . . . of the Shūf now strengthened themselves and began seeking trouble. The Druses, for their part, held constant meetings and consultations among themselves in all localities, communicating with the Druses of Ḥaurān, Ḥāsbayyā, and Syria and making secret compacts among themselves that their efforts would be united. The Ottoman authorities, with the knowledge of the English government, strengthened them and gave them arms. Both sides strengthened themselves and prepared for the outbreak of troubles.[10]

Indeed, following the armed affray between the Christians and Druzes in Bayt Mirī on 30–31 August, the outbreak of sectarian warfare in Lebanon became merely a question of time:

All through the fall and winter, both sides hastened their preparations. The government of Beirut could have stopped these movements at any moment, and prohibited the importation of arms and ammunition. But for some reason they did not interfere.[11]

In the predominantly Christian villages and towns young Christians organized themselves in armed bands, each led by a *shaykh shabāb*, and adopted a special uniform; they roamed from one place to the other displaying their weapons and boasting of their determination to exterminate the Druzes. The Christian leadership in each district went to a supreme *shaykh shabāb*, who kept a record of the names of all the men under his command and maintained contact with other district leaders. In Beirut Bishop Ṭūbiyya ʿAwn[12] organized a 'Maronite Young Men's League'[13] and taunted the Druzes in the most irresponsible manner, while 'Maronites of wealth and means raised subscriptions for the purpose of purchasing arms and ammunition, which they distributed to their co-religionists in the mountains'.[15] Meanwhile the Druzes also prepared for the oncoming conflict, but unlike the Christians they prepared in secret. Many observers, like Colonel Charles Churchill, were convinced that they did so with the obvious connivance of Khūrshīd Pasha:

> Several Druze sheiks took the unusual step of spending the winter of 1859–60 at Beyrout. Here, their conferences with the Turkish authorities were long and frequent, and almost of daily occurrence. Of the object of those meetings there could be no possible doubt; and though all the minute details discussed, remained of course unknown, the great fact transpired, that the Druzes had been called upon to prepare themselves for a most responsible and important service, that they had responded to the call in terms of absolute devotion to the Sultan, but had taken the liberty to observe that such responsibilities could not be undertaken, nor such services entered upon, without explicit sanction, and clear and definite instructions from Constantinople. Early in the spring of 1860 they returned to their homes. In the month of April, Khurshid Pasha received dispatches from Constantinople which seemed suddenly to relieve him from a disagreeable suspense. His language displayed a tone of buoyancy and assurance. It was even rumoured about the serail, that a firman had arrived which would soon bring the giaours to their senses.[15]

By early May there was widespread agitation throughout the Druze districts of Lebanon:

> The air was thick with the news of outrage and murder: two Christians killed at Owaly bridge near Sidon, four Druzes killed at Medairij on the Damascus road, three Christians at Jisr el Kadi bridge; two Moslems at Juneh north of Dog River near Beirut; muleteers carrying flour to Deir el Komr[16] stopped by the Druses, the highroad everywhere dangerous. The Druse leader, Said Beg Jumblatt,[17] held constant councils, and his adherents poured in from all quarters.[18]

The Christians, indeed, were by no means unprepared for the

now imminent conflict; their leaders had never ceased to boast of their fifty thousand men under arms who were expected to overwhelm the twelve thousand armed Druzes in the country by sheer force of numbers. Yet the agitation in the Druze districts had hardly begun when the Christians were seized with panic. Whole families abandoned their villages in order to seek refuge in such Christian strongholds as Dayr al-Qamar, Jazzīn, and Zahleh, leaving their homes to be pillaged and burnt to the ground. In a number of cases the fugitives were overtaken and robbed by armed Druzes before they could reach their destination.

In the latter half of May the Christians of the ʿUrqūb district, in the territory of the ʿImād sheikhs (*see* p. 10), left their villages in a body and fled towards Zahleh. On their way they were pursued and fired upon by the Druzes, who had lately been assembling in large numbers at Mukhtāra. In retaliation, a Christian force of three thousand men from Zahleh advanced across the Lebanon range to attack the Druzes at ʿAyn Dārā, at the northernmost tip of the ʿUrqūb, on 27 May. A small force of six hundred Druzes, led by Sheikh Khaṭṭār al-ʿImād, set out to meet them on the Damascus road, and a fierce encounter followed. By the end of the day the Christians were retreating in confusion. Thereupon the Druzes proceeded to ravage the district of the Matn, on the other side of the Damascus road, and burnt down a number of Christian villages there.

The news of the Christian defeat at ʿAyn Dārā had probably not yet reached the Kisrawān when the Christians of that region began to take precautions. On the day of the battle the peasant leader Ṭāniyūs Shāhīn, with a crowd of his followers, descended from Rayfūn and advanced along the coast towards Beirut, stopping at Anṭilyās. From there, on 28 May, a small force of some three hundred men was sent to protect the Shihāb emirs in Bʿabdā and al-Ḥadath, south-east of Beirut. By that time Khūrshīd Pasha, with five hundred Turkish troops and two hundred irregulars, had left the city and taken up a position at nearby Ḥāzmiyya, on the Damascus road. When the reinforcements sent by Ṭāniyūs Shāhīn arrived in Bʿabdā, Khūrshīd Pasha urged the Shihābs to request their immediate recall, as they were 'cutting his lines of communication'.[19] The Shihābs at once complied with the Pasha's wishes, trusting that he himself would secure their protection in the event of a Druze attack, as he had indeed promised. In any case the Kisrawānī force which had arrived in Bʿabdā, apart from being entirely undisciplined, was altogether too small to be effective. The Shihābs probably felt that its continued presence in their midst would ultimately prove a hindrance rather than a help.

However, no sooner had the Kisrawānīs withdrawn from Bʿabdā than the Druzes attacked the town and its district in force. It was said that the Turkish troops in Ḥāzmiyya signalled the right moment for the attack by firing a cannon. In response the Druze forces in the Gharb, led by the Talḥūqs and Abū Nakads, descended from their mountain on 30 May and took the Christians below by complete surprise. Within hours the villages of the Bʿabdā district were all in flames, and the entire Christian population had fled towards Beirut. Bʿabdā, al-Ḥadath and their surroundings were then given up to plunder, the Turkish irregular troops joining in the robbery and pillage and cutting down a number of Christian fugitives.

The attack on Bʿabdā and its district found the Christians there utterly unprepared. A contemporary Christian source says:

> The hamlets and towns of that district mustered no more than six hundred men. . . . And within a short time . . . the band of Christians wavered and became confused, getting bewildered and stunned, so that they were unable to persevere and swerved from right to left. And they retreated . . . but were routed in the worst of routs.[20]

Panic, indeed, had spread among the Christians of the Bʿabdā and Gharb districts several days before the Bʿabdā district was attacked; the state of the Christians of those districts is vividly described by the American missionary Henry Harris Jessup, who was living in ʿAbay, the seat of the Abū Nakads, at the time:

> On Saturday the 26th, we made an American flag to hoist over the mission premises in case the hordes from Hauran should invade this district, for we had no fear from the Lebanon Druses. The whole population were in a state of apprehension. Bodies of armed Druses, horse and foot, marched from village to village, singing their weird [war] song. . . . On Sunday, May 27th . . . we went down to the little church under Mr Calhoun's house. . . . It was my turn to preach. I looked down on a company of anxious faces. I had begun the service and was reading the first verse of 'My faith looks up to Thee', 'Araka

bil eeman', when the report of a gun nearby, followed by a scream, startled the congregation. Just then a man ran by the church door shouting, 'Abu Shehedan is killed. Rise and run for your lives!' That church was emptied in a moment. It had been agreed beforehand among the Protestants, Greeks and Maronites, that if any Christian was killed in Abeih they would all run en masse down the steep mountain descent of six miles to Moallakah, a large Maronite village on the seashore and thence twelve miles to Beirut. So no time was needed for consultation. The entire male Christian population fled, over walls, terraces, vineyards and through pine groves and the rocky slope, avoiding the roads. . . . Kasim Beg [Abū Nakad] came at once with the Druze sheikhs and explained the matter to Mr Calhoun and myself. He said that in the civil war of 1845, Abu Shehedan killed a Druse of Binnai, a small Druse village one mile over the ridge from Abeih, and the family had been watching for fifteen years an opportunity for revenge, and this morning a small body of them crept in and surprised him and shot him. He said he regretted it deeply and had driven the men away, and would guarantee that there should be no more shooting in Abeih. But his new assurances came too late. Not a Christian man or boy over ten years was left in the village. As the Druses never touch women in their wars, the Christian women and girls all remained.[21]

The Druze attack on B'abdā and its district caused considerable destruction of property, but little loss of life. A few Christian fugitives, fleeing their villages to Beirut, were waylaid and killed by Druzes or cut down by Turkish irregulars. Among those killed were some Shihāb emirs, including the retired Bashīr III, then a blind old man of eighty-five. The London *Times* of 27 July related the circumstances of his death: 'While being led away from his house by his servants he was attacked. His servants fled and left him. The marauders cut his throat and hacked his body with their swords.'[22] These, however, were exceptions. On the other hand, the burning of villages in the Matn and B'abdā districts filled Beirut with 'masses of unhappy fugitives, lying about under the trees in all directions, some bleeding, some naked, all in the last stages of destitution'.[23] The European community in Beirut were surprised by the sudden influx of fugitives and immediately organized a programme of relief work. Urgent appeals were made to Europe and the United States for funds, while on 1 June the European consuls in Beirut proceeded in a body to Ḥāzmiyya to remonstrate with Khūrshīd Pasha regarding his strange conduct.

The consuls urged the pasha to intervene and stop the conflict; the Pasha, in response,

> expressed his anxious desire to suppress the hostilities, vehemently denounced what he called the committee, established at Beyrout, for buying and distributing arms to the Christians, as the cause of the war; threatened even to arrest its members, and concluded by requesting the consuls to do all in their power to restrain the Maronites from sending assistance to their countrymen, declaring that he on his part would give orders to the Druzes to cease from their warfare.[24]

The consuls agreed to this suggestion, and from then on continually advised moderation to the Christians; these, in their fear, were only too willing to heed such advice. It is possible that Khūrshīd Pasha also kept his word and urged the Druzes to stop their assaults; if he did, he must have been in no position to enforce his demands, for the Druzes, encouraged by their first easy victories, continued their attacks with what soon became unbridled ferocity.

What was the secret behind the flagrant temerity of the Druzes at the time, and the seemingly inexplicable Christian cowardice? The Christians, it was well known, far exceeded the Druzes in number, and were generally considered their equals in military valour. The Druzes, indeed, were conscious of the numerical superiority of the Christians and greatly feared the possibility of reinforcements being sent them from the districts of the north. It was probably for this reason that they invariably attacked the Christian towns and villages by surprise, often by treachery. Fortunately for the Druzes, the Christians were poorly organized and had no trust in their selfish and incompetent leaders; these quarrelled incessantly among themselves, and were generally willing to compromise the Christian cause for personal gain. Most important of all, the Christians lacked discipline:

> The inferiority of the Christians in military organization to that of the Druses, became apparent, as usual, from the first collision. The former advanced without the slightest order, dispersed themselves right and left, and seemed each to follow his own inspirations. In the battle near Aindara, they actually fired upon each other, and while thus engaged, found themselves outflanked, and nearly surrounded by the enemy. The Druses, on the contrary, moved steadily on given points, under the direction of their chiefs, to whom they yielded the most

implicit obedience. Quarters menaced were carefully watched, and if attacked, reinforced with extraordinary celerity.[25]

It must not be forgotten, moreover, that the cowardice exhibited by the Lebanese Christians in 1860 reflected a fear prevalent at the time among all Christians in the Ottoman Empire. During the seventeenth and eighteenth centuries the Christian subjects of the sultan had generally grown rich and influential, and had established close commercial, cultural, and sometimes also political contacts with Europe (*see* p. 129). There consequently developed, in every part of the Empire, communities of well-to-do Christian townsmen whose prosperity and power aroused the envy of their Moslem neighbours. When, by the Ottoman reform decrees of 1839 and 1856, the Sultan recognized the principle of equality between his Christian and Moslem subjects, the latter were highly incensed. A wave of fanaticism spread all over the Ottoman provinces, and Christians everywhere, as a result, found their existence threatened. It seems that in Lebanon the Druzes took advantage of the prevalent Moslem fanaticism; in 1860 they tried to appear as champions of Islam. By so doing they succeeded in gaining the support of the Moslems in the country, and also the sympathy of the local Turkish garrisons and their commanders. Khūrshīd Pasha himself apparently sympathized with the Druzes, and may also have been guilty of some of the less extravagant accusations brought against him. These being the prevailing conditions, it was only natural that the Lebanese Christians, in spite of all their preparations, were dismayed. Lacking proper leadership, they could only look for help to the European consuls, and felt that only foreign intervention could save their cause.

On 1 June, the day the European consuls met with Khūrshīd Pasha at Ḥāzmiyya, the Druzes attacked Dayr al-Qamar and the district of Jazzīn. By the *Règlement* of Shakīb Efendi (*see* p. 73), the town of Dayr al-Qamar had since 1845 enjoyed an extraordinary administrative status; a Turkish governor, with headquarters in the old Shihāb palace, managed its affairs, and a special garrison was assigned to him to maintain order. In the circumstances its citizens, although well armed, preferred to remain neutral and assured the Druzes of their earnest desire to remain at peace with them. Professions of friendship between the two sides were indeed frequent; meanwhile individual attacks on some Dayr al-Qamar Christians were, in the interest of peace, left unavenged. Nevertheless, towards the end of May, the Christians of Dayr al-Qamar were surprised to find themselves blockaded by the Druzes. They scarcely had time to organize their defences and patch up internal differences when three days later, on 1 June, the joint forces of the Janbalāṭs, 'Imāds, and Abū Nakads fell on the town. The battle raged all day, the Christians putting up a desperate defence against the Druze attack while the Turkish governor and the town garrison, refusing to interfere, stood by and watched. Despite treason within their ranks, the Christians inflicted considerable losses on the Druzes; the next day, however, Dayr al-Qamar surrendered. On 3 June Ṭāhir Pasha, commander of the Turkish troops in Beirut, arrived in the town to restore order. The Druze sheikhs, upon his request, agreed to withdraw their forces from Dayr al-Qamar; but before the last Druze had left the town one hundred and thirty houses were already in flames.

The Druze attack on the Jazzīn district was carried out on a larger scale. Here an armed band of two thousand Druzes, advancing southwards from the Shūf, took the Christian peasants of the district by complete surprise. On the very morning of the attack word had arrived from Sa'īd Janbalāṭ, the supreme Druze leader, assuring the Jazzīn Christians of their safety. Relying on these assurances, they had all gone about their daily work and were busy attending to their silk crop, when the Druze attack caught them off their guard. Within hours the Druzes had overrun the whole district, plundering, killing, and burning without discrimination. The Christians, unable to resist the attack, hurriedly left their homes and fields and fled with their families towards Sidon. They were pursued and cut down by their assailants. Some one thousand five hundred, it is said, were massacred on that day, three hundred of them outside Sidon. Here the survivors, weary and starved, were refused admittance to the town. As they waited for help to arrive, they were attacked and robbed by a mixed horde of Sunnites and Shi'ites.

During the week that followed the rout of the Christians the district of Jazzīn was completely given over to plunder and violence. In every village, homes which had been deserted by their inhabitants were set on fire, while bands of armed Druzes roamed the countryside robbing and murdering Christian stragglers. Monasteries and nunneries which the Druze sheikhs, not many decades before, had helped the Christians build were now attacked, pillaged, and burned; monks who had stayed behind were slaughtered, and nuns were turned out nearly naked into the fields. In Sidon the Moslems, taking courage from the Druze example, began to taunt the defenceless Christians living among them and threaten them with massacre. These Christians, struck by the fate of their co-religionists in the hinterland, were overcome with terror; but the timely arrival of a British warship outside Sidon restored their confidence and imposed order on the town.

Meanwhile trouble had started across the Biqāʿ in the region of Wādī al-Taym, which fell at the time within the vilayet of Damascus. This region, with its mixed Druze and Christian (mostly Greek Orthodox) population, had for centuries been the feudal domain of the Sunnite Shihābs. Lately, however, a Druze upstart by the name of Salīm Shams had risen to dispute the Shihāb authority there, and his provocative behaviour quickly caused the Shihābs grave annoyance. From his headquarters in the Shūf, Saʿīd Janbalāṭ, who was himself a bitter opponent of the Shihābs, supported the claims of Salīm Shams in Wādī al-Taym and recognized the sheikhly title he had assumed. A kinsman to Salīm, Amīn Shams, had married Nayifa Janbalāṭ, Saʿīd's sister; Salīm, in turn, had married their daughter, and so become the husband of Saʿīd Janbalāṭ's niece. Thus allied to the powerful lords of the Shūf, Salīm Shams found himself well placed to oppose the Shihābs in Wādī al-Taym, especially as the Druze community there was solidly behind him.

In the spring of 1859 Saʿd al-Dīn Shihāb of Ḥāṣbayyā, the head of his family, complained against Salīm Shams before Aḥmad Pasha of Damascus (*see* p. 107), and at his request eight hundred Turkish troops were sent to Ḥaṣbayyā and Rāshayyā to maintain order. With the arrival of these troops the anti-Shihāb activity of the Druzes ceased. But when, in the early summer, the Turkish garrison was temporarily withdrawn from Wādī al-Taym, the Druzes seized the opportunity to stage a rebellion. Circumstances were particularly favourable because the Shihābs, reluctant to stay in Wādī al-Taym without protection, had followed the Turkish troops to Damascus. The Druzes now approached the local Christian leaders and suggested that the two communities should unite to destroy the Shihāb supremacy in the region.

As it turned out, the Druze rebellion as planned came to naught. The Christians, rejecting the Druze suggestions, remained loyal to the Shihābs and refused to renounce their authority. The Druzes alone could do little. In the late summer the Turkish troops, accompanied by the Shihābs, returned to Wādī al-Taym. Meanwhile Salīm Shams, sensing danger, fled to the Shūf, leaving the leadership of the Druzes to his mother-in-law Nāyifa Janbalāṭ.

The failure of the revolt of Salīm Shams increased the indignation of the Wādī al-Taym Druzes, and the return of the Turkish troops to the region aroused their bitterest hostility against the Shihābs and their Christian supporters. Aḥmad Bey, the officer in command of the Turkish garrison, lost no time in making the presence of his troops felt, and no sooner had he arrived than he 'seized a number of Druzes who had supported the rebellion and threw them into jail, humiliating them and treating them with contempt'.[26] The Shihāb triumph, however, was short-lived. Before long Aḥmad Bey, who had been sent from Damascus with the express purpose of supporting the Shihābs, had been completely won over to the Druze side, partly by the engaging manners of Nāyifa Janbalāṭ, and partly by the rich presents he received from her brother Sa'īd. When, in the autumn of 1859, Aḥmad Bey was recalled from Wādī al-Taym because of the 'irregularities of his conduct' and replaced there by 'Uthmān (Osman) Bey, the Druzes immediately began 'to cultivate the good opinion of the new Bey and to approach him with ready money and promises'.[27]

In the meantime, relations between the Christians and Druzes of the region were steadily deteriorating. By refusing to renounce the authority of the Shihābs, the Christians had aroused the suspicions of the Druzes, who also blamed the Christians for the failure of their rebellion in the early summer. Later, when Aḥmad Bey was taking repressive measures against the Druze rebels, the Druze leaders pleaded with the Christians to petition for the removal of the Turkish garrison from Wādī al-Taym, seeing that it was no longer necessary; the Christians, suspecting their motives, refused to do so. Meanwhile Emir Sa'd al-Dīn Shihāb, in an effort to counterbalance the growing power of the Druzes, had formed around himself 'a party of Christians . . . to ensure his continuance in the office of governor. And in this manner began the discord and the conflict and the mischief between the Christians and the Druzes in this region'.[28] Hostility between the two groups was already intense when the Druzes one day intercepted a letter, sent by the Greek Orthodox Bishop of Tyre and Sidon to the Christians of Rāshayyā, urging them to take a common stand with the other Christian groups in Lebanon against the Druze enemy:

> There has been a general meeting in the mountain of Lebanon [so the letter announced] of the chiefs of the people of Zahleh, Deir el-Kamar, Keserawan, Jezzin and the neighbouring places; and they will be as one hand against this nation [the Druzes], small in numbers and weak, in destroying them from out of the land which before was that of your forefathers. . . .[29]

To the Druzes, there could no longer be any doubt as to the Christian intent. 'Their rage knew no bounds. "This then is a war of religion, said they; so let it be . . . The country is ours or theirs".'[30]

Fortunately for the Druzes, 'Uthmān Bey, the new Turkish commander, was more willing to co-operate with them than his predecessor. Indeed, his meetings with Nāyifa Janbalāṭ, which were frequently attended by Druze leaders from other regions, soon began to attract notice. When Christians expressed misgivings about these meetings, 'he gave them the most solemn assurances of his friendship and support'.[31] It was clear, however, where his real sympathies lay. By the early spring of 1860, three weeks before any clash between the Christians and Druzes in the Shūf had taken place, the Druzes of Wādī al-Taym began to prepare for war. Christians who inquired about the meaning of their preparations were assured that there was no need for alarm. Nevertheless, when the Druze preparations went on with unabating vigour, the Christians began to take precautions. During the last week of May hundreds of them, with their cattle and belongings, came pouring into Ḥāṣbayyā from the various villages of Wādī al-Taym, most of them crowding into the grand quadrangle of the town fortress. The presence of the Turkish garrison in the town made them feel somewhat secure.

The panic among the Wādī al-Taym Christians was still at its height when, on 3 June, the people of Ḥāṣbayyā woke to find the Druzes surrounding their town. Hurriedly the town elders decided to leave the task of defence entirely to the Turkish garrison, and summoned the townspeople to the fortress where the Shihāb emirs were already taking shelter. A few hundred young men refused to follow the advice of their elders; leaderless and inexperienced, they sallied forth to meet the Druze attack. Half an hour later they were in full flight, while the Druzes, 'making directly on a given point *en masse*, carried everything before them'.[32] As the routed Christian force re-entered the town and rushed to seek admittance to the fortress, they were hotly pursued by their triumphant foes. 'Uthmān Bey forthwith admitted the Christians to the fortress and, for the sake of appearances, fired two rounds of cannon shot at their pursuers. Some Druzes and a few retreating Christians were killed. By now, however, the Druzes had become full masters of the town; within two hours the Christian homes of Ḥāṣbayyā were mostly in flames:

> Osman Bey then went up to Sitt Naaify[33] and asked her wishes. She demanded an unconditional surrender on the part of the Christians and the delivering up of their arms. With her consent, Osman Bey gave them a written guarantee, pledging the faith of the government for their personal safety. . . . The helpless Christians consented perforce to the mournful arrangement. Their arms were all heaped together in the middle of the grand court. The best among them were selected by the Druzes and the Turks. The remainder, about eight hundred stand, were packed on mules and consigned to Druze carriers, ostensibly to be taken to Damascus. These, likewise, were afterwards taken by the Druzes.[34]

On 4 June, the day the Christians of Ḥāṣbayyā surrendered their arms, a force of one thousand five hundred Druzes attacked Rāshayyā, to the north. Here the Christians put up a courageous resistance. Although taken by surprise they successfully gathered their forces, set up barricades, and held out for a whole day, inflicting heavy losses on their assailants. Towards evening they ran out of ammunition. In despair they rushed to join the Shihāb emirs in the town fortress, where the Turkish garrison 'swore to defend them at the hazard of their lives'.[35] By the following day the Druzes had occupied the town, and were surrounding the fortress in which the Christians were now helpless prisoners.

For several days the Christians in Ḥāṣbayyā and Rāshayyā remained locked up with their families in the town fortresses, shattered by hunger and anxiety. The Turks did not permit them to venture out, nor was it safe for them to do so; the Druzes, unsatisfied by their victory, were eager to attack their defenceless enemies and vent their rage on them. Meanwhile the Greek Orthodox clergy and European consuls in Damascus pleaded with Aḥmad Pasha there, earnestly requesting him to intervene in Wādī al-Taym and restore order. When he did not readily respond to these requests, they begged him at least to have the Christians in Ḥāṣbayyā and Rāshayyā released and sent under escort to Damascus. Aḥmad Pasha forthwith issued an order to this effect and sent it by special messenger to Ḥāṣbayyā, where it arrived at about mid-day on 10 June. Immediately upon receiving it, ʿUthmān Bey had it read before the Christians in the fortress.

The Christians were overjoyed to hear the Pasha's order. Right away they began to collect their belongings and prepare for departure. It was not long, however, before the fortress in which they were gathered was surrounded by a wild crowd of Druzes, determined not to allow a single Christian to leave the place alive. Later it was alleged that the Druzes, on that day, were acting upon the orders of Nāyifa Janbalāṭ, who in her turn was carrying out the instructions of her brother Saʿīd. More probably, the crowd was being driven by its own passions. Meanwhile ʿUthmān Bey, ostensibly acting upon Aḥmad Pasha's orders, commanded his soldiers to drive all the Christians inside the fortress into the central court, then mount their horses and stand guard around the walls. The gates of the fortress were then thrown open:

The Druzes rushed in with a loud yell. . . . And now the butchery began. The Druzes, from their standing place, first fired a general volley, and then sprung on the Christians with yatagans, hatchets and bill-hooks. The first victim was Yoosuf Reis, the confidential secretary of the Emir Saad-e-deen. . . . The Emir Saad-e-deen was next decapitated, and his head sent as a trophy to Said Bey forthwith.[36] By degrees the moving mass was hewn into. . . . A few Christians, at first, tried to escape by the gate. The Turkish soldiers seized them . . . and delivered them over to the Druzes; in more than one instance indeed dispatching them themselves.[37]

By the time the carnage ended a minimum estimate of nine hundred and seventy Christians, including some women, had been killed.

While the massacre in Ḥāṣbayyā went on, the Ḥawrān chieftain Ismāʿīl al-Aṭrash was advancing across the Anti-Lebanon into Wādī al-Taym, cutting down a number of Christian villagers on his way. On 11 June he reached Rāshayyā, where one hundred and fifty Christians and the greater part of the Shihāb family were still being detained inside the fortress. A large crowd of Druzes was already gathered around the fortress when Ismāʿīl al-Aṭrash and his men arrived, and the joint Druze forces pushed on to the fortress gates. After some negotiation with the Turkish officer in charge, the gates of the fortress were thrown open and the Druzes were allowed to enter unopposed. Of the Christians and the Shihābs inside not one was left alive. Then the joint forces of the Wādī al-Taym and Ḥawrān Druzes, five thousand strong, proceeded to ravage and burn the Christian villages of the Biqāʿ, killing whatever Christians they found, while the Sunnites and the Shiʿite tribesmen of the region readily joined them in the work of destruction.

By mid-June, less than three weeks after the first clash between Christians and Druzes had taken place, the Druzes were complete masters of the situation. The Shūf, Wādī al-Taym, and the Biqāʿ were entirely under their control, Dayr al-Qamar and the Bʿabdā district were completely at their mercy, while the Christians of the Gharb and Jurd were happy to accept the protection of their Druze feudal sheikhs against payments of money. Of the Christian strongholds south of the Kisrawān only Zahleh, 'the shield of the Christians, the terror of the Druzes', remained unconquered. According to a contemporary American missionary, the Greek Catholic people of Zahleh were 'as tyrannical, as unjust and almost as bloodthirsty as the haughty Moslems',[38] and their reputation for bravery made them feared by their non-Christian neighbours. 'Within a certain radius from its habitations, no Christian, no matter whence he came, could ever be insulted with impunity.'[39]

The Druzes of the Ḥawrān and Wādī al-Taym could indeed still remember how, in 1841, the warriors of Zahleh had twice crushed their forces in the Biqāʿ. On 27 May the men of Zahleh had advanced against the Druzes at ʿAyn Dārā only to be repelled with heavy losses. Nevertheless, Zahleh still stood defiant of its enemies, and while it stood the Druzes could not consider their triumph complete.

After the massacres of Ḥāṣbayyā and Rāshayyā, while the Druzes were ravaging the Biqāʿ, the people of Zahleh began to prepare their defences and appealed to the Christians of north Lebanon for help. Here leaders like Ṭāniyūs Shāhīn and Yūsuf Karam (*see* p. 68) had large Christian forces at their disposal; as yet, however, not one of them had shown the least intention of crossing the border line into the Druze districts. Ṭāniyūs Shāhīn, still uncertain of his position in the Kisrawān, was reluctant to leave his home district, and his hesitation did not encourage lesser leaders, like Yūsuf al-Shantīrī of the Matn, to do so. As for Yūsuf Karam, the sheikh of Ihdin, it seems that he was already dreaming of an appointment to the Christian Kaymakamate; he was consequently unwilling to take any action which would compromise his position with the Turks. When Zahleh appealed for help, Yūsuf Karam answered the call and advanced to the Matn with a large Christian force. Taking courage from his example, Yūsuf al-Shantīrī also mustered his forces and prepared to advance across the mountain to rescue Zahleh. But when, upon arriving in the Matn, Yūsuf Karam stopped his advance, pleading that he was doing so upon the orders of the French Consul, Yūsuf al-Shantīrī immediately changed his plans. Instead of moving on across the mountain, he remained in the Matn, like Yūsuf Karam, while the joint Druze forces of the Shūf, the Ḥawrān, and Wādī al-Taym, with their Shiʿite and other allies, advanced in a body against Zahleh.

Trusting to the help which seemed at hand, the people of Zahleh did not wait to be attacked. On 14 June they set out into the Biqāʿ to meet the enemy, as they had done before in 1841. A fierce encounter with the Druzes followed, and the Zahleh people were badly beaten. On the following day they again sallied forth against the advancing enemy, this time with a larger force; again, however, they were defeated. Failing to check the enemy advance, they now retired inside their town and waited for the Druzes to attack. In the meantime, they hoped, Yūsuf Karam and his forces would have arrived. There were four thousand armed men in Zahleh. With some help coming from the Christian districts the town stood a good chance against its assailants, whose total forces numbered close to eight thousand. Yūsuf Karam, however, only arrived in Zahleh when it was too late. When the Druzes attacked on 18 June, the Zahleh people had to defend their town single-handed:

When the inhabitants of Zahlah saw their enemies pressing them . . . they sent three of the notables of the town to Yūsuf Karam, requesting that he should come to them since no other chance of succour was left to them. And he promised them to come on the second day, which was a Sunday. So the next morning a party went out to meet him on the road. . . . The townspeople killed animals of their flocks and cooked food for him and his army and remained waiting for him with burning hearts. And when the appointed time passed and he failed to come, their anxiety and vexation increased, and they sent again to inform him of the danger they were in. . . . Whereupon he apologized for his delay on that day and promised to come on the second day with auxiliaries and allies. So their hearts cheered up and their anxiety abated. . . . But on the second day, which was Monday, the eighteenth of the month of June, the Druzes closed in upon them from all sides and places, confronted by the Christians with hearts of flint, man dashing against man. And the fight between them was desperate. . . . The action continued like this for the space of four hours. . . . And still the people of Zaḥlah put their trust in the advance of Yūsuf Bey Karam, according to his appointment. So they did not attend to the proper watching of the side from which he was to arrive with his force. And this came to the knowledge of Sheikh Khaṭṭār al-ʿAmād (*see* p. 90) who took a troop of his bravest men and spread out [waved] in front of it Christian flags. . . . As he approached in this manner on that neglected flank, they thought it was Yūsuf Bey Karam who came to their aid with men and ammunition. So, reviving their hope of being relieved, the good news circulated among them and they concentrated their attention on the other side. And while they were . . . cherishing this illusion the fire of war broke out in the high quarter of the town. . . . And the clamor of men forcing their way rose with the noise of the gunpowder. And when they found that the sky showered men upon them from outside and inside the town . . . they drove their families before them . . . defending them against . . . their enemies, and abandoned their homes and habitations. And they took the road to Biskintā and the neighbouring villages of al-Matn, and some of them reached by degrees the seashore.[40]

By their courageous stand on that day, the people of Zahleh saved their town from massacre and the Christian cause in Lebanon from utter ignominy. The fall of Zahleh, however, made the Druze triumph complete. Druze bands now roamed the countryside as they pleased, meeting no opposition whatever. As for the Christians of the mixed districts, they were now mostly refugees in Sidon, Beirut, the Kisrawān, or Damascus. Only in the Gharb and the Jurd did the Christians remain unmolested, their safety fully assured by the Talḥūq and ʿAbd al-Malik sheikhs. Elsewhere in the Druze Kaymakamate, scarcely any Christians were left.

Of the larger Christian centres in the mixed districts Dayr al-Qamar alone had escaped plunder. Having surrendered on terms on 2 June, its people had not been forced to leave their homes. They remained in the town at the mercy of their Druze neighbours, 'their strength . . . broken and their determination crumbled. . . . They seemed as if their blood had become frozen in their veins and stagnant in their arteries. . . .'[41] To some Druzes, however, a victory over the Christians was bound to remain incomplete unless Dayr al-Qamar was retaken and sacked. The town was the richest in the mountain, and promised to yield considerable spoils. Besides, there were many old scores to settle between its Christian townsmen and the neighbouring Druzes, some dating back twenty years. The Abū Nakad sheikhs in particular had not forgotten the disrespect with which the people of Dayr al-Qamar had treated them; how, in 1854, they had forbidden them to build a house on their own property outside the town.

On 20 June, the Druzes returning in triumph from Zahleh attacked Dayr al-Qamar. The attack was completely unprovoked, and the assailants met with no resistance:

A Druze would enter a Dayr al-Qamar home and find two or three men seated with their family on a carpet. He would pull it [from underneath them, and the master of the house] would tell him: 'Take it. There is no difference between us.' Then [the Druze] would tell him, 'Give me your rifle.' He would thereupon yield his arms, handing them over to his Druze foe.[42]

The plunder of the town, indeed, was easier than the Druzes had ever imagined: The Druzes would

> kill everyone they found in the houses, men and male children indifferently . . . hacking their bodies to pieces with their swords and axes. . . . And whenever they had finished plundering a house, they set fire to it.[43]

Many Christians, with their families and belongings, flocked for refuge to the old Shihāb palace, where the Turkish governor had his headquarters. When, however, the palace was in its turn attacked, the governor made no attempt to defend it, and a fearful massacre followed. By the evening more than two thousand Dayr al-Qamar Christians had been killed.

CHAPTER VI

GOVERNMENT OF MOUNT LEBANON 1860–1920

WITH THE massacre of Dayr al-Qamar the violent phase of the 1860 disturbances in Lebanon came to an end. In less than four weeks an estimated total of eleven thousand Christians had been killed, four thousand more had perished of destitution, and nearly a hundred thousand had become homeless fugitives. The Druzes had also lost a number of dead, but otherwise their triumph had been amazing. Now they spoke of crossing over into the northern Kaymakamate and invading the purely Maronite district of the Kisrawān, and it seemed that nothing could stop them. Meanwhile in Beirut, Moslem taunts and threats caused many Christian families to leave the city; some escaped to the Maronite districts in the north, while those who could afford it fled by sea to Greece or Egypt.

Finally, on 6 July, Khūrshīd Pasha summoned the Christian and Druze leaders to Beirut and presented them with peace proposals which were forthwith accepted. The past, it was agreed, was to be forgotten. Neither side was to claim compensations. The principal blame for the events of the earlier weeks was laid on the ineffectiveness of the double Kaymakamate administration; Khūrshīd Pasha was therefore entreated to take direct charge of affairs and re-establish order and justice. The peace convention was to be drawn up in four copies, two of which were to be kept by the Turkish authorities and the other two by the Druze and Christian kaymakams respectively. None of the European consuls in Beirut received copies, nor were they officially notified of the terms of the convention. Khūrshīd Pasha had resolved the crisis as a purely internal affair. For the time being he could congratulate himself on having barred the way to European intervention.

Ever since 7 June, when the news of the civil war in Lebanon first reached Istanbul, the European embassies there had been urging the Porte to take action. As a result, a Turkish frigate and two battalions of Turkish troops were sent to Beirut; but as these reinforcements only left Istanbul on 19 June, they arrived in Beirut when everything was over. Meanwhile the news of the Christian massacres in Lebanon had reached Europe – there to cause widespread indignation. In France, in particular, popular feeling demanded immediate intervention; the French government was indeed negotiating a plan for such intervention with Britain, when Khūrshīd Pasha announced that the warring sects in Lebanon had agreed to peace. The terms of the Lebanese peace convention clearly endorsed the Druze victory and gave the Turks increased control over the country. The Christian leaders, however, appeared content; as they made no remonstrance, the European Powers had no excuse to intervene.

The Lebanese crisis seemed indeed settled, when fresh troubles broke out in the Syrian interior. On 9 July, three days after the Christian-Druze convention in Lebanon had been signed, the Moslem populace of Damascus suddenly fell upon the Christian quarter of the city, and in one day nearly 5,500 Damascene Christians were massacred. The Ottoman governor of the Damascus vilayet, Aḥmad Pasha (*see* pp. 96, 100), made no attempt to stop the carnage; Turkish troops under his command, in fact, assisted in the massacre. Throughout Syria, Moslems now believed that the Sultan had issued special orders to exterminate the infidels, so that the Christian population everywhere stood threatened. In Palestine, it is said, whole villages of Christians embraced Islam as the only means of escaping certain death.

On 16 July the news of the massacre of Damascus reached Paris. Immediately the French Government ordered seven thousand French troops to be sent to Beirut under General de Beaufort d'Hautpoul, ostensibly to help the Porte re-establish order. The Porte, expecting armed intervention from Europe, had meanwhile sent to Syria its Foreign Minister Fu'ād Pasha with full powers to settle affairs in Damascus and Mount Lebanon on the spot. Fu'ād Pasha arrived in Beirut on 17 July; British, French, and other European warships had by then been cruising about the Lebanese coast for more than two weeks. Finally, on 16 August, the first French contingents under General d'Hautpoul landed in Lebanon and set up camp in the pine forest outside Beirut.

Before the arrival of the French forces in Beirut, Fu'ād Pasha had one month in which to settle the affairs of Syria. Immediately upon reaching Beirut himself, he promised the people of Lebanon swift justice and began the distribution of relief funds to the homeless Christians. Then, having heard that a French expedition was on its way to Syria, he hastened to Damascus to re-establish order there. The French were to have no excuse to intervene in the Syrian interior; Fu'ād Pasha consequently proceeded to deal with the perpetrators of the Damascus troubles with the utmost severity. Among the Turkish soldiers and officers, 111 were tried and shot for participation in the massacres or gross neglect of duty; these included the former commanders of the Ḥāṣbayyā and Rāshayyā garrisons (*see* pp. 97–101). Aḥmad Pasha and fifty-six other public officials and civilian offenders were also hanged, and hundreds of others received lesser sentences. As a final blow, that part of the male population of Damascus which was elegible for conscription was forcibly recruited into the Ottoman army. Damascus at last was quiet, and on 11 September Fu'ād Pasha returned to Beirut to meet General d'Hautpoul and settle the affairs of Lebanon.

It is possible that Fu'ād Pasha at first intended to deal as sternly with the leading offenders in Lebanon as he had done in Damascus. Circumstances, however, did not permit him to do so. In Damascus armed Moslems, led by some well-known ruffians, had without provocation attacked and massacred unarmed Christians. In Lebanon a civil war between Christians and Druzes, for which the two groups were perhaps equally responsible, had resulted in atrocities for which the Druze leaders were not directly to blame. To punish the mob leaders of Damascus was possible; to punish the Druzes meant calling to account a whole community for its conduct in the civil war, and this could not easily be done. Fu'ād Pasha, indeed, did investigate the Lebanese situation with an attempt to determine responsibility. On his return to Beirut he immediately placed Khūrshīd Pasha and his leading officers and civil officials under arrest, and proceeded to summon the forty-seven leading Druze chieftains to Beirut. Of these only Sa'īd Janbalāṭ, the kaymakam Muḥammad Arslān, and twelve others answered the summons; they were duly placed under arrest. The remaining thirty-three fled to the Ḥawrān. Fu'ād Pasha next proceeded to have the prisoners tried, and all of them were convicted. The Turks were sentenced to life imprisonment, the Druzes to death. Later the death sentences were all commuted to life imprisonment, and even the prison sentences were in the end allowed to lapse. On 11 May 1861 Sa'īd Janbalāṭ died in prison of tuberculosis. Except for him, all the Turkish and Druze prisoners ultimately regained their freedom.

While it was to some extent possible to determine the responsibility of the Druze emirs and sheikhs in the Lebanese massacres, it was impossible to establish the guilt of the lesser Druze leaders. Probably to demonstrate the impracticability of such a project, Fu'ād Pasha asked a special Christian commission to furnish him with a list of the principal Druze offenders. The commission presented him with the names of 4,600 Druzes and 360 Sunnites and Shi'ites. Fu'ād Pasha insisted that the number of the accused was too large, whereupon a revised list was prepared assigning the prime guilt to only 1,200 Druzes. These were immediately arrested and a special tribunal was established at Mukhtāra for their trial. When the court, however, called for witnesses, none appeared. Even the members of the Christian commission which had drawn up the list of Druze offenders were unwilling publicly to testify against them. In the circumstances no proper trials could be held, so that in the end most of the Druze prisoners were released. The remainder, 245 in all, were temporarily exiled to Tripolitania, returning to Lebanon after order was finally re-established. Fu'ād Pasha, meanwhile, announced that no further complaints by Christians against Druzes would be heard. At the judicial level the issue was settled.

Politically, however, the settlement took a longer time to achieve. While General d'Hautpoul and his French troops, starting in the early autumn, occupied the Shūf and concentrated on relief work, an international commission representing Britain, France, Russia, Austria, and Prussia was established in Beirut under the presidency of Fu'ād Pasha to consider the reorganization of Lebanon. The commission held its first meeting on 5 October, but agreement was only reached after eight months of discussion. France proposed the restoration of the Lebanese Emirate, possibly with a Shihāb emir at the helm. Russia half-heartedly supported the French proposal; Britain, Austria and Turkey completely rejected it. British proposals to turn the whole of Syria into a vice royalty like the Egyptian Khedivate, or to divide Lebanon into three Kaymakamates – one Maronite, one Druze, and one Greek Orthodox – were also discussed and rejected. Finally, on 9 June 1861, an organic statute for Lebanon to which all the commissioners in Beirut had agreed was formally signed in Istanbul. This statute, known as the *Règlement Organique*, constituted Lebanon as an autonomous Ottoman province under the guarantee of the six signatory Powers. In 1867 Italy adhered to the statute as a seventh guarantor. On 5 June 1861, four days before the *Règlement Organique* was finally signed, General d'Hautpoul and the French troops left Lebanon.

The *Règlement Organique*, with its seventeen articles, gave Lebanon an entirely new organization. The country, stripped of Beirut, the Biqāʿ, and the Tripoli and Sidon regions, was now to be governed by a Catholic Christian plenipotentiary, or muteṣarrif, appointed by the Porte and responsible directly to Istanbul. The mutesarrif had to be an Ottoman subject, but not a Lebanese, and his appointment had to be approved by the signatory Powers. In the government of Lebanon he was to be assisted by a local administrative council of twelve elected members representing the different religious communities: four Maronites, three Druzes, two Greek Orthodox, one Greek Catholic, one Sunnite, and one Shiʿite. The territory of the Mutesarrifate was to be divided into seven administrative districts, or cazas, in each of which the mutesarrif was to appoint a kaymakam of the prevalent religious group. Special administrative officials were also to be appointed in the sub-districts, or nahies (*nāḥiya*), into which each caza (*qaḍā*') was divided; in every village, finally, the local people were to elect a village headsman, or sheikh, who then received formal appointment from the mutesarrif. It was these village sheikhs who, in their turn, elected the members of the administrative council.

By the terms of the *Règlement Organique*, a special corps of Lebanese gendarmerie was to assist the mutesarrif in the maintenance of order and serve as a judicial police. Taxes collected in Lebanon were to serve as a basis for the Lebanese budget, and only the surplus, if any, was to be turned over to Istanbul; any deficiency in the Lebanese budget was to be paid by the central Ottoman treasury. The judicial function was to be vested in courts of first instance and a court of appeal. Feudalism, finally, was to be abolished, and all Lebanese individuals were declared equal before the law. The *Règlement Organique* was put into force tentatively for three years. In 1864 it was re-examined and amended to assume its final form.

At the suggestion of the French Government, the first mutesarrif appointed to Lebanon in 1861 was Dāwūd Efendi: an Armenian Catholic of Istanbul, formerly an attaché at the Ottoman Embassy in Berlin, and for some years the Director of Posts and Telegraphs in the Turkish capital, who was now sent to Lebanon as plenipotentiary with the title of Pasha. Hardly could a better choice have been made. The new governor of Lebanon was one of the most capable and enlightened officials of the Ottoman Empire, and he took up the government of the Mutesarrifate with energy and devotion. On his initiative, there was established for Lebanon, in record time, an up-to-date administrative machinery of an honesty and efficiency that was as yet unknown in the country. The Lebanese gendarmerie corps, organized by two French officers under his supervision, was for its time a model of discipline. Shortly after he had arrived in Lebanon, Dāwūd Pasha brought for the Lebanese Government the Shihāb palaces of Bayt al-Dīn and Dayr al-Qamar. Bayt al-Dīn became the official residence of the mutesarrif for the summer months; in winter the seat of the government was moved to Bʿabdā. In Bayt al-Dīn, Dāwūd Pasha also established a government press which, for the first time, published a Lebanese official gazette.

By his keen sense of justice Dāwūd Pasha succeeded in bringing about a swift reconciliation between the various Lebanese communities. Shortly after he took office calm returned to the mixed districts of Lebanon, and soon co-operation was possible again between the country's Christians and Druzes. As the abolition of feudalism by the *Règlement Organique* threatened to turn the Lebanese feudal families into a class of troublemakers, Dāwūd Pasha undertook to keep them content by arranging for their gradual absorption into the new administration. During the seven years of his Mutesarrifate no less than sixteen feudal emirs or sheikhs were appointed to the leading government positions; the later muteṣarrifs followed Dāwūd Pasha's policy in this respect. In addition to his political and administrative achievement, Dāwūd Pasha paid great attention to the promotion of Lebanon's social and economic prosperity, began the establishment of a carriage road system for the country, and encouraged agriculture and trade. The government school he established in 1862 in 'Abay, al-Madrasa al-Dāwūdiyya, continues to bear his name until this day (*see* p. 140).

As governor of Mount Lebanon Dāwūd Pasha was most successful in the southern districts, where the harm suffered during the civil war made people particularly anxious to co-operate with the new régime. In the north, which had escaped the civil war, the Mutesarrif was faced with a strong opposition from the Maronite leader Yūsuf Karam, of whom mention has already been made in connexion with the events of 1845 and 1860. In the early months of the French occupation, while the international commission for the reorganization of Lebanon was holding its first meetings in Beirut, Fu'ād Pasha had sent for Yūsuf Karam and appointed him Christian kaymakam in the place of Bashīr Aḥmad Abū'l-Lam'. During his brief kaymakamate Karam had successfully invaded the Kisrawān and had subdued the peasant leader Ṭāniyūs Shāhīn who still controlled the district. Order was thus restored throughout the northern Kaymakamate, and although Ṭāniyūs Shāhīn was permitted to maintain control in the Kisrawān as a local commissioner, the feudal families, who had been ousted from the district by the peasants in 1858, were now allowed to return to their homes. Generally popular among the Maronites, and supported by influential circles in France, Karam was now encouraged to expect appointment as governor of the whole of Lebanon, and looked forward to at least his confirmation as Christian kaymakam. As the months went by, however, he became gradually disillusioned. General d'Hautpoul, commanding the French forces of occupation, was no admirer of his; the general's candidate for the future government of Lebanon was Majīd Shihāb, a grandson of Bashīr II, whom he hoped to see instated as Emir.

Opposed by d'Hautpoul, Yūsuf Karam resigned from the Christian kaymakamate shortly before the international commission in

Beirut had completed its work. He probably hoped to be reappointed to the same or to a better post once the French forces of occupation were out of the country. To his disappointment, however, Dāwūd Pasha arrived in Beirut to be publicly invested with the Lebanese Mutesarrifate on 22 June 1861. Dāwūd Pasha, indeed, tried hard to gain Karam's goodwill by offering him various high posts and treating him as an equal of the highest-ranking emirs and sheikhs. After refusing an offer to the gendarmerie command, he was prevailed upon to accept appointment to the kaymakamate of the Jazzīn district in the extreme south. He held the office for three days, after which he tendered his resignation and returned to his native Ihdin in the north. There, shortly after, he attempted rebellion, whereupon he was summoned by Fu'ād Pasha, who was still in Beirut, and sent into exile in Egypt.

On 6 September 1864 the *Règlement Organique* was revised, giving Dāwūd Pasha an additional five-year term. Shortly after, in November, Yūsuf Karam was permitted to return to Ihdin on condition that he would completely submit to Dāwūd Pasha's government. Karam agreed to this condition, and for more than a year after his return he remained at peace with the Mutesarrif. By January 1866, however, he was again in revolt. In the previous year the refusal of some of Karam's partisans in the Kisrawān to pay their taxes had forced Dāwūd Pasha to take disciplinary action against them. The rebels appealed to Karam for help, whereupon he advanced to the Kisrawān to assist them. Warfare now broke out between the rebel Maronites and the forces of the Mutesarrifate. At Dāwūd Pasha's request, Turkish troops were sent to assist him in suppressing the rebels. Skirmishes between the two sides continued for a whole year. Finally, defeated in battle, Karam surrendered to the Turkish authorities in Beirut and was sent into permanent exile in Europe on 31 January 1867. After many vain requests for permission to return to Lebanon, he died in exile in Italy on 7 April 1889, aged sixty-seven.

The revolt of Yūsuf Karam ended in complete failure, and after 1867 the power of the Mutesarrifate was firmly established in the whole territory of Mount Lebanon. Nevertheless, an undercurrent of dissatisfaction, harking back to the Yūsuf Karam episode, continued in the Maronite districts of the north throughout the Mutesarrifate period. In the early summer of 1868 Dāwūd

Pasha, discouraged by silent Maronite opposition to his rule, resigned his post as mutesarrif and left for Istanbul. Among his successors were several men of exceptional ability under whose rule Lebanon knew examplary order and prosperity. To the Maronites, however, the 'static politics' of the Mutesarrifate continued to be a cause for grave complaint. France had only agreed to the establishment of the Mutesarrifate as a compromise solution to the Lebanese question. French political circles which had originally opposed the establishment of the Mutesarrifate encouraged Maronite ambitions for a greater degree of political independence; Yūsuf Karam was held up by such circles as the supreme example of the Lebanese national hero. Thus it was, among the Maronites, that the idea of a Lebanese Christian nationalism developed, centring around the figure of Karam. The growth of this idea and its encouragement by religious and political circles in France was, in fact, a feature of this period.

The tenure of the mutesarrif was not fixed by the *Règlement Organique*. It was only specified that his appointment should not be for life, and that he was subject to dismissal. Dāwūd Pasha was appointed for a three-year term in 1861, which was renewed for five years in 1864. Naṣrī Franco Pasha, a Greek Catholic of Aleppo, succeeded Dāwūd Pasha on his resignation and was in 1868 appointed for a term of ten years; he died in 1873, after holding the office for less than five years. The next Mutesarrif, the Italian-born Rustum Pasha, was also appointed for a term of ten years. So, in 1883, was his successor, the Roman Catholic Albanian Wāṣā Pasha. On Wāṣā's death in 1892, Na'ūm Pasha, a Greek Catholic of Aleppo and a nephew and son-in-law of Naṣrī Franco Pasha, was appointed mutesarrif for five years; in 1897 his term was renewed for another five years. Muẓaffar Pasha, a Roman Catholic and a Pole, succeeded Na'ūm Pasha in 1902 and died in 1907 just before completing his five-year term. Yūsuf Franco Pasha (1907–12), the son of Naṣrī Franco, and the Armenian Catholic Ohannes Kuyumjian Pasha (1912–15) were also both appointed for five-year terms, although the latter's tenure of office was abruptly terminated by the Porte shortly after Turkey's entry into the First World War. Turkish forces were by then in occupation of Mount Lebanon. The *Règlement Organique* was thus thrown aside, and for the next three years the country, now an integral part of the Ottoman Empire, was governed by Moslem mutesarrifs. ʿAlī Munīf Bey, a Sunnite Turk, succeeded Ohannes Kuyumjian until 1917; he was then in turn succeeded by the Shiʿite Ismāʿīl Ḥaqqī Bey (1917–18). During the last months of the war the Mutesarrif of Lebanon was the Sunnite Turk, Mumtāz Bey (July–September 1918).

Among the Christian mutesarrifs of Lebanon by far the most outstanding were the first, Dāwūd Pasha, and the third, Rustum Pasha. The others, however, were also able to govern the country well. Naṣrī Franco Pasha, the second Mutesarrif, was Superintendent of Customs in Istanbul before his appointment to the Mutesarrifate. In Lebanon he paid particular attention to agriculture, promoted forestry, and generally managed to keep the country in order. The stern Rustum Pasha, perhaps the greatest of the mutesarrifs, was Turkish Ambassador at St Petersburg at the time of his appointment, and after leaving Lebanon he was sent as Turkish Ambassador to London. As Mutesarrif, he established in Lebanon a standard of honest government which was never surpassed, and which contributed to the maintenance of administrative efficiency in the country until the end of the Mutesarrifate. Wāṣā Pasha, it seems, was also a man of considerable ability; he distinguished himself in particular by his public works, including a considerable extension of the Lebanese road system. The period of his office, however, was marked by an alarming growth of corruption; in particular his Armenian son-in-law, Kupelian Efendi, and a few of the latter's Lebanese associates, took advantage of this family connexion to enrich themselves. Naʿūm Pasha, who succeeded Wāsā, is generally remembered as a good ruler. Like his predecessor, he was interested in public works, and particularly in the construction of roads. Later the Turkish Government recognized his ability and appointed him Ambassador to Paris. Muẓaffar Pasha, a military man, did not achieve particular distinction in the Mutesarrifate; a nineteen-point reform programme which he outlined on his assumption of office remained for the most part unimplemented. A well-meaning governor, he was unable to enforce his will in the face of local Christian opposition, which by his time had become particularly strong. Yūsuf Franco Pasha, who assumed the government of Mount Lebanon shortly before the Young Turk Revolution of

1908, was the least distinguished of the Lebanese mutesarrifs, and his attempts to please the Porte at Lebanese expense were deeply resented in the country. Ohannes Kuyumjian Pasha, the last of the Christian mutesarrifs, was a kind and well-meaning governor, but he was old and lacked the energy of his more able predecessors, and his career was cut short in 1915 when Lebanon's autonomy was suspended.

On the whole the period of the Mutesarrifate was one of general development and prosperity. It was noted in particular for the cultural awakening which took place in Lebanon at the time and which was reflected in every aspect of life.[1] This awakening, it is true, was largely the outcome of European and American missionary work and of private Lebanese initiative; the mutesarrifs were not directly responsible for it. But it was the peace and order which the mutesarrifs established that made it possible. In other spheres the achievement of the Mutessarrifate spoke for itself. From the time it was established until the First World War, Mount Lebanon was widely recognized to be 'the best governed, the most prosperous, peaceful and contented country in the Near East'.[2] Its governors endowed it with good roads and bridges, excellent public buildings, a number of efficient public services, and a general security which became proverbial. Under the supervision of the mutesarrifs agriculture flourished. The culture of silk, in particular, was encouraged by French firms which established factories in a number of villages for the production of silk thread. Local firms, in imitation of the French, also established silk factories, employing large numbers of workers and making silk production the primary feature of Lebanon's economy at the time. As the population of Lebanon steadily increased, a movement of emigration to the American continent began. This started in earnest in the last decade of the nineteenth century. By the end of the Mutesarrifate period thousands of Lebanese emigrants in North and South America were sending remittances to their families at home; others had returned with their small fortunes to build the white stone houses with their red-tiled roofs which still dot the Lebanese countryside. Emigration, which was initially the concomitant of deserted mountain villages, soon became a leading factor in Lebanon's prosperity.

In 1917, when he took over the government of Mount Lebanon,

Ismāʿīl Ḥaqqī Bey could feel justly proud of what the Mutesarrifate had achieved. Ḥaqqī himself was deeply interested in Lebanon, possibly because of his Shiʿite connexions, and he made his one year in office memorable by the publication of a general social and economic survey of the country.[3] This survey, published in Beirut in the last year of Ottoman rule, was prepared by a group of specialists representing the best scholarship available in Lebanon at the time. Considering the speed with which it was done and the war circumstances in which it was issued, it was a truly remarkable work; it remains until today the only complete survey of Lebanon ever made, and is a monument to the brief rule of an enlightened and devoted mutesarrif.

In addition to all its other achievements, the Mutesarrifate gave Lebanon a basis of modern administration. It also trained a class of Lebanese civil officials who could later take over the government of the country. This Lebanese administrative tradition, which started under the Mutesarrifate, was particularly strong in the Matn and in the districts of the former Druze Kaymakamate now reorganized as the cazas of the Shūf and Jazzīn. It was also fairly strong in the Kisrawān, where the former sheikhly families, particularly the Khāzins, became closely associated with it. In northern Lebanon, on the other hand, co-operation with the Mutesarrifate administration remained generally weak. The region, as a result, continued to be administratively backward. The leading families of Lebanon, to which the holders of the highest offices in the Mutesarrifate usually belonged, were mostly families of the Kisrawān and the southern regions, with names that recalled the earlier periods of Lebanon's history. Through this administrative aristocracy, a political continuity was maintained in Lebanon's government, linking the period of the Mutesarrifate with the earlier periods of the Emirate and double Kaymakamate and preparing the way for later developments.

It was, indeed, among the members of this administrative aristocracy rather than in north Lebanon that the local opposition to the Mutesarrifate was most coherent. While the Maronites of the Batrūn and Bsharrī districts, faithful to the memory of Yūsuf Karam, refused the Mutesarrifate their whole-hearted co-operation, those of the south, like the Druzes, maintained a steady political association with the mutesarrifs. The political experience which they consequently gained made it possible for them to aspire to a greater degree of self-rule. The Mutesarrifate had originally been established to guarantee the autonomy of Lebanon, which was particularly in the interest of Lebanese Christians. In time, however, Maronites and other Christians with political ambitions became highly critical of its administration, and resented in particular the fact that the mutesarrif could not be Lebanese. They also resented the reduction of Lebanese territory, and insisted on the reintegration in Lebanon of the Biqāʿ, Beirut, and the regions of Tripoli and Sidon. The Maronite lawyer Paul Nujaym, writing in Paris in 1908 under the pseudonym M Jouplain, sums up the aspirations of the Lebanese Christian nationalists at the time:

> [For Lebanon] to play the great role which nature and history assign to it in Syria, great and profound reforms are necessary, in the first place territorial readjustments. The statutes of 1861 and 1864 have mutilated Lebanon and robbed it of some of its most fertile districts. Most of all, they have deprived it of its great port of Beirut, which has been placed under the direct administration of the Porte. Lebanese commerce, very active and flourishing, has no opening on the sea, as the Porte does not permit the creation of a port on the Lebanese coast.[4] The Lebanese, highly prolific, find themselves crowded in their little country. . . . Every year, thousands of mountaineers are condemned to expatriation. Grave problems have thus to be resolved in Lebanon; political reforms are necessary. Society becomes more and more democratic; institutions in harmony with the social evolution must be established. . . . These reforms are particularly urgent as Young Turkey tries to abolish Lebanese autonomy. . . . It is necessary that the guaranteeing Powers should intervene to defend the autonomy and accomplish the necessary reforms. But the most serious and most urgent problem of all is the extension of the Lebanese frontiers. . . . The live forces of the Lebanese nation must be made use of in Syria itself, rather than be dispersed in all parts of the world; and for this, first Beirut and the fertile Biqāʿ, then Bilād Bishāra, ʿAkkār, the Ḥūla, and Marj-ʿUyūn,[5] must be incorporated in the autonomous province.[6]

The Druzes, it seems, did not openly share the nationalist enthusiasm of Maronites like Paul Nujaym. Reconciled after 1861 to their status as a minority, they were in general content to make the best advantage of their position by a close co-operation with the Mutesarrifate government. The nationalism of the Maronites, with its strong Christian tone, was, in fact, unattractive to the Druzes. Christian nationalists thought of Lebanon as a Christian refuge, and were encouraged in this by Western writers like the Jesuit Father Henri Lammens who wrote of *l'asile du Liban.*[7] The Druzes, indeed, were often assigned a special position in Lebanon by Christian nationalists, but it was a secondary position which did not flatter their pride. True, the Druzes under the Mutesarrifate exercised great tact in dealing with their Christian countrymen; they were careful not to alienate the Christian nationalists. On the other hand, they remained suspicious of these nationalists and wary of their aims, particularly because they associated Christian nationalism in Lebanon with French expansionist ambitions.

The Christian nationalists of Lebanon were actually proud of their connexion with France and made no attempt to hide it. Maronite peasants, remembering French kindness to them in 1860, frequently referred to France as the 'Kind Mother'. Even in 1915, during the World War, the Maronite Patriarch publicly acknowledged the debt his people owed to France, although France at the time was technically an enemy power. To Paul Nujaym and other Lebanese patriots, it was France who was trusted ultimately to fulfil the Lebanese national aspirations:

> The Lebanese are conscious of the great role which their glorious past imposes upon them. Placed under the collective control of Europe, they demand that the [Ottoman] Empire should not prevent them from fulfilling [this role], but rather assist them. . . . Above all, they appeal to France, their protectress over the centuries, to that French nation with which they have so much cultural affinity . . . to assure a normal, legitimate solution to the question of Lebanon. . . .[8]

It was therefore amid wide Christian rejoicing, especially among the Maronites, that the French in 1918 occupied Lebanon, bringing to an end the period of Ottoman rule. Two years later, on the establishment of the French Mandate in the Levant, France fulfilled the Lebanese nationalist aspirations by extending the frontiers of the country to the limits they reach today. On 1 September 1920 General Henri Gouraud, the first French High Commissioner in Beirut, formally proclaimed the State of Greater Lebanon.

CHAPTER VII

THE LEBANESE AWAKENING

THE POLITICAL involvements of Bashīr II, the two decades of trouble which followed his downfall, the collapse of the Emirate, the disintegration of the Lebanese feudal régime and the establishment of the Mutessarrifate under international guarantee tell only a part of the story of nineteenth-century Lebanon. Another part, in some respects more important, involves the radical changes which took place at the time in the country's social and cultural life, accounting for much of what distinguishes Lebanon in the Near East at the present day. The two parts of the story are, indeed, closely related. The special social and cultural development of Lebanon was to a large extent made possible by the peculiar political status which the country enjoyed in the Ottoman Empire, first under the Emirate and then under the Mutesarrifate. The presence in the country of large groups of Maronite and other Uniate Christians, who maintained regular contact with Europe, was also important. Yet it must be remembered that the social and cultural changes in Lebanon during the nineteenth century were also part of a general movement of modernization and reform in which the whole Ottoman Empire was involved.

By the end of the eighteenth century the world of Islam was becoming seriously conscious of the impact of Europe. The successive defeats which the Ottomans had suffered since the late seventeenth century at the hands of European enemies had impressed them with the military superiority of the West and the necessity of adopting some of its methods. In 1798 Napoleon Bonaparte and his expedition landed in Egypt, bringing with them samples of the West's scientific and technological achievements which greatly aroused Moslem interest. Responsible Moslems now clearly realized that unless a degree of westernization was accepted, at least at the scientific and material level, the Islamic world would not be able to meet the challenge of Europe. In

Turkey and Egypt, in particular, important changes soon began to occur, sometimes introduced by government initiative and at other times developing spontaneously. Other provinces of the Ottoman Empire were bound to feel these changes, and Lebanon was no exception.

In Lebanon, indeed, conditions were especially favourable for advancement and change. The situation prevailing there under the emirs assured for the Lebanese a degree of freedom unknown elsewhere in the Ottoman Empire. Volney, writing in the late eighteenth century, was struck by the fact that the country, though small and rocky, had a population of considerable size, of a density equal to that of the most prosperous French provinces: 'How can this profusion of men on so small a territory be explained? Having considered all, I can see no other cause than the ray of freedom which shines there.'[1] This 'ray of freedom' guaranteed security of life and property not only for the Lebanese subjects of the emirs,[2] but also for foreign visitors and residents, including European travellers, missionaries, traders, and political agents. As a result Lebanon became open to outside influence in a way that no other Ottoman province was, and the attitude of friendship and reliance which the Christians of the country showed towards the West made Lebanon particularly receptive to European ideas and ways.

Direct relations had long been established between Christian Lebanon and Europe. It was in the late twelfth century, while the Franks were in occupation of coastal Syria, that the Maronites, as their allies, became formally attached to the Roman Catholic Church. After 1291 when the last Crusaders were expelled from Syria, the ecclesiastical union between the Maronites and Rome tended to weaken, although it was never formally abandoned. During the fourteenth and fifteenth centuries the Franciscan missionaries, re-established in Syria, were specifically instructed to restore the effectiveness of the Maronite union with Rome, and it was largely due to their efforts that a close relationship was once more brought about and maintained between the Maronites and the Latin Church. Under the influence of these missionaries the Maronite Patriarch Yūḥannā al-Jājī answered the summons of Pope Eugene IV in 1439 and travelled to Italy to attend the Council of Florence.[3] But by then it had become clear that Latin missionary work alone could not indefinitely and fully secure the attachment of the Maronites to the Holy See. The best guarantee clearly lay in the training of the Maronite clergy themselves in Roman orthodoxy and in handing over to them the prime responsibility for maintaining the union, with the Latin missionaries merely as helpers. Consequently, in the decades that followed the Council of Florence, the Popes not only enjoined the Roman Catholic orders in Syria to pay special attention to the Maronites, but also encouraged the education in Italy of the more promising young Maronites destined for the priesthood. Three such Maronites went to study in Italy in 1470; one of them, Jibrā'īl Ibn al-Qilā'ī, returned to Lebanon later as a missionary to his own people.[4] Late in the following century, in 1584, Pope Gregory XIII, renowned for his reform of the Calendar, established the Maronite College (Collegium Maronitarum) in Rome as a special seminary to train young Maronites for the clergy.

Among the graduates of the Maronite College in the seventeenth and eighteenth centuries the most distinguished remained, for the most part, in Europe where they helped lay the foundations of orientalism. Gabriel Sionita (Jibrā'īl al-Ṣahyūnī, 1577–1648) taught Syriac and Arabic in Rome, and later at the University of Paris where he came to occupy the Chair of Semitic Languages. His contemporary Abraham Ecchellensis (Ibrāhīm al-Ḥāqilānī, 1605–64) also taught in Rome and in Paris; and both were called upon to help in the compilation of the Polyglot Bible. More distinguished than either was Joseph Simonius Assemanus (Yūsuf Sim'ān al-Sim'ānī, 1687–1768), author of the *Bibliotheca Orientalis* (Rome, 1719–28) – an annotated catalogue of oriental manuscripts in the Vatican Library, where he was for many years the librarian. There were also other Maronite graduates of Rome who stayed on in Europe – Italy, France, or Spain – to make their mark there in orientalist scholarship. It seems that with few exceptions only the least distinguished among the graduates of the Maronite College returned home to help their own people; or, perhaps, that the return to the Near East had a dulling effect on young intellects freshly awakened in Europe. Of those who returned, indeed, only the brilliant Isṭifān al-Duwayhī (1629–1704), who became Maronite Patriarch in 1670, deserves special note as a historian and a reformer of the Maronite church.[5] By the eighteenth century the influence of the Roman graduates was being reflected in Lebanon in the few schools which were being established at the time in some parts of the country to give instruction beyond the primary level. Yet even in the later years of that century the achievement of these graduates left the observant Volney unimpressed:

> The see of Rome . . . gave [the Maronites] a hospice in Rome, where they can send several young men who are brought up there free of charge. It would seem that by this means the arts and ideas of Europe should have been introduced among them; but the graduates of this school, limited to a purely monastic education, bring back to their country only Italian, which becomes useless to them, and a theological learning which leads them to nothing. It is also not long before they fall back into the common ranks.[6]

What were the schools established in Lebanon in the seventeenth and eighteenth centuries? It is possible that a number of Maronite clerics, returning from Europe, started simple schools for primary instruction in the villages to which they were assigned as priests. One such school was started by Isṭifān al-Duwayhī when, on his return from Rome, he served as a priest in his native Ihdin.[7] There were more advanced schools which were being established in some Maronite monasteries as early as 1624. In that year a monastic school was founded in the village of Ḥūqā, in north Lebanon, by Patriarch Yūḥannā Makhlūf who was himself a graduate of Rome. The school closed down on its founder's death in 1633. But this same patriarch was also the founder of another monastic school in north Lebanon, this one in the village of Bqarqāshā. The Bqarqāshā school apparently survived Yāḥannā Makhlūf, and was later transferred to a monastery in the vicinity of Bsharrī. Following the death of Makhlūf, however, no new schools of importance were opened for the rest of the century. It was not until 1728 that the next advance was made. In that year another graduate of Rome, the priest Buṭrus Mubārak, founded and endowed a school in the Kisrawān, in the village of 'Ayn Ṭūrā, and placed it, in 1734, under the administration of the Jesuits on joining their order. When the Jesuit order was suppressed in 1773 the school was closed down; but it was re-opened in 1834 by the Lazarist Fathers, who continue to run it today. Following the example of Buṭrus Mubārak, another Maronite Jesuit, Jirjis

Binyamīn, founded and endowed a school in Zghartā, in the Tripoli region, in 1735. This school was also placed under Jesuit administration, and apparently ceased to function long before the end of the century.

It seems, indeed, that during the first half of the eighteenth century the Maronite church had come fully to realize the importance of lay education for boys. At the Synod of Luwayza, held in 1736 to consider the reorganization of the Maronite church, the establishment of schools for male children was considered among the necessary church reforms. One feels the influence of the great Joseph Assemanus, who was present at the Synod as the delegate of the Pope, in the act regarding education:

> Since the nature of young men inclines them to the pleasures of the world if they do not receive a good education, and since they do not attain perfection nor become steadfast according to the teaching of the Church unless at an early age their hearts are made to absorb the love of piety and of worship . . . we command that schools be established in the towns, villages, and larger monasteries, and that care be taken for their upkeep, so that in them the boys of a town or of neighbouring villages may learn the essential matters. . . . We command those teachers whom we would have the bishops and heads of monasteries appoint . . . to observe the general regulations and teach the young first reading and writing in Syriac and Arabic, then the Psalms, then the Book of the Mass, the Daily Office of Prayer, and the New Testament. Then, should they note special scholarly ability in some, they should teach these the rules of Syriac and Arabic grammar and syntax, then music and the Church calendar, then promote them to the study of the higher branches of knowledge: rhetoric, prosody, philosophy, arithmetic, surveying, astronomy, and similar mathematical subjects. We urge the graduates [of Rome] and the school-teachers to . . . prepare textbooks in Arabic . . . or at least translate them from Latin into Arabic. Let them also translate and publish the writings of the Church Fathers, the Acts of the Councils, the History of the Church, and other works worthy of reading which are neither found in Syriac nor in Arabic. . . . We further command the monks to appoint copyists in every monastery . . . to copy works of ecclesiastical literature and place them in the library of the monastery for the benefit of all.[8]

In spite of all this stress on the establishment of schools and on higher instruction, no new schools for advanced study were, in fact, opened in Lebanon after the Synod of Luwayza until 1787, when Patriarch Yūsuf Isṭifān transformed the monastery of Saint Anthony at ʿAyn Waraqa, in the Kisrawān, into a clerical seminary. Two years later this seminary was converted into a secular high school by the influence of Ghandūr al-Saʿd, a prominent Maronite feudal sheikh and a friend of the now deposed Emir Yūsuf Shihāb, who had served that emir as his manager and who also served as French Consul in Beirut. It was probably about that time that another school for higher instruction, this one Greek Catholic, was established in ʿAyn Trāz, the family seat of Ghandūr al-Saʿd, in the Jurd district. However, of all the Maronite educational institutions founded in Lebanon during the eighteenth century none was to rival in importance the college of ʿAyn Waraqa, whose graduates during the nineteenth century ranked among the principal leaders of the movement for cultural revival.[9]

It would be wrong to imagine that, before the nineteenth century, the establishment of Maronite schools in Lebanon had led to any general spread of literacy or advanced knowledge in the country. By the end of the eighteenth century only the colleges of ʿAyn Waraqa and ʿAyn Trāz were still open, providing some higher education for the sons of a few well-to-do Maronite and Greek Catholic families. Students leaving these schools would often find employment in the court of the governing emir, or enter the service of other emirs or sheikhs as clerks or household tutors. For the rest, ignorance prevailed – even among the Maronite and Druze feudal aristocracy who were often barely literate. In Sidon, Beirut, and more particularly Tripoli, mosque schools continued to teach Koran-reading to Moslem boys and the tradition of Islamic learning was carried on, albeit to a limited extent. Otherwise the only form of instruction available was by private tutoring, and this only a few could afford. The Greek Orthodox See of Antioch, long suffering from clerical indiscipline, maintained as yet no schools for its flock in Lebanon, and its hold over its followers was so weak that many of them had slipped away since the late seventeenth century to join the younger and more vigorous Greek Catholic church. A number of Greek Orthodox and Greek Catholic families living in the larger towns, like the Maronite and Druze feudal families, could afford to hire private tutors for their children. But of all the communities of

Mount Lebanon those who had least opportunity for education were the Greek Orthodox and Druze peasantry, who lived for the most part in the districts of the Matn, the Gharb, the Jurd, and the Shūf. Here the Greek Orthodox priesthood, in general an ignorant lot, completely neglected the instruction of their parishioners, while the Druze *'uqqāl*, who could scarcely manage to read their sacred texts, carefully guarded the secrets of literacy from the *juhhāl*.

During the early nineteenth century the Maronite church was awakened again to the necessity of establishing more schools. On the initiative of Patriarch Yūḥannā al-Ḥulū (1809–23) two monasteries were, in the manner of 'Ayn Waraqa, converted into schools: one in 1812 in the village of Kafarḥay (district of Batrūn), and the other in 1817 at Rūmiya (the Matn). The next patriarch, Yūsuf Ḥubaysh, went on to convert three other monasteries into schools, all of them in the Kisrawān: at Ṣarbā (1827), Mār 'Abdā Hirhrayyā (1830), and Rayfūn (1832). Following the example of the Maronites, the Greek Orthodox church now established its first school in Lebanon in the monastery of Balamand, near Tripoli, in 1833. But still, popular education made little progress. As'ad Khayyāṭ, born in Beirut in 1811 of a Greek Orthodox merchant family, had to serve as a boy in the shop of a tobacconist who was to teach him reading: 'At the time . . .' he remarks, 'education was considered dangerous, and was difficult to be obtained, even when most desired. . . . Even . . . reading in common Arabic was difficult to be obtained.'[10] As late as 1849 Sulaymān Ṣalībī, a Greek Orthodox villager from the Gharb where American missionaries were already established, would complain about his fellow-villagers in Bḥawwāra being 'most ignorantly blind[11]. Ṣalībī himself, at the time a student in an American missionary school, became literate by accident: in 1837 two Moslems escaping probably from Beirut to avoid conscription by Ibrāhīm Pasha sought refuge in his father's house and taught the boy the Arabic alphabet.[12]

The slowness of educational development in Lebanon during the eighteenth and early nineteenth century was due in a large part to the scarcity of books. Until the fifth decade of the nineteenth century, and even later, books were still being copied by hand, although by then the Syriac (*Karshūnī*) script in which

Christians had written Arabic since medieval times had been definitely superseded by the Arabic script. The employment of educated Maronites as clerks by the governing emirs and the feudal aristocracy forced them to abandon the old clerical script, which was clearly unsuitable for general correspondence. However, while the Arabic printing-press remained 'practically non-existent',[13] ideas were slow to spread and literacy did not really develop.

Book printing, indeed, had long been known in the Ottoman Empire, although its use had remained limited. The first printing-press was brought to Istanbul in 1493 or 1494 by Jewish refugees from Spain, and in time Jewish presses were established in other cities of the Empire, particularly Salonika. The Arabic script, associated with the Koran, was considered sacred by Moslems, and for a long time the Porte banned the printing of Arabic and Turkish, both of which used the Arabic characters. But there was no ban on printing in non-Arabic characters, and the non-Moslem peoples of the Empire were free to print in their own languages. Hence the Armenians established their first printing-press in Istanbul in 1567, and the Greeks in 1627. In Mount Lebanon, a press using *Karshūnī* characters was established in the early seventeenth century in the monastery of Qazḥayyā (district of Bsharrī), probably by some Maronite graduate of Rome, and this press issued a book of the Arabic Psalms in 1610. Meanwhile, printing in Arabic characters had been developing in Europe for nearly a century. The first Arabic press in history, that of Fano in Italy, was printing Arabic prayer-books for the Papal See as early as 1514.

It was not until the early eighteenth century that printing in Arabic type was introduced into the Ottoman Empire. In 1702 Athanasius al-Dabbās, Melchite Patriarch of Antioch, established a press in Aleppo with Arabic characters, the fount for which was cast by the deacon ʿAbdallāh Zākhir (1684–1748). In 1733 Zākhir, who had become a Greek Catholic (*see* pp. xxii-xxiii), left Aleppo to settle in Lebanon, and started a new press in the Greek Catholic monastery of al-Shwayr, in the Matn district. The Shwayr press served as a model for a later press which was established in a Greek Orthodox monastery in Beirut, issuing its first book (again the Psalms) in 1751. Unlike the Maronites, the Greek

Orthodox and Greek Catholics were not familiar with *Karshūnī* writing because they used the Greek liturgy rather than the Syriac, and therefore wrote Arabic in the Arabic script. It was natural that they should have been the first to print in Arabic characters. Meanwhile, the Porte had relaxed its ban on printing in Arabic type. On 5 July 1727, an imperial firman was issued permitting the establishment in Istanbul of a press to print books in Turkish on subjects other than religion. The Istanbul press issued its first book in 1729, was closed down in 1742, and finally reopened in 1784. Since then the development of printing in Turkey has proceeded rapidly.[14] Despite the progress made, however, books printed in Arabic remained scarce. The Istanbul press printed mostly in Turkish, while the output of the Arabic presses in Aleppo and Mount Lebanon remained small and almost entirely limited to books of prayer.[15]

With the schools being few and books scarce, it is no wonder that the cultural movement in eighteenth-century Lebanon did not have much effect at the popular level. Yet there is no doubt that such a movement did exist. Among the Maronites the careful historical scholarship of Patriarch Isṭifān al-Duwayhī, who was active in the last decades of the seventeenth century, was to serve during the eighteenth century as a model for a number of writers. Indeed, the Maronite literary output of the period is of an impressive size, although it nowhere approaches in quality the high scholarly standards set by Duwayhī.[16] The renown which Maronite scholars like Joseph Assemanus were achieving in Europe was certainly an inspiration to contemporaries at home, prompting them in their literary efforts. But the Maronites were not the only scholars to be active in Lebanon at the time. Towards the end of the seventeenth century the split took place in the Melchite church of Syria between the Greek Orthodox and the Greek Catholics (*see* pp. xxii-xxiii), and the theological disputes associated with this schism provided stimulus for a literary revival among both communions.[17] This revival was not confined to Lebanon, but circumstances helped to make Lebanon its centre. Of the two Melchite groups, the Greek Catholics, who had connexions with the College of Propaganda in Rome, were culturally the more advanced, and their persecution by the Greek Orthodox in some parts of Syria drove many of them (like the printer ʿAbdallāh

Zākhir) to seek refuge in Lebanon. Here, the presence of the Greek Catholic fugitives was to reinforce considerably the Maronite literary revival and to place Lebanon in the lead of the Christian cultural movement in Syria.

This cultural movement among the Christians of Syria reflected social changes of the time. As the Ottoman Empire during the seventeenth and eighteenth centuries declined in strength, the revival of commerce in the Eastern Mediterranean combined with other factors to increase the 'prosperity and strength' of some of its Christian communities.[18] In each case the growth of material prosperity led to educational development and cultural awakening, as happened among the Greeks and Armenians. So also was the case with the Christians of Syria. The great prosperity of the trade of Aleppo in the seventeenth and early eighteenth century brought considerable profit to the Christians of the city, many of whom amassed great fortunes. Later, a number of Aleppo Christians went to Italy and established themselves in Leghorn, which was becoming the chief centre of the trade between Europe and the Levant. There was also a movement of emigration to Egypt, 'where Greek Catholics persecuted by the Greek Orthodox in Damascus and Aleppo found an atmosphere less charged with theological odium, and where, after Ali Bey had ruined the Jews, Syrians took over the farm and the customs'.[19] Meanwhile, the settlement of a large number of Greek Catholic families on the territory of the Lebanese emirs brought to Lebanon a prosperity which further strengthened the Christian position there, and presaged the commercial revival of the nineteenth century.

At the beginning of that century ignorance and illiteracy may well have prevailed in Lebanon, but the country was not culturally stagnant. At the court of Bashīr II at Dayr al-Qamar, and later Bayt al-Dīn, flourished a poet of some renown: Niqūlā al-Turk (1763–1828). The poet's father was a Greek Catholic who came originally from Istanbul to settle in Dayr al-Qamar, hence the surname. In 1798, when Napoleon Bonaparte arrived in Egypt, Bashīr II sent al-Turk there on an intelligence mission, and the poet remained in Egypt until 1804. Today he is best remembered for his eye-witness account of the French expedition to Egypt, which became known in Europe in a French translation as early as 1839.[20] The poetry of Niqūlā al-Turk was of no exceptional merit, but the prestige he enjoyed as court poet must have awakened ambitions among his younger contemporaries.

Al-Turk in Lebanon represented the wider literary movement among the Greek Catholics in Syria and Egypt – a movement led at the time by various members of the Ṣabbāgh family, which had risen to fortune some decades earlier as a result of its connexions with the court of Dāhir al-'Umar in Acre (*see* pp. 15–16).[21] Another representative of this movement in Lebanon was the monk Ḥanāniyyā al-Munayyar (1757–1820), noted in his day as a scholar and the author of some verse. Among the known works of al-Munayyar are a history of the Shihāb dynasty, an essay on the Druze religion, and a collection of four thousand Lebanese proverbs. His history of the Shihābs was used as a source by later historians.[22] In 1811 Niqūlā al-Turk introduced to the Shihāb court another poet of Greek Catholic origin, Buṭrus Karāma (1774–1851). Born in Homs, Karāma was converted to Greek Orthodoxy in Acre before coming finally to Lebanon. At the court of Bashīr II he rose in time to occupy a position of great power, not only as court poet but also as chief secretary and finance manager.[23] His success, as in the case of Niqūlā al-Turk, pointed out to his contemporaries the high status which a scholar or man of letters could hope to attain.

Among the Maronite scholars of the period the most distinguished was no doubt the emir Ḥaydar Aḥmad Shihāb (1760–1835), a cousin of Bashīr II. The son of an unsuccessful former pretender to the Lebanese Emirate, Ḥaydar al-Shihābī (as he is commonly known) lived in complete retirement from politics and devoted himself to scholarship, employing a number of younger scholars as copyists and assistants in his research. Apart from collecting a valuable library, al-Shihābī left a three-volume history of Syria with particular reference to Lebanon, from the Moslem conquests to his own time. Some of the scholars who assisted him in this work were later to achieve distinction.[24]

By 1820, as the first Protestant missionaries began to arrive in Beirut, the slow beginnings of a cultural awakening could already be noticed in Lebanon. Throughout the country, it seems, there were young men restless for instruction, eagerly seeking the advantages of an education still difficult to obtain. It was with such young men that the earliest American missionaries established their first connexions: As'ad al-Shidyāq (*c.* 1798–1829), formerly a student of 'Ayn Waraqa, who was employed as a teacher of Arabic (*see* p. 56), and the precocious As'ad Khayyāṭ, barely twelve years old when the first missionaries arrived, who wanted to learn Italian to improve his prospects as 'interpreter and broker' with foreign traders. Khayyāṭ vividly describes his first contacts with the missionaries:

> Walking one day, I saw two strangers, whom I followed till I reached their house at a short distance from the town. I entered it after them. With an expression of mild benignity, one of them inquired my business. 'I wish to learn your language,' was my answer. The strangers proved to be two devoted, pious missionaries, the Rev Isaac Bird, and the Rev William Goodell, of the American Board of Missions. Good and ever kind, Mr Bird told me to come on the morrow, and bring some of my friends with me, and he would teach me. My uncle accompanied me, and he was almost their first friend in Beyrout: they gained his heart and mine also, and presented us each with a copy of the Bible in Arabic, printed by the excellent British and Foreign Bible Society. At once I began Italian with dear Mr Bird: he and his pious and accomplished lady were like parents to me, and I was the first pupil of that mission. In a short time, I acquired so much Italian that I was appointed teacher in the school, when other Syrian[25] boys were attracted there, by seeing how great a *man-boy*[26] I was become from knowing these languages. I left the money-making business . . . contenting myself with . . . the salary which Mr Bird allowed me, of five dollars, or £1 per month . . . I continued teaching in the school, thus improving my own Italian; but with this I was not satisfied. I wished to add the English language to my other acquirements. The Rev Pliny Fisk, who lived with the Rev William Goodell, kindly undertook to teach me; and so eager was I, that I often got to their house before they were up. I remember, the first English sentence I ever heard was from Mr Goodell, when he knocked at Mr Fisk's door, and said, 'Fisk, Assaad is come!'[27]

It is to the credit of the early American missionaries that they quickly sensed the mood of the time in Lebanon. 'The purely religious aspect which featured [their] early . . . endeavour fell short of . . . success mainly because it failed to express its mission in terms of values meaningful and appreciable to the people to whom the mission was addressed. The religious aspect was therefore relegated to a secondary place below the educational.'[28] Except for the Jesuits who until 1733 had run the locally-founded schools of 'Ayn Ṭūrā and Zghartā, the Roman Catholic missionaries until the fourth decade of the nineteenth century paid practically no attention to education. Their activities were confined to preaching and to developing relations with the Eastern churches. It was not until 1834, when the American missionaries started their educational work in earnest, that the Roman Catholics were attracted to the idea. In that year the school of 'Ayn Ṭūrā was reopened by the Lazaris Fathers; soon after the Jesuits who had been permitted to return to Lebanon in 1831 resumed their educational activity in the country.

Meanwhile, important developments had been taking place elsewhere in the Near East. Muḥammad 'Alī Pasha, master of Egypt since 1805, had embarked on the first successful attempt at educational westernization in the world of Islam. The ultimate goal of Muḥammad 'Alī's reforms was neither social nor cultural:

> By improving economic conditions in Egypt to increase his revenue, he hoped to establish his own power and to perpetuate the rule of his dynasty in the Nile valley, and if possible in Syria and Arabia. This is why he concentrated in his reforms on military organization, agricultural development, and public works. But Muḥammad 'Alī was shrewd enough to realize that no reform would be really effective and lasting without a broad social basis. The Egyptian viceroy was himself illiterate, but he patronized learning, started a ministry of public instruction, created an educational council, and founded in his country the first modern schools of engineering and medicine, with French professors and physicians. French military and educational missions were invited to Egypt, and no less than 311 Egyptian students were sent to Europe to study and receive training in western technology.[29]

When Syria was conquered by Ibrāhīm Pasha in 1831–32, the influence of Muḥammad 'Alī's reforms was extended there. In 1834, the year in which the rivalry between the Protestants and the Catholics in the field of education began, Ibrāhīm Pasha started a military school in Damascus, followed by another for artillery officers in Aleppo. Regimental schools were instituted to teach reading and writing to Syrian conscripts, among whom only the literate were promoted beyond the rank of *onbashi* (corporal).

Schooling facilities were also provided for the male children of these conscripts.[30] 'The scholastic system introduced by Ibrāhīm, although short-lived, gave a powerful stimulus to national education, particularly among the Moslem community. . . .'[31] Furthermore, during the period of Egyptian occupation, hospitals were established in the larger towns like Acre, Sidon, Damascus, and Aleppo, while mobile medical units served the smaller centres. Clot Bey, the French surgeon who organized these medical services for Ibrāhīm Pasha, surveyed the state of public health in the occupied territory and, in 1837, arranged for ten young men, among them four Lebanese Christians, to be sent to study medicine in Cairo.[32]

It seems, indeed, that the activity of Ibrāhīm Pasha in Syria overshadowed the early educational experiments of the American missionaries in Beirut and Mount Lebanon, which were, nevertheless, in themselves important. In 1834 Mrs Eli Smith, wife of an American missionary, started in Beirut 'a promising little school for girls in one of the rooms of the mission house'.[33] This school, which had some forty pupils in its first year, was probably the first institution of its kind in the Ottoman Empire. During the following summer another 'small school for Druze girls' was started in the mountains.[34] Meanwhile 'a boys' boarding-school was opened with six pupils, which it was intended should be enlarged to become in time an institution for the supply of schoolmasters and preachers of the gospel'.[35] This boarding-school was founded in Beirut apparently in 1835, by which time five 'common schools' with some three hundred pupils were already in operation.[36] But the work of all these schools was interrupted in 1840 by the troubles of that year: the revolt in the mountains, the British bombardment of Beirut, the landing of British and Ottoman troops in Junieh, and the allied war operations which ended with the expulsion of Ibrāhīm Pasha from Syria. Once the war was over:

> [the missionaries] made haste to return to their station, but their schools were all disbanded, and it was a considerable space before their operations reverted to their former regular course. The greatest damage had been inflicted upon the boarding boys' seminary, from which a number of the more advanced youths, allured by offers of high wages, had been induced to join the army in the capacity of interpreters.[37]

It was not long, however, before the Syria Mission (as the American mission in Beirut was called) was active again. In the autumn of 1840 the boys' seminary was reopened, this time with 'a well-educated teacher from the patriarch's own college at Ain Waraka' – the later famous Buṭrus al-Bustānī[38] (*see* pp. 144–5). Three years later the Mission established another station at 'Abay, in the mountains overlooking Beirut, where they started 'a good school . . . numbering fifty pupils . . . taught by a Maronite who had lately embraced evangelical sentiments'. This school soon grew to be the leading Protestant seminary where students were 'trained to work as evangelists', and special buildings were erected for it in 1849.[39] Meanwhile in the spring of 1841, the American Press, established in Beirut since 1834, began to print in 'the most beautiful fount of Arabic type the world had ever seen' – a fount specially cast in Leipzig at the orders of the Syria Mission.[40] With its older and less attractive fount, the American Press had been printing the Scriptures and other literature for the missionaries in Arabic since it was first started in Malta in 1822, twelve years before it was transferred to Beirut. Now, with the new fount, its output greatly increased, and soon it was printing textbooks for use in the missionary schools.

By mid-century the American missionaries in Lebanon had made a good start in education, with several day schools and a seminary in Beirut, another seminary in 'Abay, and several other schools in the mountains 'containing between three and four hundred pupils'.[41] Soon their efforts were to receive reinforcement from a new and mainly local quarter. Towards the time that the 'Abay seminary was being built, a 'venerable Christian gentleman from the neighbourhood of Carlisle' called John Lowthian came to settle in Lebanon not far from 'Abay, in the village of Bḥawwāra in the Gharb – a village owned at the time by a fellow-Englishman, Colonel Charles Churchill.[42] Lowthian came to the country 'chiefly for the purpose of spending the close of his life in advancing its spiritual needs'; and, unattached to any missionary group, he took up residence in the home of a villager, Jirjis Ṣalībī, whose second son Sulaymān (*see* p. 126) had gone to study with the American missionaries at 'Abay. Before leaving home, Sulaymān had taught his younger brother Ilyās to read Arabic; and soon Lowthian took an interest in the boy and began to teach him

English. By the time Sulaymān returned from the ʿAbay seminary, his brother Ilyās had been taught 'not only . . . a little of the English language, but also to write a little, and some knowledge of figures'. As for Sulaymān, he had returned as 'a missionary to his own numerous tribe, preaching to them every Sunday in his father's house, with a school under the same roof every day in the week; and also a night school . . . at which many of the grown-up people attended'. Lowthian was impressed by Sulaymān's enthusiasm; and when he returned to England for a few months in 1852 he took Ilyās with him 'to receive a little further instruction, and in hopes of being able to raise a small sum of money to assist in their desire of extending schools in the neighbourhood'. The two returned to Lebanon in March 1853 having raised the sum of £80, which was duly offered to the American missionaries.

> This offer was declined, and the wish expressed that they should themselves spend the money in doing good. Mr Lowthian and the Saleebeys then proceeded to build a school in Howarah (Bḥawwāra), ground for the purpose having been granted and regularly conveyed by the Hon Colonel Churchill. . . . The new schoolroom was opened on 1st January 1854.

Meanwhile, in the autumn of 1853 Lowthian and his friends had established a school in ʿAramūn, in the Gharb, and another in Bṭallūn, in the Jurd. Encouraged by the success of these schools, Ilyās Ṣalībī left for England again in the spring of 1854 to raise more money, while his brother Sulaymān and John Lowthian stayed behind to direct the schools.[42]

Shortly before Ilyās left, the group had started a fourth school in Btātir, principal village of the Jurd and seat of its Druze chiefs, the ʿAbd al-Maliks. These chiefs were so pleased with the school that they sent their own children to attend it, and during the first year more than twenty young ʿAbd al-Maliks were enrolled among its pupils. Eager to keep up with their neighbours in the Jurd, the Talḥūqs of the Gharb now invited Sulaymān Ṣalībī to establish a school in ʿĀlay, their own village of residence. A school, indeed, was started there in 1855 'in compliance with their written application'. But most important of all was the school started in that year in nearby Sūq al-Gharb, where Sulaymān and his family established themselves towards the end of 1854. Here a large schoolroom was erected by public subscription on ground donated by the Ṣalībīs and John Lowthian. The whole property was to be held free by the Protestant inhabitants of the village; 'and such was the interest taken in this building by the people, that those who had no money, gave from eight to ten days of their labour without any payment'. In Glasgow, Ilyās Ṣalībī was able to raise a special fund of £40 a year for the upkeep of this school; and in time the 'Glasgow School', as it was sometimes called, was to grow to become the rival of the American seminary at ʿAbay.[44]

In the autumn of 1855, while Ilyās was still away, a special committee was formed including the British and American consuls in Beirut, John Lowthian, the Ṣalībī brothers, a representative of the American mission, and two other members, with Buṭrus al-Bustānī as secretary, to direct the five schools hence to be known as the Lebanon Schools. On his return from Britain, Ilyās Ṣalībī was charged with the general superintendence of the schools, while his brother Sulaymān taught at Sūq al-Gharb.[45]

In the years that followed the Lebanon Schools increased in number. In 1856 a sixth school was started in the village of Btikhnay, in the Matn. By 1858 three more had been added in other villages, including a girls' school in Btātir. The schools were temporarily closed in 1860 because of the troubles of that year, but in 1861 there were fifteen schools operating in various villages of the Gharb, the Jurd, and the Matn, attended by some six hundred pupils. In 1867 William Benton, an American missionary who took a special interest in the Lebanon Schools, reported that 'the Schools have numbered twenty-one, beside the training School,[46] in twenty different villages, affording employment to thirty-two teachers and assistants . . . and instruction to more than eight hundred different pupils of both sexes . . .'[47]; these pupils were mostly Greek Orthodox or Druze, but there were also a number of Maronites, Greek Catholics, Shiʿites, and Sunnites who attended. The instruction they received was elementary:

In all the schools, so far as means and circumstances permit, a uniform course of instruction is pursued. It consists of reading, grammar, geography, writing, and arithmetic; all the instruction, with the exception of the English class at 'Glasgow' school, being in Arabic, the universal language of the country. Among the books in Arabic, daily used in the schools, are the Shorter Catechism, and Bunyan's Pilgrim's Progress; the chief and most constantly taught of all being the Bible.

> . . . For the more ordinary school books, the schools are indebted to the kindness of the American brethren, who at first, to encourage the work, granted them without charge, and now that the schools are more numerous, supply them at half price. . . . It is believed that there are few missionary operations, of the kind, carried on at so small an expense in proportion to their extent. . . .[48]

The co-operation between the American missionaries and the founders of the Lebanon Schools was a fruitful one. For the first time in Lebanon a co-ordinated system of village schools, competently taught and regularly inspected, was bringing primary instruction within the easy reach of ordinary laymen. William Benton in January 1860 wrote:

> These schools are doing much good not merely to the children, but also to their parents, and all the villages where they have been established. Two hundred of them are needed today in as many different villages of Lebanon, as I hear some of my native friends say to one another.[49]

As it was, the number of Lebanon Schools did not increase much beyond twenty-four or twenty-five. Following the retirement of John Lowthian from Lebanon in 1858, and his death in England three years later, the development of the schools was frequently embarrassed by conflict between the local founders and the American missionaries. These were often distrustful of the local Protestants, who, in their turn, resented the superior airs assumed by the missionaries. As a result, it was not uncommon for relations between the two sides to be strained; the resulting clashes slowed down the pace of the Protestant missionary endeavour. Nevertheless, Sulaymān and Ilyās Ṣalībī continued to manage the Lebanon Schools together until Sulaymān died in 1866, and Ilyās finally retired in the face of strong missionary opposition in 1873.[50] The schools they had founded afterwards fell into neglect, or were taken over and developed by American or other foreign missionaries.

By the time Ilyās Ṣalībi retired, however, the various Protestant missions in Lebanon had embarked on more extensive and ambitious educational schemes which diverted attention away from the earlier and humbler efforts. A boarding-school for girls was established in Sūq al-Gharb in 1858, then transferred to Sidon in 1862. A similar school was started in Tripoli in 1872. In 1881 the American day-school for boys in Sidon was turned into a boarding school, and became the Gerard Institute. Two years later the Lebanon School at Sūq al-Gharb, closed since 1872, was reopened as a boarding-school by the Scotch Mission, then sold to the Syria Mission in 1889. Another Lebanon School, that of Shwayr in the Matn, was taken over by the American missionaries and transformed into a boarding-school in 1899.[51] Meanwhile other missionaries had been active, establishing a number of boarding-schools for boys and girls among which those founded by the Society of Friends in Brummānā, in 1877, deserve special note. All the boarding-schools so far mentioned were of the secondary level. Most of them had extensive grounds and well-equipped modern buildings. But the crowning achievement of Protestant missionary work in Lebanon was the establishment in Beirut of the Syrian Protestant College, which later became the American University of Beirut. The Syria Mission had voted to establish a college in Beirut as early as 1862. In the following year the Syrian Protestant College was incorporated by the Legislature of the State of New York. The College was formally opened in October 1866, under the presidency of its founder Daniel Bliss (1823–1916), and it soon took its place as a leading centre of advanced learning in the Ottoman Empire. The corner-stone of its first building was laid on 7 December 1871.

The educational activity of the Protestant missionaries had from the very start provoked the Roman Catholic missionaries to follow their example. These began their educational work in earnest in 1834, when the Lazarist Fathers reopened the school of ʿAyn Ṭūrā. Five years later the Jesuits started a school in Beirut. In 1843 a second Jesuit school was founded in Ghazīr (the Kisrawān), followed by a third in Zahleh in 1844. The Jesuits also established schools in Bikfayyā (the Matn), Taʿnāyil (the Biqā), Jazzīn, Dayr al-Qamar, and Sidon. Again following the example of the Americans, they established a press, operated on the lithographic process, in 1847, and six years later they began to print with movable type. By the end of the century the Catholic press, as the Jesuit press in Beirut was called, was the leading Press in the country, both in its output of scholarly works and in its excellent production.

The Jesuits in Lebanon were certainly the most active of the Roman Catholic missionaries in education, but they were not the only ones. Besides the Lazarists, there were the Sisters of Charity and a number of other orders who established schools for boys and girls throughout the country. It was not long also before the local Catholic churches and pious foundations took up the challenge and began to compete with the foreign missionaries in educational work. In 1853 two orders of Maronite nuns were founded, which specialized in establishing schools for girls in the various Lebanese villages. By 1914 these two orders had thirty schools with six thousand pupils under their management. Meanwhile, Maronite and Greek Catholic schools for boys, established in almost every part of the country, were meeting with considerable success. Among these were two important schools in Beirut: the École Patriarcale founded in 1865 by the Greek Catholics, and the École de la Sagesse founded in 1874 by the Maronite Bishop of Beirut. The Collège Oriental, founded in 1898 by the Greek Catholics in Zahleh, also deserves mention. By the last quarter of the nineteenth century the educational system brought into being by local and foreign (mostly French) Catholic agencies had grown into an impressive structure. To crown it, the Jesuits in 1875 transferred to Beirut the seminary which they had founded in Ghazir, transforming it into an institution of higher learning to rival the Syrian Protestant College. This was the start of the Université St Joseph, which continues until this day as one of the two leading universities in Lebanon.

Apart from the Protestants and Catholics, the educational contribution of other Lebanese communities during the nineteenth century must not be forgotten, although it was certainly on a smaller scale. Like the Maronites and Greek Catholics, the Greek Orthodox took some initiative in founding schools. A school for boys was established in 1833 in the convent of Balamand, near Tripoli (*see* p. 126). Another was established in 1852 in Sūq al-Gharb, then transferred to Beirut to become the Collège des Trois Docteurs. Later, in 1880, a Greek Orthodox lady in Beirut, Emily Sursuq, founded a school for girls called Zahrat al-Iḥsān (Flower of Charity). These two schools were established along with others outside Beirut. Meanwhile, on 31 July 1878, a group of prominent Sunnites of Beirut founded a charitable society which was to become, in time, the richest and most active organization of its kind in Lebanon: the Moslem Society of Benevolent Intentions (*Jam'iyyat al-Maqāṣid al-Khayriyya al-Islāmiyya*). The first aim of this society was to spread instruction among young Moslems of both sexes; and soon after its foundation the first Maqāsid schools for boys and girls were opened in Beirut, Sidon, and Tripoli. Later, in 1897, a Sunnite of Beirut, Aḥmad 'Abbās al-Azharī (1853–1927), founded a school called al-Madrasa al-'Uthmāniyya (Ottoman School) which was closed down during the First World War by the Ottoman authorities. Of all the Lebanese communities only the Shi'ites and the Druzes took no part in the educational movement of the time. The Shi'ites, living in the more remote parts of the country, were not even exposed to the educational influence of the other communities or of the foreign missionaries. The Druzes were better off in this respect. While they did not establish schools themselves, they sent their children to the Christian schools in their districts, particularly the Protestant schools. The first mutesarrif of Lebanon, Dāwūd Pasha, moreover sponsored a special school for the Druzes at 'Abay, which was established as a Druze pious foundation and continues to be so run today[52] (*see* p. 112).

By the end of the nineteenth century Lebanon was easily the most advanced part of the Ottoman Empire in the field of popular education. Literacy was widespread in the country, particularly in Mount Lebanon and in Beirut, Sidon, and Tripoli. Anyone could easily obtain primary instruction, and a good secondary education was available for those who could afford it. Two colleges in Beirut offered courses of advanced study in the arts and sciences, as well as training in medicine. The American Press, the Catholic Press, and thirteen other printing-presses in Beirut and Mount Lebanon published books in Arabic on a wide variety of subjects, mostly literary, and issued no less than forty periodical publications, including fifteen newspapers, between 1870 and 1900.[53] Of these the newspaper *Lisān al-Ḥāl* (1877) and the Jesuit learned journal *Al-Mashriq* (1898) are still published and widely read today.

These developments in Lebanon had come about at a time when the Ottoman Empire as a whole was undergoing profound changes. In Turkey, the nineteenth century was the age of the *tanzimat* or reforms, and nowhere were the *tanzimat* more successful than in education. In the Turkish schools and colleges established at the time, notably the Imperial Ottoman Lycée at Galatasaray (1868), 'a new educated *élite* was evolved, with a new spirit, and a new and clearer perception of realities'.[54] Increased contact with Europe was meanwhile bringing about a revolution in ideas, as writers like Ibrāhīm Shināsī (1826–71), Ziyā Pasha (1825–80), and Nāmiq Kamāl (1840–88) grappled with the problems of liberalizing the Ottoman Empire and of adapting Islam and Moslem society to the West. Likewise in Egypt, where the successors of Muḥammad 'Alī were eagerly continuing his work of westernization, an intellectual movement developed, led by men like Jamāl al-Dīn al-Afghānī (1839–97) and Muḥammad 'Abduh (1842–1905), which stressed the necessity of modernizing Islam to meet the challenge of Europe. Turkey and Egypt were both Moslem countries, and what disturbed Turkish and Egyptian intellectuals most at the time was the political and material superiority of the West and its growing dominance over the Moslem world, particularly after the British occupation of Egypt in 1882. To face the impact of the West, it was necessary for Moslem society to discover and adopt from the West those elements which were at the basis of its power and prosperity. This implied a considerable degree of westernization, which was not possible unless a great deal of that which was fundamental to the Moslem heritage was neglected or abandoned. Such a course no Moslem in the nineteenth century was willing to consider or advise, and the modernization of Islam under the circumstances could not advance beyond half measures. Consequently, the leaders of the modernist movement in Turkey and Egypt, who were fascinated by the new ideas from the West, could not permit themselves to accept such ideas before they were first justified in accordance with Islam. This placed limits on the progress of modernism in both countries as well as in other countries of the Near East which fell under their influence.

While Turkish and Egyptian intellectuals were engrossed in attempts to justify modernism in the light of Islam, or Islam in the light of modernism, no such consideration disturbed the Christian intellectual in Lebanon. True, the traditional social background of the Eastern Christian, in Lebanon and elsewhere, differed little from that of the Moslem. Yet the Lebanese who identified himself as a Christian could easily accept the West, with none of the Moslem's religious or political reservations. Not only was the Westerner a Christian like himself, but he also appeared to him as a champion and a protector. After the troubles of 1860, Western Powers were the agents which guaranteed for the Lebanese Christian the autonomy of his country and the safety of his community. As a result, the intellectual movement in Lebanon during the nineteenth century, in that it was led by Christians, was in sharp contrast to contemporary developments in Turkey, Egypt, and other Moslem countries. Unlike the Turk or Egyptian, the Lebanese Christian did not feel responsibility for the reform and perpetuation of a declining empire threatened from without and within, nor for the expulsion from his country of a foreign master of alien faith, who was holding him in subservience. Although as an Oriental he was conservative by habit, he was not in principle opposed to social change along western lines. When necessary, he accepted western ways with no misgivings and often with enthusiasm. The West, which the Moslem feared or resented, was his friend.

Meanwhile, the Lebanon of the Mutesarrifate was enjoying a security and prosperity which it had never known before. Compared to other Ottoman subjects then, the Lebanese people had reason, indeed, to be happy with their lot. The oppressive feudalism of former days had almost completely disappeared, and Christian and Druze peasants in Mount Lebanon were gradually acquiring real estate and becoming landowners. In the larger mountain villages and towns prosperous communities of artisans and tradesmen, mostly Christian, had already developed and gained importance. In Beirut and Tripoli the commercial revival that followed the withdrawal of Ibrāhīm Pasha from Syria opened the opportunity for a number of families, mostly Greek Orthodox, to rise to great wealth. Greek Orthodox merchant princes like the Sursuqs, Buṭruses, Twaynīs and Ṭrāds in Beirut lived outside the town in the fashionable suburb of Ashrafiyya, in large Italianate mansions furnished and decorated mostly in European style. Such families formed in their day the select westernized society, whose manners were imitated by a growing class of Christian *bourgeoisie*

– a class which rapidly developed as villagers flocked to the coastal towns, mainly Beirut, to make use of the new opportunities.

Living in relatively easy circumstances, and having no fundamental hostility towards the West, the Christian intellectual in Lebanon during the nineteenth century felt none of the tension experienced by the Turk, Egyptian, Syrian, or even by the Lebanese Moslem. While controversy and apologetic or romantic fervour characterized and often obstructed the activity of the Moslem writer or thinker, the Lebanese Christian intellectual was at ease to explore such fields as history, linguistics, and literature with a cool and positive scholarly interest. Politics, which sapped the energies of Moslem colleagues, interested him little. In westernization he saw progress, not conflict. So it was that the age which in the Moslem world produced fiery revolutionaries like Nāmiq Kamāl and Jamāl al-Dīn al-Afghānī, produced in Lebanon scholars and linguists like Nāṣīf al-Yāzijī, Buṭrus al-Bustānī and Fāris al-Shidyāq, writers like Jurjī Zaydān, and enterprising journalists like Ya'qūb Ṣarrūf, Fāris Nimr, and Salīm and Bishāra Taqlā. Such Lebanese Christians were the vanguard of an Arabic literary revival which, in time, was to spread from Lebanon to every other country where Arabic was spoken. By their efforts 'Arabic became once again a pliable tool of thought and learning',[55] the Arabic literary heritage was rediscovered and studied, and the broad lines for future developments in literature and journalism were set. It is hardly possible to exaggerate the importance of their contribution in these respects.

The beginnings of the Arabic literary revival in Lebanon were closely connected with the activity of the American missionaries, and particularly of two exceptionally gifted men: Eli Smith (1801–57) and Cornelius Van Dyck (1818–95). In 1844 these two men undertook to make a new translation of the Bible into Arabic – a project first envisaged by the American missionaries in 1837. The work of translation was begun in 1847 under the direction of Eli Smith, and it was continued after Smith's death in 1857 by Cornelius Van Dyck. The original idea was to make the translation 'in the best modern form of spoken Arabic'. When the actual translation began Smith 'attempted to remain true to classical Arabic usage, but also to use only that part of the old language which is understood by the unlearned'. Van Dyck continued to work in the same manner, and the result was an Arabic version of the Bible, completed and printed in 1865, which was locally acclaimed to be 'so pure, so exact, so clear, and so classical, as to be acceptable to all classes and all sects'.[56]

As the work on the Bible translation went on, Smith and Van Dyck came into close intellectual contact with three local scholars who assisted them in the work: Nāṣif al-Yāzijī (1800–71), Buṭrus al-Bustānī (1819–83), and Yūsuf Al-Asīr (1815–89). Yāzijī came from a Greek Catholic family, and was already a scholar and writer of great reputation when he was called upon to assist in translating the Bible. In his youth he had been in the circle of the historian-emir Ḥaydar al-Shihābī, and he had later served Bashīr II as a secretary. After 1840 he established himself in Beirut where he soon became associated with the American missionaries as a tutor in Arabic. In his later years he taught Arabic in a school started by his associate Buṭrus al-Bustānī, and afterwards in the Syrian Protestant College. The works of Yāzijī include books and essays on philosophy, style, rhetoric, poetry, and other subjects. He also began a commentary on the works of the Arabic poet al-Mutannabbī (AD 915–55), and this commentary was completed after his death and published by his son Ibrāhīm (1847–1906). Furthermore, Nāṣif al-Yāzijī wrote original prose and verse in imitation of the classical Arabic style, which set a fashion followed by other writers. Ibrāhīm al-Yāzijī, his son, was also to distinguish himself as a grammarian and man of letters, and left among other works an essay on journalistic style (1901) and a dictionary of Arabic synonyms (1904). Ibrāhīm taught at the École Patriarcale in Beirut, and beginning in 1872, he helped in the Jesuit translation of the Bible into Arabic which was completed in 1880.

Buṭrus al-Bustānī, a graduate of 'Ayn Waraqa, was a Maronite turned Protestant. He first came into contact with the American missionaries in 1839 or 1840, when he was employed as a teacher at their seminary in Beirut. From that time on Bustānī remained in continuous association with the American missionaries, working with them in full harmony and enjoying their confidence and high esteem. A school which he started in his home in 1863, the National School (al-Madrasa al-Waṭaniyya), was later incorporated in the Syrian Protestant College where he taught for a number of years. He also held for a time the post of dragoman at the American

Consulate. When he died in 1883 he was considered 'the most learned, industrious, and successful, as well as the most influential man of modern Syria'.[57] Among the many works he left is his well-known Arabic dictionary *Muḥīt al-muḥīt* (Beirut, 1870), a standard work unexcelled until this day, and six volumes of an encyclopaedia, *Dā'irat al-ma'ārif* (Beirut, 1876–82), of which five more volumes were issued after his death by his son Salīm and his kinsman Sulaymān al-Bustānī. Although incomplete, this encyclopaedia continues to stand as 'a monument of industry and literary ability'.[58] In 1860, following the massacres of that year in Lebanon and Damascus, Buṭrus al-Bustānī pioneered in Arabic journalism with his weekly 'sheet of advice' *Nafīr Sūriyya* (Bugle of Syria), in which he called his people 'to union and co-operation in reconstructing their distracted and almost ruined country'.[59] Later he founded other periodicals: the semi-weekly *Al-Janna* (1870) edited by his son Salīm, and the fortnightly *Al-Jinān* (1870) and daily *Al-Junayna* (1871) edited by his kinsman Sulaymān.

Unlike Nāṣīf al-Yāzijī and Buṭrus al-Bustānī who were Christians, the third local scholar who assisted in the Bible translation was a Moslem sharī'a expert from Sidon. Yūsuf al-Asīr was a graduate of Al-Azhar in Cairo, and at various times held the position of judge in Tripoli, mufti in Acre, and attorney-general for Lebanon under Dāwūd Pasha. For a time he taught Arabic at Istanbul, after which he returned to Beirut where he taught at the École Patriarcale and the Syrian Protestant College. As a scholar and writer Yūsuf al-Asīr did not attain the stature of Yāzijī and Bustānī, but he nevertheless became the chief collaborator in the completion of the Arabic Bible after 1857, when Van Dyck took over. Like Yāzijī and Bustānī, Asīr was among those who had taught Van Dyck Arabic, and Van Dyck had a high opinion of his scholarship and literary ability. Most important, Asīr was the first Moslem in Lebanon to associate himself with the Christian-led Arabic literary revival which was in time to influence other Moslems in the country. Among his writings are some works in verse which include several contributions to the Arabic Protestant hymnal, and a commentary on the Ottoman Code which was published posthumously. He was also the founder of a newspaper *Thamarat al-Funūn* (1875) – the first newspaper in Lebanon to be published by a Moslem.[60]

The influence which Eli Smith and Cornelius Van Dyck exercised over Yāzijī, Bustānī, and Asīr was indeed great. The American scholars set their Lebanese colleagues an example of scholarly diligence and determination which was carefully followed, and which one finds reflected particularly in the work of Bustānī. These were not, however, the only Lebanese scholars and writers whose careers were connected with the American missionaries. Of the others whom they influenced, the most brilliant beyond doubt was Fāris al-Shidyāq (1805–87), brother of the Protestant martyr As'ad al-Shidyāq, and like him a graduate of 'Ayn Waraqa. On leaving school Fāris al-Shidyāq was employed by the historian Ḥaydar al-Shihābī as a copyist and assistant. The persecutions suffered by his brother As'ad at the hands of the Maronite clergy so infuriated Fāris that he broke away from the Maronite church in 1826 and became himself a convert to Protestantism. The American missionaries sent him first to Egypt where he pursued his linguistic and literary studies with eminent masters, then in 1834 to Malta where he taught at the mission school and edited the publications of the American press until 1848. Shidyāq afterwards travelled in Europe, and went to England where he helped in a never-published Arabic translation of the Bible under the auspices of the British and Foreign Bible Society. In 1854 he was invited by the Bey of Tunisia to enter his service and edit the official Tunisian journal *Al-Rā'id al-Tūnisī*. While in Tunisia he became a convert to Islam and adopted the name Aḥmad Fāris. Later, in 1860, he was invited by the Porte to settle in Istanbul, and there, Shidyāq began to publish an Arabic newspaper *Al-Jawā'ib* – perhaps the most influential Arabic periodical published during the century. *Al-Jawā'ib* continued publication until 1884, printing articles by its editor on a wide variety of political and cultural subjects and setting a standard for contemporary Arabic journalism. After Shidyāq's retirement the editorship of *Al-Jawā'ib* was taken over by his son Salīm. Fāris al-Shidyāq died in 1887, in Istanbul, leaving many works of linguistic and literary criticism, original writings in prose and verse, and accounts of his numerous travels in Europe and the Near East. Critics have ranked him with Nāṣīf al-Yāzijī as the chief creator of modern literary Arabic.

Yāzijī, Bustānī, and Shidyāq dominated the Arabic scholarly and literary revival of the nineteenth century. Of the three, Shidyāq flourished outside Lebanon, and his influence was felt during his own lifetime throughout the Near East as well as in North Africa. During the last decades of the century, as education spread in Lebanon with the establishment of the schools and colleges, a number of other scholars and writers appeared, many of whom, like Shidyāq, flourished outside their native land. Egypt under the khedives, and later under British rule, attracted those who were to become the leading figures. Salīm Taqlā (1849–92), a Greek Catholic from Kafarshīmā (near Beirut), studied at the ʻAbay seminary and at Bustānī's National School, taught for some time at the École Patriarcale in Beirut, and finally emigrated to Egypt. There, in 1875, he founded a weekly newspaper *Al-Ahrām* which later became a daily publication, and which remains until this day the leading newspaper in Egypt. In editing *Al-Ahrām*, Salīm Taqlā had as an assistant his brother Bishāra (1852–1911), a graduate of ʻAyn Ṭūrā. One year after *Al-Ahrām* had started publication in Cairo, Yaʻqūb Ṣarrūf (1852–1927) and Fāris Nimr (*c.* 1860–1952) began publishing in Beirut a monthly periodical *Al-Muqtaṭaf*. The editors of this scientific-literary journal were both of Greek Orthodox stock. Ṣarrūf, who became a Protestant, was from al-Ḥadath, near Beirut, and Nimr came originally from Ḥāṣbayyā, in Wādī al-Taym. Both studied at the Syrian Protestant College, became teachers there upon their graduation, and formed with other students and teachers an intellectual circle dominated by Cornelius Van Dyck. *Al-Muqtaṭaf* grew out of the activity of this circle, with the encouragement of Van Dyck who chose the name 'The Selection' for the journal. When Sarrūf and Nimr left Beirut and emigrated to Egypt in 1883 they took their journal with them, and within a year *Al-Muqtaṭaf* was established in Cairo as a leading forum of free opinion. In its pages, between 1884 and 1886, two other graduates of the Syrian Protestant College, Shiblī al-Shumayyil (1860–1917) and Ibrāhīm al-Ḥawrānī (1844–1916), debated the theories of Charles Darwin, the latter attacking them while the former wrote in their defence. Shumayyil, a Greek Catholic from Kafarshīmā, rose to fame in Egypt as a physician and wrote extensively on science. Ḥawrānī, originally a Greek Orthodox Christian from Homs, became a convert to Protestantism, settled in Lebanon, and taught mathematics and astronomy at the Syrian Protestant College. He wrote on science, philosophy, theology, sociology, and other subjects and gained some distinction as a poet and man of letters. Ṣarrūf and Nimr, however, did not only publish *Al-Muqtaṭaf*. In 1889 they launched in Cairo their newspaper *Al-Muqaṭṭam* which became for many years the rival of *Al-Ahrām* in influence and popularity. Both *Al-Muqtaṭaf* and *Al-Muqaṭṭam* continued publication until 1952, the year Nimr died. Meanwhile, another Lebanese emigrant to Egypt, Jurjī Zaydān, founded in 1892 in Cairo the monthly magazine *Al-Hilāl*. Modelled after *Al-Muqtaṭaf*, this magazine soon rose to share the prestige of the older publication as a leading Arabic scientific and literary journal, and it continues publication today in a more popular form. Zaydān himself was a Greek Orthodox Christian from Beirut and a former medical student at the Syrian Protestant College. Apart from editing *Al-Hilāl* and becoming the founder of a major publishing house in Egypt, he wrote brilliantly on history and on Arabic philology and literature and was the author of a number of historical novels set in various periods of the Moslem past. His histories of Arabic literature (*Ta'rīkh al-ādāb al-'Arabiyya*) and of Moslem civilization (*Ta'rīkh al-tamaddun al-Islāmī*) are classics which, along with his historical novels, are still widely read.

Part II

GREATER LEBANON

Un pays que la tradition doit
défendre contre la force. . . .

MICHEL CHIHA

CHAPTER VIII

GREATER LEBANON

Closely connected with the general development of Lebanon under the Mutesarrifate was the emergence of certain social and political ideas which were to be of fundamental importance in the subsequent history of the country. These ideas, varying and often in conflict, represented attempts by Lebanese intellectuals to understand the special nature of their country and its peculiar relationship to the surrounding Near Eastern world. Christian intellectuals, in particular, tried to determine some principle of Moslem-Christian co-operation which would secure the safety and dignity of Syrian and especially Lebanese Christians in predominently Moslem surroundings. To such Christians the European idea of nationalism, with its secular connotations, seemed to provide a useful clue; but the adaptation of this idea to the special circumstances of Lebanon was not to prove an easy task.

By 1861, when the Lebanese Mutesarrifate was established, the idea of nationalism was already gaining wide currency in the Ottoman Empire. It had first become manifest four decades earlier in the European provinces, when the Serbs and Greeks revolted against Turkish rule and began their struggle for independence. Other Balkan peoples later followed their example; and in every case, as Greeks and other Balkan Christians revolted against a Turkish domination which was essentially Moslem, their nationalism, as Christians, already bore a religious colouring. In reaction, there developed among the Moslems of the Empire – Turks, Arabs, and others – an intense desire to vindicate the political ascendancy of Islam, if necessary by violence. The Ottoman government did not always approve of such fanaticism. Between 1839 and 1876, during the *Tanzimat* period (*see* p. 44), sincere efforts were indeed made to allay the disaffection of the Sultan's non-Moslem subjects and associate them more closely in the Ottoman State. Reformers at the time tried hard to secure a general loyalty to the Empire by promoting the idea of a secular Ottoman nationalism which would transcend religious loyalties and embrace Moslem and non-Moslem Ottomans alike. In practice, however, Ottomanism did not prove a success. Moslem zealots found its secularism repugnant and refused to accept non-Moslems as their political associates. As for the Christians, they seriously doubted the motives behind the Ottomanist reforms and tended to regard Ottomanism as a mere device to strengthen the predominance of Islam.

To the Christians of the Empire, indeed, Islamism and Ottomanism appeared to be equally threatening. While the former doctrine frankly aimed at perpetuating their inferior status, the latter threatened to deprive them of valuable privileges which they had always enjoyed as protected minorities. Ottomanism, moreover, sought to intensify centralization; consequently, remote Christian provinces, which had traditionally enjoyed a considerable measure of self-rule, were now menaced with the unwelcome prospect of direct Turkish government. True, the Ottomanist reformers promised to compensate for any loss of traditional privilege or local autonomy by allowing the minorities a fuller share in the general management of the Empire. The Christians, however, were not reassured; they realized that no real equality between Christians and Moslems was possible, whatever promises were made, in a predominantly Moslem empire. While they remained within the Ottoman Empire, the Christian nationalities in the Balkans, Armenia, and Syria insisted on retaining their old privileges along with any new ones they might secure. Beyond that, they generally looked forward to the acquisition of a larger measure of autonomy as a first step towards complete independence.

Separatism, indeed, acquired increasing momentum among Ottoman Christians in the nineteenth century; the various groups differed, however, in their ability to pursue their aims. In the Balkan countries, the Serbians, Bulgarians, and Rumanians formed, as did the Greeks, distinct Christian national groups identifiable by language. Proximity to Europe and the ready availability of outside help made it comparatively easy for these nationalities, one after the other, to revolt and achieve their independence. The Armenians, like the Balkan Christians, also had the advantage of being a distinct group with a language and separate church organization of their own; their two homelands of Cilicia and Greater Armenia, however, were both in Asia Minor, surrounded by Moslem territory and geographically out of contact with Europe. Armenian nationalism, consequently, could not challenge Turkish rule with impunity, and when revolt was finally attempted, it was suppressed with the utmost severity.

Like the Armenians, the Arabic-speaking Christians of Syria belonged to the Asiatic part of the Ottoman Empire and lacked the Balkan advantage of proximity to Europe. Furthermore, by contrast with both the Balkan Christians and the Armenians, they had neither a country nor a national language which was exclusively their own. Hence they could only be distinguished from the Arabic-speaking Moslems of Syria by religion, and were in no position to claim a separate independence. In the Mutesarrifate of Lebanon, it is true, the majority of the population were Christians, mostly Maronites. But the Druzes had an equal claim to Lebanon as a national homeland; and Christian attempts to establish an autonomous Lebanon which took no account of Druze aspirations were doomed to failure.

Thus, when the Maronites after 1840 sought to assert their supremacy in the country, Druze reactions were set in motion which culminated in the massacres of 1860. The lesson of that year was not forgotten. In the purely Maronite districts of the north many Maronites continued, even after 1860, to think of Lebanon mainly as a Christian homeland, and they were sometimes encouraged to do so by Roman Catholic missionaries. In the mixed districts of the south such an attitude was not possible. Here, even the staunchest Christian nationalists realized that survival involved compromise. As a possible solution to the problem of establishing a viable Lebanese state, some of them called for an extension of its existing frontiers; but the more perceptive probably realized that even this solution would be ineffective in the long run without close Christian-Moslem co-operation. The coastal towns and the Biqāʿ, so important to Lebanon, were predominantly Moslem in population; hence, their incorporation in a Greater Lebanon was bound to make the country much less of a Christian homeland.

If the Maronite patriots of the Mutesarrifate period were mainly concerned with the enlargement of Lebanon, the loyalty of other

Christian groups went far beyond to include the whole of Syria. Lebanese Greek Orthodox and Greek Catholics could not ignore the fact that many of their co-religionists lived in predominantly Moslem surroundings outside Lebanon, in the Syrian interior and in Palestine. The Maronites also had some co-religionists in the larger Syrian towns, particularly in Aleppo where a large Maronite community thrived. In the case of each of the three sects, the church organization centring round the See of Antioch covered the whole of Syria excluding only the Palestinian See of Jerusalem. This in itself unified the Christian cause throughout the Syrian vilayets. Hence, while the Maronites in general continued to be principally devoted to Lebanon, some prominent men among them joined the mass of Greek Orthodox and Greek Catholics in thinking of all Syria as their homeland. As the years passed, there developed among this group of Christian patriots the idea of a Syrian nationality which transcended religious and sectarian identities and could, therefore, include the Arabic-speaking Moslems of Syria along with the Christians. This secular nationalism, based on the Arabic language and cultural heritage in which all Syrian communities shared, promised to provide the Christians of Syria with the much-needed formula for Christian-Moslem co-operation, and to make possible a Syrian-Arab nationalism of the linguistic and cultural kind, such as had arisen by natural processes in the Balkans.

The emergence of this nationalism, based on the Arabic language and cultural tradition, was closely connected with the Arabic literary revival which was taking place at the time in Lebanon. One of its earliest exponents was Buṭrus al-Bustānī, the Maronite convert to Protestantism whose career as a scholar and educator has already been referred to in the previous chapter (*see* p. 144–5). In the weekly publication *Nafīr Sūriyya* (Clarion of Syria), the first issue of which appeared in 1860, Bustānī called for fraternity between the Moslems and Christians of Syria. For a later publication, the fortnightly *al-Jinān*, Bustānī used the motto 'Love of homeland is part of the Faith'. To Bustānī and his associates the 'homeland' in question was Syria, but it was a Syria inseparable from its Arabic cultural tradition. The Arabism of Syria was given great emphasis in the latter part of the nineteenth century in the literary and scientific circles which grew around the

Syrian Protestant College in Beirut, and which were intellectually dominated by the eminent American missionary and scholar Cornelius Van Dyck (*see* p. 147). It was probably under the influence of Van Dyck, with his deep interest in the Arab heritage, that the Syrianism of Bustānī evolved by imperceptible degrees into the Arabism of younger Christian intellectuals like Ibrāhīm al-Yāzijī, Ya'qūb Ṣarrūf and Fāris Nimr.

It was in the last decades of the nineteenth century that the Arab nationalist idea first emerged and gained clarity among young Christians in Lebanon. The idea, as it was conceived at the time, was not clearly distinguishable from the earlier Syrian nationalism, which only differed from the new Arabism in being generally more vague. Nor was the Arab nationalism of Ibrāhīm al-Yāzijī and his associates in any real conflict with the Lebanese nationalism prevalent among Maronite patriots. The idea canvassed by the Christian Arab nationalists of Lebanon challenged the claims of Ottomanism and Pan-Islamism, but presented, as yet, no threat to the Lebanese nationalists. The Arabs, according to the Arab nationalist theory, had once been a great nation with a glorious history and a splendid civilization; in time, however, they had fallen under the domination of the Turks and had gone into decline. To reverse this historical process and restore the Arab nation to its greatness, early Christian Arab nationalists invited their Moslem compatriots throughout Syria to join them in a general Arab movement to oppose Turkish claims. Ottomanism, which threatened to impose complete centralization, was to be rejected; also to be rejected was the pan-Islamist idea, which threatened to perpetuate the disunity of the Arab nation by dividing its Christians and Moslems. Pan-Islamism was pointed out to be dangerous for yet another reason – it confirmed Turkish dominion over Arabs in the name of Moslem unity. This being the position of the Christian Arab nationalists of the nineteenth century, it is no wonder that they frequently collaborated with the Lebanese Christian nationalists, as both aimed primarily at securing the Christian position in Syria.

One cannot really claim that Arab nationalism, by origin, was a purely Lebanese Christian invention. The idea, as set forth by Ibrāhīm al-Yāzijī and his Christian group, did not fail to find expression in the work of some contemporary Moslem writers, notably ʿAbd al-Raḥmān al-Kawākibī of Aleppo (1825–1902). Until the early years of the twentieth century Arab Moslems, it is true, remained supremely conscious of their religious and political unity with Turkish Moslems, and their loyalty to the Ottoman Sultan seldom wavered. Arab dislike for the Turks was, nevertheless, common, and there was no lack of mutual prejudice and tension between the two races which the early Arab nationalists could exploit. The circumstances of the late nineteenth century did not, however, favour the spread of Arab nationalism among the Syrian Moslems. ʿAbd al-Ḥamīd II, who succeeded to the Sultanate in 1876, was deeply disappointed at the Christian reaction to the secularist reforms of that period. As the Christian nationalities under his rule persisted in their separatism, he gradually turned away from the secularism of the Ottomanist reformers and began to seek his main support among his loyal Moslem subjects. Stressing his authority as Caliph of Islam, ʿAbd al-Ḥamīd II championed the widely popular pan-Islamic movement and showed special favour to the Empire's non-Turkish Moslems, particularly the Arabs who formed, among them, the most important group. In the circumstances, Arab Moslems in Syria and elsewhere stood to gain little by opposing their Sultan-Caliph, and were certainly not tempted to join their Christian countrymen in clamouring for partial or complete separation from a Moslem Ottoman empire in which they enjoyed privileged status. While ʿAbd al-Ḥamīd II remained Sultan, Arab nationalism remained a largely Christian separatist movement in Syria, attracting little, if any, Moslem support.

In 1908, however, the situation in the Ottoman Empire underwent a radical change. Working in conjunction with the army, the Young Turks, heirs of the nineteenth-century reform group, staged a successful revolution against ʿAbd al-Ḥamīd II, and in the following year deposed the Sultan and placed his weak brother, Muḥammad V, on the throne. In the late nineteenth century the Young Turks and ʿAbd al-Ḥamīd II had alike been disillusioned with Ottomanism. However, while the Sultan abandoned this secular idea for pan-Islamism, the Young Turks continued to think in mainly secular terms and developed a Turkish nationalism, proclaiming the Turks a distinct race with a special mission of leadership in the Ottoman Empire and in Islam. This Turkish nationalism, opposed to Christian separatism and unwilling to accord separate recognition to the Arabs or to other non-Turkish Moslems, began to overshadow pan-Islamism in Ottoman policies and attitudes when the Young Turks, after 1909, took over the Ottoman Government. Soon it became clear that the centralization of the Ottoman Empire, which the reformers of the nineteenth century had promoted, was henceforth to be accompanied by an attempt at the deliberate Turkification of all Ottoman peoples, Moslems and non-Moslems alike.

The new policy introduced by the Young Turks was to provoke a strong reaction among the Moslem Arabs of Syria, who, until then, had regarded the Turks primarily as brothers in Islam. As the Young Turk régime in Istanbul emphasized Turkish supremacy, abandoned the Ḥamīdian form of Pan-Islamism, and often showed contempt for its subject peoples, young Moslem Arabs everywhere felt alienated and resentful. Many among them, especially in Syria, began to turn against the Turks, some altogether abandoning their old loyalty to the Ottoman State. Within a short time a vigorous Arab nationalist movement began to gain ground among the Moslems of Syria, with active centres in Damascus, Aleppo, and Beirut. This Moslem Arab nationalism was akin to that of the Christians in its emphasis on the Arabic language and heritage as a basis for unity; Moslem and Christian Arab nationalists could, therefore, co-operate to a great extent in their efforts to propagate their nationalist ideal. To some Christians, however, a major difficulty soon became apparent. While their Moslem colleagues, in theory, stressed the secularism of the Arab nationalist movement, it was nearly impossible for them, in practice, to dissociate Arabism from Islam.

The rapid Moslem adherence to Arab nationalism after 1909 radically changed the nature and course of the Arab nationalist movement. For three decades or more the movement had owed its main inspiration to Christian separatism and had been, for the most part, opposed to pan-Islamism. As long as it made no headway among the Moslems, its chances of ultimate success seemed poor. After 1909 the situation completely changed. Arab nationalism, now under Moslem leadership, became an important force with which the Young Turk Government in Istanbul had to reckon. Secret societies in the leading towns of Syria established political contacts with foreign powers and began to make serious plans for the separation of the Arabs from the Ottoman Empire. With the Christians among them now in the minority, the new Arab nationalists ceased to be seriously concerned with secularist opposition to pan-Islamism. Their efforts, instead, were directed against the Young Turk policy of Turkification and centralization. Looking beyond the united Syria, envisaged by the earlier nationalists, they spoke of the establishment of a far-flung and independent Arab empire, which would include all Moslem countries where Arabic was spoken.

As Arab nationalism, under Moslem direction, began to assume its new form, the Christian attitude towards it naturally changed. In the Syrian interior the Christians, being clearly a minority, saw no wisdom in opposing the new trend, in spite of the distinct Moslem colouring it had acquired. The Moslem nationalists there insisted that their movement was purely secular, and this gave their Christian colleagues no cause to withdraw their support. In Lebanon, however, the prevailing attitude among the Christian majority was entirely different. Never truly happy with the Arab nationalist formula, Lebanese Christian nationalists, who were mainly Maronites and Greek Catholics, became increasingly suspicious of it when Arab nationalism developed into a predominantly Moslem movement. Like the Moslem Arab nationalists, the Lebanese Christians were opposed to Ottoman rule and looked forward to the achievement of full independence for their country. On this immediate issue Lebanese and Arab nationalists were at one. For Lebanese patriots, however, the ultimate aim of Moslem Arab nationalists threatened to produce a situation to which even continued Ottoman rule was preferable. In the Ottoman Empire the Lebanese enjoyed a privileged autonomy which they were anxious at least to preserve. There was no guarantee that such an autonomy could be maintained in an Arab empire. Lebanese Christians, in the event of the dissolution of the Ottoman Empire, were not prepared to accept another form of Moslem overlordship; in particular, they feared that the Arabs, in the name of Arab secularism, would impose their own Moslem dominance in Lebanon far more completely than had the Turks.

The first breach between Lebanese and Arab nationalism may have occurred shortly after 1909. It was only in the latter years of the First World War, however, that it became important. In the early war years Lebanese and Arab nationalists, in common opposition to the Turks, were forced to continue working in collaboration. In 1915 and 1916, a total of thirty-three leaders of both groups were convicted of high treason because of their connexions with the Allies, and publicly hanged in Beirut and Damascus. The common martyrdom of these leaders, who came from among the most prominent families in Lebanon and Syria, created, for a while, the illusion that Lebanese and Arab nationalists were fighting for a common cause. In June 1916 the revolt of Sharīf Ḥusayn in the Hijāz completely changed the situation. Prompted by the British, who encouraged the breach between Arabs and Turks as part of their war strategy, Sharīf Ḥusayn started his revolt on 5 June by declaring the Arabs independent of Turkish rule. On 5 November he proclaimed himself 'King of the Arab Countries'. By this time it was widely rumoured that after the war the Sharīf, with British help, would fulfil the pan-Arab dream of a great Arab empire. Among Arab nationalist circles in Syria enthusiasm for the Sharīfian revolt knew no bounds. Moslems in Damascus, Beirut and other leading Syrian towns soon began to look upon Sharīf Ḥusayn and, more particularly, his gallant son Fayṣal as living embodiments of Arab nationalism and saviours of the Arab nation from the Turks. Among those who stood ready to acclaim the establishment of a Sharīfian Arab empire were a number of Christians, mainly Greek Orthodox or Protestant. In Lebanon, however, the Maronites and Greek Catholics, along with the majority of other Christians, stood firmly against any incorporation of their country in a greater Arab state. While the supporters of the Sharifian movement counted on the help of Britain, the Lebanese separatists turned for support to France, their traditional protector, imploring her to assist them in securing an independent Lebanon.

France needed no prompting where her traditional interests in Syria were concerned. In April-May 1916, shortly before the outbreak of the Sharīfian revolt, her former Consul in Beirut, François Georges-Picot, had negotiated a special agreement with Sir Mark Sykes, representing Britain, which guaranteed for France a pre-eminent position in Syria after the war. By the terms of the Sykes-Picot Agreement[1] the whole Syrian territory west of Aleppo, Hama, Homs, and Damascus, excluding Palestine, was to be included in a special area where France would be free to establish any form of administration she pleased. The Syrian interior, together with the Mosul region in northern Iraq, were, furthermore, to form a French zone of influence, although they were not to be actually placed under French control. Several months before the Sykes-Picot Agreement was concluded, Britain, who had full knowledge of the French interest in Syria, had already warned Sharīf Ḥusayn of it. In the negotiations with the Sharīf which ultimately led to the Arab revolt, the British High Commissioner in Egypt, Sir Henry McMahon, made it plain that Western Syria could not be considered purely Arab; for this reason and also because of the interest of her ally France there, Britain could not agree to the inclusion of this area in the Arab kingdom which the Sharīf was proposing to establish. The Sharīf, for his part, persistently maintained that Western Syria, whose population he regarded as essentially Arab, could under no condition be excluded from the proposed Arab kingdom. His point of view certainly reflected the attitude of the Arab nationalists in Syria. Nevertheless, in his anxiety to conclude the negotiations, the Sharīf finally agreed to ally himself with Britain and revolt against the Turks, without securing any assurances on this important point.[2]

By January 1917 Sharīf Ḥusayn's revolt in the Ḥijaz was clearly successful; by the following July his Arab forces, led by his son Fayṣal, were protecting General Allenby's right flank as he slowly advanced through Palestine. Allenby took Jerusalem on 9 December; it was not until the following summer that he managed to make the next important advance. On 18 September 1918, at the battle of Megiddo in northern Palestine, the Turks were decisively defeated and began rapidly to retreat. By the end of October the whole of Syria had fallen to the British. Meanwhile Fayṣal, whose forces had entered Damascus on 1 October, had formed an Arab military government there which, in the name of the Sharīf, claimed authority over the whole occupied region. In Beirut the collapse of Ottoman control preceded the Allied occupation by several days. On 1 October, the outgoing Turkish governor, Mumtāz Bey (*see* p. 115), handed over authority to a local Moslem notable, 'Umar al-Dā'ūq. An Arab government was forthwith proclaimed in Beirut, hoisting the Sharīfian flag over the public buildings, while Shukrī Pasha al-Ayyūbī, one of Fayṣal's men, was sent with a token force to occupy the town.

These developments in Lebanon and Syria pleased neither the French nor the Christian nationalists in Lebanon. France, however, had taken precautions. During the war, while representatives of the British Government were cultivating the friendship of Sharīf Ḥusayn and the Arab nationalists, the French Foreign Office was maintaining close contact with Lebanese nationalists both in and out of Lebanon. As it became known that Britain was encouraging the Arab nationalists, committees of Lebanese and Catholic Syrian emigrants were formed throughout the world, which persistently pleaded with the Allies to oppose the pan-Arab claims. These committees, with their predominantly Francophile sentiment, willingly co-operated with France and supported her claims in Syria. France, consequently, encouraged them, and in 1917 a central committee, the *Comité Central Syrien*, was formed in Paris to co-ordinate their activities. Meanwhile, the French Naval Division of the Levant, established on the island of Arwād off the Syrian coast, kept watch over developments in Syria and maintained direct contact with Christian nationalists in Lebanon.[3] The British, bound by the Sykes-Picot Agreement to respect the French claim in Syria, did not interfere in these activities.

The Sharīfian occupation of Beirut was, indeed, a shock to the French, as it was to Lebanese Christian nationalist opinion. The Christian nationalists and the French were even more shocked when Shukrī Pasha al-Ayyūbī left Beirut to visit B'abdā, the seat of the Lebanese Mutesarrifate, where he hoisted the Arab flag and, in the name of the Sharīfian Government, convened the Lebanese Administrative Council which had been disbanded by the Turks in 1915. Ḥabīb Pasha al-Sa'd, the Maronite President of the Council, was thereupon called to assume the government of Lebanon in the name of King Ḥusayn. However, Sharifian rule in Lebanon lasted barely a week. On 7 October, by agreement with General Allenby, a small landing party from French ships made its appearance in Beirut. The following day Allenby himself entered Beirut with his British forces, accompanied by a French detachment under Colonel de Piepape. On Allenby's orders

Shukrī Pasha al-Ayyūbī was forced to leave Beirut, the Arab flag was removed from the public buildings, and the Arab Government of 'Umar al-Dā'ūq handed over authority to Colonel de Piepape as Military Governor. Only the Administrative Council of Mount Lebanon, which Shukrī Pasha had reconvened, was allowed to remain as a local governing body, since its allegiance to the Sharīfian Government in Damascus had been purely a matter of temporary convenience. It was not until the end of the month that Tripoli, the last important Lebanese town, fell to the Allies. Meanwhile, on 24 October, Allenby laid down the broad lines for the military administration of Syria. As Occupied Enemy Territory, the area was to be divided into three zones: a British South Zone (Palestine), an Arab East Zone (the Syrian interior) and a French North Zone (Lebanon and coastal Syria). When on 18 December Cilicia came to be called the North Zone, coastal Syria and Lebanon to the south became the West Zone, and continued to be called this until 1920.

The history of modern Lebanon may be said to have begun in 1918 with the French occupation. When Allenby announced the division of occupied Syria into three zones Colonel de Piepape, until then Military Governor of Beirut, became Chief Administrator of the French Zone. Meanwhile François Georges-Picot, who had been appointed High Commissioner of France in the Levant as early as April 1917, could now assume the functions of his office on the spot; but as Georges-Picot was not able to establish himself permanently in Beirut until the early weeks of 1919, he first sent a deputy, Robert Coulondre, to take charge of affairs until his own arrival. In the meantime, a French warship brought home to Beirut the prominent Maronite lawyer Emile Eddé,[4] an ardent Lebanese nationalist and Francophile who had spent the war years in France under Turkish sentence of death. For a few weeks Eddé became the chief local adviser to Coulondre and quickly acquired great prestige.

Georges-Picot had not yet arrived in Beirut when violent clashes between Coulondre and Eddé caused the latter to abandon his office at the headquarters of the French High Commission. The initial favour shown to Eddé, however, had indicated from the very start the kind of policy the French had planned for

Lebanon. The French Administration in the so-called West Zone, from the moment it was established, showed its determination to fulfil all the legitimate aspirations of the Lebanese nationalists. Coulondre, during his brief stay in Beirut, made no secret of the French intentions, and on one occasion publicly announced that France had come to Lebanon primarily to protect her Maronite friends and uphold their interests. Consequently, wherever the representatives of France went in occupied Lebanon, they were met by welcoming crowds of Maronites who discharged their pistols in the air and greeted them with loud cheers. French and Maronite interests clearly converged. If France needed a friendly Lebanon with a Christian majority as a base for her Syrian policy, Maronite and other Lebanese Christians needed French protection for their country against pan-Arab claims. Solidarity between the two sides was particularly urgent as Fayṣal and his Arab Government were still in control of the East Zone and were clamouring for a united Arab Syria.

The Maronites immediately proved useful to the French as allies. In 1919, while American and British circles in Paris supported Fayṣal's pan-Arab claims at the Peace Conference, Maronite delegations, one of them led by Patriarch Ilyās al-Ḥuwayyik in person, went to Versailles to press for a separate and enlarged Lebanon under French protection. The *Comité Central Syrien* and other Lebanese committees abroad also supported the Lebanese separatist claims; so did the delegation sent by the Lebanese Administrative Council which was eager to please France and make up for its short-lived connexion with the Sharifians at Damascus. This last delegation was composed of three Christian members, a Moslem, and a Druze, with Emile Eddé as a prominent Christian member. Meanwhile at the Peace Conference, the Supreme Council had decided to establish mandates for all occupied territories formerly under Turkish or German rule. These territories, it was suggested, were by no means ready for independence. Some, like the German colonies in Africa and the Far East, were clearly primitive and needed long periods of tutelage under mandatory powers before they would be ready to manage their own affairs. Lebanon, Syria, Palestine, and Iraq could in no way be compared to these backward areas. As relatively advanced countries, they were capable of a considerable measure of self-rule. Nevertheless, it was urged that the establishment of French and British mandates in these countries was needed in order to prepare them for full independence. In Syria, Arab nationalist circles strongly protested against the proposal for mandatory rule. Fayṣal and his government refused to consider it in any form. In the West Zone, however, Maronites and Greek Catholics found the idea congenial and felt that a French Mandate for the time being was perhaps the best possible guarantee for a separate and independent Lebanon.

On 28 April 1920, despite the strong protests from Damascus, the Allied Supreme Council, meeting at San Remo, offered the Mandate for 'Syria and Lebanon' to France. The news came to Damascus as a shock; in Lebanon most Christians received it with satisfaction. The fulfilment of all Lebanon's aspirations seemed now at hand. General Henri Gouraud, who had arrived in Beirut on 21 November 1919 as French Commander-in-Chief and High Commissioner, was a devout Catholic whose very presence in Lebanon reassured the Christians. In the summer of 1920 Gouraud took the necessary measures to make the Mandate effective throughout Syria. On 22 July the French forces under his command defeated Fayṣal's Arab forces at Maysalūn Pass, across the Anti-Lebanon, and proceeded to occupy Damascus. By the end of the month Fayṣal had left Syria; the East Zone, along with the West Zone, was now completely in French hands. It was now possible for Gouraud to make the necessary constitutional arrangements which would turn the two occupied zones, starting with Lebanon, into States under French Mandate. On 31 August 1920 the High Commissioner published a decree establishing a State of Greater Lebanon, which would include the former territory of the Lebanese Mutesarrifate along with Beirut and the Biqaʿ, Tripoli, Sidon and Tyre regions. On the following day the State of Greater Lebanon was formally proclaimed and a provisional statute was decreed for its government.

During the next six years Greater Lebanon, declared an independent State under French Mandate, was governed by a succession of four French governors appointed by the High Commissioner in office: Captain Georges Trabaud (1920–23), M. Privat-Aubouard (1923–24), General Vandenberg (1924–25), and Leon Cayla (1925–26). Until 1922 Trabaud, as governor, was assisted by an Advisory Council of seventeen members, nominated by Gouraud to represent the various sects in the country. On 8 March 1922, however, Gouraud decreed the institution of a Representative Council for Greater Lebanon, which was elected by universal male suffrage in April; seats in the Representative Council, as in the Advisory Council, were distributed along confessional lines, but the election was by mixed constituencies. The Representative Council met for the first time on 25 May and elected as its first president the veteran Maronite politician Ḥabīb Pasha al-Saʿd, whom the French had thus far tended to neglect because of his fleeting association in 1918 with Fayṣal. In the two years that followed two other Maronites succeeded Ḥabīb al-Saʿd in the presidency of the Council, Naʿūm Labakī in 1923 and Emile Eddé in 1924. Finally, in January 1925, the Council was dissolved by the High Commissioner, General Maurice Sarrail (January-November 1925), who called for elections in July. The next Representative Council was to see the birth of the Lebanese Republic in 1926 and to become thereupon its first Chamber of Deputies.

The establishment of a Lebanese Constitutional Republic in 1926 was indeed the final outcome of a process of political and administrative development in Lebanon which began shortly after the arrival of Gouraud in the country as High Commissioner. In Syria Gouraud and his immediate successor General Maxime Weygand (1923–24) met with such obstinate resistance that it was difficult for them to introduce any effective constitutional system there; under General Sarrail Syrian opposition to the French Mandate reached its climax in the revolt of the Druzes of the Ḥawrān, which developed in the end into a general Syrian revolt lasting from 1925 until 1927. Meanwhile in Lebanon political life continued vigorously, as Christian, Druze, and even some Moslem leaders co-operated, despite certain reservations, with the mandatory authorities. The Lebanese in general demanded a larger measure of self-rule and, in particular, pressed for a Lebanese to assume the functions of the French governor. They were not prejudiced, however, against the many important reforms which the French introduced. Robert de Caix, the capable Secretary-General who accompanied General Gouraud to Lebanon in 1919, was the man principally responsible for these reforms.

From the time of his arrival and until 1923, while he served under Gouraud and Weygand, de Caix laid the foundations of a new Lebanese administration, selecting among the graduates of the French and Roman Catholic missionary schools a number of assistants who became the first civil servants of modern Lebanon. Many of these civil servants continued to hold office throughout the mandatory period and the early years of independence. Some of them have remained in high positions to this day. De Caix introduced other innovations which also outlasted the Mandate, such as the Lebanese electoral law and the real estate laws which regulated land tenure in the country. In March 1920, probably at his suggestion, the High Commissioner introduced a special currency for Syria and Lebanon, the Syro-Lebanese pound; a subsidiary of the Imperial Ottoman Bank was given the exclusive right to issue this currency, and so became the Banque de Syrie et du Liban. Meanwhile, starting in 1919, the Lebanese gendarmerie corps of the Mutesarrifate period was completely reorganized as was also the police corps of Beirut, a remnant of Turkish times. A serious effort was furthermore made to restore public security and put an end to the wave of crime and banditry which swept the country in the years immediately following the War.

The revolt in Syria was still in its first year when Henry de Jouvenel, a prominent senator and editor in Paris, arrived in Beirut in December 1925 as the first civilian High Commissioner in the mandated states. His predecessor General Sarrail, by his singular lack of common sense, had done much to provoke the Syrian revolt; he had also alienated Maronite and other Christian circles in Lebanon by his violent anti-clericalism. De Jouvenel immediately set out to remedy the situation. While taking initial measures to restore order in Syria, he turned his main attention first to the constitutional development of Lebanon. As early as October 1924 General Weygand, as High Commissioner, had promised Lebanon constitutional progress. Weygand, however, left office before the end of the year, and no steps in this direction were taken under his successor Sarrail. Upon his arrival de Jouvenel immediately convened the Lebanese Representative Council to draft a constitution. The Council, elected in July 1925, thereupon assumed the functions of a constituent assembly, formed a drafting committee, and on 23 May 1926 approved the text of a Constitution which transformed the State of Greater Lebanon into the Lebanese Republic. De Jouvenel gave this Constitution his blessing and forthwith called for the election of a Lebanese President of the Republic. Meanwhile, in accordance with the new arrangements, he recognized the elected Representative Council as a Chamber of Deputies and appointed the sixteen members of the newly established Senate. On 26 May the two chambers met jointly to elect Charles Dabbās, a prominent Greek Orthodox lawyer and former journalist, as first President of Lebanon.

The Lebanese Constitution served to provide Lebanese political life with a firm basis. Despite supervision, it was principally the creation of its drafting committee, among whose members the Roman Catholic banker Michel Chiha[5] (*d.* 1954) was perhaps the most active. A staunch Christian and ardent Lebanese patriot, Chiha was also a practical man with a keen insight into his country's affairs. In his opinion the maintenance of Greater Lebanon, so important for the Lebanese national survival, was only possible if the traditional relations between the various Lebanese sects were properly understood and maintained. Lebanon, he said, was 'a country which tradition must defend against force'.[6] Consequently, while the Constitution which Chiha helped to draft clearly declared the boundaries of Lebanon to be unalterable, and required the elected President of the Republic to swear loyalty to the 'Lebanese nation', it did not attempt to lay down hard and fast principles for co-operation between the various confessions, but preferred to leave the traditional process of give-and-take to operate spontaneously. Thus the constitution provided for the equitable representation of the various sects in public office; it did not, however, fix a ratio for such proportional representation, nor did it reserve specific government positions for each sect. Such matters were left to be settled by unwritten agreement, according to circumstances.

From the moment the Lebanese Constitution was proclaimed, impatient nationalists denounced the provisions it contained regarding the prerogatives of the French Mandate. According to the text the Lebanese Government was to be entirely free in the management of Lebanon's internal affairs. The control of foreign relations, however, was reserved for France. Furthermore, the French High Commissioner was to have the right of veto over all fundamental legislation, and he could also dissolve the legislature, suspend the Constitution, and rule by decree. In practice the powers of the High Commissioner were even more extensive. By appointing French advisers to the various government offices he could exercise control at every administrative level. The Lebanese Republic, as proclaimed in 1926, was in effect under complete French tutelage – a condition symbolized in the Constitution by its designation of the Lebanese national flag as the French tricolor with the Lebanese cedar superimposed, and of French as a second official language of the Republic.

The special provisions in the Lebanese Constitution regarding the mandatory prerogatives remained in force until 1943, when the Mandate was finally terminated (*see* p. 189). Meanwhile, during the first three years of the Republic, the basic structure of the Lebanese government as defined in the original terms of the Constitution had proved impracticable and had been revised. According to the original text, the Lebanese legislature was to consist of two houses: an elected Chamber of Deputies which sat for four years, and a Senate in which the President appointed seven out of sixteen members, and which sat for six years. The President, elected by both houses in joint session, was to hold office for a renewable term of three years. For a small state like Lebanon these provisions soon proved 'too elaborate . . . and too easily mishandled by politicians to the detriment of good administration'.[7] Consequently, in October 1927, a first constitutional amendment abolished the Senate. A second amendment in April 1929 extended the presidential term to six years and made it non-renewable.

By the end of the first decade of the French Mandate the Lebanese Republic already enjoyed a workable system of government. Critics of the mandatory régime could still object to the 'undefined but all-pervasive French powers of interference',[8] but they could not deny that political progress had been made. As far as mere technicalities of government were concerned, Lebanon by 1930 was well on its way to becoming a modern state. One important problem which remained unsolved, however, was entirely unconnected with government technicalities. It concerned the attitude towards Lebanon of the Lebanese Moslems.

In 1920, when the territory of Lebanon was enlarged to include the coastal towns, the Tyre region, and the Biqāʿ, the Moslem majority in the annexed districts found itself at a disadvantage. As Moslems or as Arab nationalists, Sunnites and Shiʿites saw that their incorporation in a Lebanese State under Christian domination meant their permanent separation from the Arab Moslem world. Consequently, Greater Lebanon had no sooner been proclaimed than the two groups raised loud cries of remonstrance, protesting against the new territorial arrangement and clamouring for the immediate union of their districts with Syria. In opposing the establishment of an enlarged and separate Lebanon the Sunnites and Shiʿites could count on some help from the Greek Orthodox, among whom the Christian Arab nationalism of the nineteenth century could still arouse some enthusiasm. They also found support among the Lebanese Druzes, especially at the time of the Syrian revolt (1925–27) when the Druzes of the Ḥawrān were fighting the French across the Lebanese frontier (*see* p. 165). The Druzes in Greater Lebanon were too few to have an effective share in leadership; they consequently tried to assert their political importance in opposition. Moreover the Druzes, like the Greek Orthodox, resented the special favour shown by the French to the Maronites, and were disinclined to show loyalty to a state in which the Maronites were the dominant section.

Greek Orthodox and Druze opposition to Greater Lebanon, even at the outset, was comparatively mild. In time a large proportion of the Shiʿites likewise ceased to oppose the new state, as they gradually realized that the status of a large minority in Lebanon was better for their community than that of a small minority in a predominantly Sunnite Syria. The marked resistance of the Sunnites, however, which was first manifested in 1920, remained undiminished until the end of the Mandate. For a long time prominent Sunnites refused to take part in the management of Lebanese affairs, and those who did were viewed by their co-religionists with great suspicion. In December 1925 there was widespread Moslem agitation, particularly among the Sunnites, when Henri de Jouvenel summoned the Representative Council to draft a constitution for Lebanon. Moslem leaders protested at the time because they had no desire for a Lebanese constitution which would confirm the country's new frontiers. Later, in the summer of 1928, prominent Lebanese Moslems visited Damascus while the Syrian Constituent Assembly was in session, demanding that a claim to the Moslem districts of Lebanon should be included in the Syrian Constitution then being drafted. Such demonstrations of Syrian unionist sentiment, while they produced no positive results, nevertheless seriously disturbed the French mandatory authorities and gave the Christians in Lebanon a feeling of considerable insecurity.

It was mainly to allay Moslem opposition in the country that the French in 1926 proposed the candidature of Charles Dabbās to the presidency. To Lebanon's Moslems Dabbās, a Greek Orthodox, was far more acceptable as Head of State than any Maronite leader. The French further approved of him because he was a Francophile; the Maronites liked him because he was a veteran Lebanese nationalist of the Paris Committee; and his election as President was bound to please his own Greek Orthodox community. Smaller Lebanese sects like the Druzes were also certain to prefer him to a Maronite president. Accordingly, the French High Commission found no difficulty in securing his election by the Lebanese Senate and Chamber of Deputies in 1926 and his re-election in March 1929 for another three-year term. During the whole of these two terms Dabbās proved an able president and managed to remain popular with the French and the Lebanese alike.

On first election as President, Dabbās entrusted the formation of the first Lebanese Cabinet to Auguste Adīb Pasha, a Maronite with long financial experience in Egypt who had already held office as Secretary-General to the French governors of Greater Lebanon. The first Cabinet of Auguste Adīb lasted for less than a year; Adīb himself, however, was recalled in March 1930 to head two more Cabinets, remaining in office until May 1932 when the second term of Dabbās expired. Meanwhile three other Maronites had been called upon to head the Lebanese Government. One of them was the former president of the Lebanese Administrative Council, Ḥabīb Pasha al-Saʿd (*see* p. 165), who became prime minister in August 1928 and remained in office until May 1929.

The two other premiers of the period, both of whom aspired to the Presidency, were of greater significance. One of them was Emile Eddé, the man whom the French had brought back to Lebanon in 1918 as chief adviser to the French High Commissioner (*see* p. 162). The other was Sheikh Bishāra al-Khūrī, a distant cousin of Ḥabīb al-Sa'd and like him the descendant of an old Maronite feudal family. Eddé, a member of the Lebanese Legislature since 1922, formed his first and only cabinet in October 1929, remaining premier for barely more than five months. His rival Khūrī was more successful, forming three cabinets between 1927 and 1929, and remaining premier for a total of nearly two years.

It was indeed the rivalry between Emile Eddé and Bishāra al-Khūrī which dominated the internal politics of Lebanon in the early years of the Republic. Eddé, the elder of the two men, was already a well-known lawyer and political figure in 1918, when the French appointed him for a short time as adviser at the High Commission. It was in Eddé's law office, in 1912, that young Bishāra al-Khūrī had done his own training as a graduate lawyer. Since then, however, Khūrī had also distinguished himself in public life. In February 1920, upon the recommendation of a prominent Jesuit Father at the St Joseph University, General Gouraud had appointed Khūrī Secretary-General to the Government of Mount Lebanon. Later in the same year, when Greater Lebanon came into being, Khūrī was appointed a member in the new Administrative Council and continued to hold this position until the first Representative Council was elected in April 1922. After some years in private law practice, he was back in politics in 1926 as Minister of the Interior in the first Cabinet of Auguste Adīb. In the following year he formed his own first cabinet, entering also the Lebanese Legislature for the first time as an appointed member of the Senate. By 1927, Khūrī was already a serious rival to Eddé, his rapid rise being due partly to his exceptional political skill and partly to his close connexions with the powerful Beirut banking families of Chiha and Pharaon. In April 1922, shortly after his first retirement from politics, Khūrī had married Laure Chiha, sister of Michel Chiha, the prominent Lebanese banker and intellectual.

Between Eddé and Khūrī there was a marked difference in background and temperament, which was reflected in differences of political attitude and outlook. Eddé, whose family came originally from a village in the Jubayl district, was thoroughly French in culture, as much at home in Paris as in Beirut and far more fluent in French than in Arabic. In Beirut he was mainly surrounded by the Christian merchant aristocracy of the Ashrafiyya quarter (*see* p. 142) and by the few Moslem families who moved in their circle, most of whom shared his French tastes and background. As an individual Eddé was arrogant, short-tempered, and lacking in resilience. In politics he tended to be outspoken and could rarely appreciate a point of view other than his own. In all these respects Khūrī appeared as Eddé's exact opposite. Originally from the Jurd, in the Druze region[9] (*see* p. 10), Khūrī was the son of a leading Lebanese civil official of the Mutesarrifate period, acquainted since his earliest years with the intricacies of Lebanese mountain politics. Like Eddé he had studied law in Paris and could speak French well. Unlike Eddé, however, Khūrī's cultural background remained Arabic rather than French; in fact, he excelled in the use of the Arabic language. In his outward personality Khūrī differed from Eddé in being quiet and reserved, with the gift of appearing perpetually undisturbed. Also, while Eddé tended to limit his social contacts to the French High Commission and the select society of Ashrafiyya, Khūrī was careful to maintain wide social and political connexions, and took special pains to develop friendly relations with Moslem and Druze circles. Among his own intimate group he enjoyed the distinct advantage of having as a close friend and adviser his brother-in-law Michel Chiha, the leading Lebanese political writer of his day whose prominent part in drafting the Lebanese Constitution has already been mentioned.

Eddé, like most Maronites of the north, tended to think of Lebanon as primarily a Christian homeland. The fact that it had ceased to be so after 1920 seemed frequently to escape him. It was difficult for him to grasp the full significance of the changes which had resulted from the establishment of Greater Lebanon, when the Moslems became for the first time major partners in the Lebanese State. Eddé's natural inclination was to regard the Moslems as a danger to Lebanon. With their Arab nationalism he was completely out of sympathy. Lebanon, he felt, must be considered as part of the Mediterranean world to which France belonged rather than as part of an Arab world which he is said to have associated with the desert. Such views, naturally, were appealing to many Frenchmen, who saw in Eddé's idea of Lebanon a guarantee of continued French influence in the Near East. Among his own countrymen, however, Eddé was only popular among Christians. His inability to gain substantial Moslem support remained a major obstacle throughout his political career.

Khūrī, unlike Eddé, was more of a practical politician than an ideologist. As a Maronite he was devoted to the Lebanese entity; nevertheless, he could see that while an independent Lesser Lebanon stood little chance of survival, a Greater Lebanon could survive only through political and social partnership between Christians and Moslems. Like Eddé, Khūrī was no Arab nationalist, and he liked to think of Lebanon as part of a Mediterranean world. As a realist, however, he could not ignore the fact that his country was geographically inseparable from its Arabic-speaking surroundings. Consequently, he saw no wisdom in denouncing Arab nationalism but rather tried hard to come to terms with it. Arab nationalists, he felt, should be encouraged to recognize a separate Lebanon; once they had done so, Arab nationalism would cease to appear as a threat and become instead a means of co-operation between Lebanon and the Arab world. In his attitude towards the Mandate Khūrī also differed radically from Eddé. The two men were alike friends of France and admirers of French culture; but whereas Eddé saw in the Mandate a necessary guarantee of the independence of Lebanon, Khūrī saw in it a distinct hindrance to that Christian-Moslem co-operation which, in his judgment, could alone assure Lebanese independence. The Moslems in Lebanon withheld their loyalty to the country on two grounds: first, they felt that their citizenship in an independent Lebanon threatened to separate them from the Arab-Moslem world; second, Greater Lebanon was associated in their minds with French political control, which they hated. The first reason was clearly the more important one. However, if Christians could take the lead in opposing continued French control, there was some chance that their Moslem compatriots would appreciate the gesture and abandon, in return, their demands for union with Syria.

It was only in the latter years of the Mandate that Khūrī's political attitude became a consistent party doctrine. Until 1932, his conflict with Eddé was pursued on a purely personal level. Meanwhile, in Beirut, a number of prominent Moslems, some of them from Tripoli, Sidon and elsewhere, had established themselves in positions of political leadership, many of them participating in the management of the State. During the two terms of his Presidency Charles Dabbās could rely for consistent Moslem support on Sheikh Muḥammad al-Jisr, a Sunnite jurist from Tripoli, who held the Presidency of the Senate, and later of the Chamber of Deputies, continuously from 1926 until 1932. Many Moslems criticized Jisr for his participation in the Lebanese Government and his co-operation with the French High Commission. Jisr's success, however, and the considerable power he came to enjoy as President of the Chamber, tempted other ambitious Moslems to follow his example. While 'Abd al-Hamīd Karāmī of Tripoli and Salīm Salām of Beirut limited their political activity to repeated demands for union with Syria, a younger generation of Lebanese Sunnites went a step further and clamoured for the establishment of a widespread Arab empire. Such, to all appearances, was the political stand of Khayr al-Dīn al-Aḥdab, originally of Tripoli, who was established in Beirut as the editor of an Arab nationalist newspaper. Such also was the stand of al-Aḥdab's close companion Riyāḍ al-Ṣulḥ, and of other members of the Ṣulḥ family, who came from Sidon to settle in Beirut and establish themselves there as the cheif competitors of the local Moslem notables. These Beirut notables, in their insistence on union with Syria, could not bring themselves to accept co-operation with the Lebanese Republic and the French Mandate. Being constantly in opposition, they were unable to render services to their community, and their command over their followers remained weak. This was not the case with Sheikh Muḥammad al-Jisr nor, after his death, with Aḥdab and the Ṣulḥs, all of whom came from outside Beirut. Jisr, a veteran politician of Ottoman days, easily took advantage of the apathy of other Moslem leaders towards Lebanon, and so established himself for a time as the only important representative of his community in the Lebanese Republic.

While Jisr stood for no particular nationalist ideology, Aḥdab and the Ṣulḥs established themselves as the principal defenders of pan-Arabism in Lebanon; this, however, did not prevent them from taking a keen interest in local Lebanese politics. Despite sharp differences of political opinion, they managed in time to develop valuable friendships with important Christian leaders in the country, quite apart from the contacts they established for themselves with members of the French High Commission and among French political circles in Paris.

Between 1926 and 1932 the Lebanese political scene was dominated by the struggle between Eddé and Khūrī. This struggle became particularly acute after the re-election of President Dabbās in 1929, as each of the two Maronite leaders could now look forward to succeeding him at the end of his second term. Meanwhile no Moslem rose to dispute the presidency of the Chamber with Muḥammad al-Jisr. With the support of Dabbās, and to the satisfaction of the French who were anxious to see the Moslems share in power, he retained an unbroken hold on this important office. Towards the middle of 1931 the Eddé–Khūrī rivalry became an open contest for the presidency of the Republic, as the election was due to be held in the following year. The French High Commission, it is commonly believed, disapproved of Khūrī as a candidate, preferring to lend its support to Eddé. The latter, however, stood little chance of being elected. During his brief tenure of the premiership in 1929–30 he had made himself extremely unpopular among the Moslems and their Greek Orthodox allies by his generally anti-Arab policy. In the field of education in particular, he had strengthened the influence of foreign Roman Catholic missions whom the Arab nationalists greatly distrusted. He had also defied the Arab nationalists by encouraging the propagation of the ideas of his friend Charles Corm,[10] who claimed for the Lebanese people a Phoenician origin. If Eddé's chances of becoming President were poor, those of other Maronite candidates like Ḥabīb Pasha al-Saʿd were still poorer. What was needed to keep Khūrī from winning the Presidency was a candidate who would deprive him of the Moslem votes on which he counted. Consequently, in the early months of 1932, Eddé and the other Maronite candidates withdrew from the presidential campaign. With their support, Sheikh Muḥammad al-Jisr now suddenly presented himself on the scene as a Moslem candidate; this was in contradiction to the unwritten understanding that only a Christian could become President of Lebanon. With the Moslems, the Greek Orthodox, and a number of Maronite deputies on his side, Jisr was certain of success. The Maronite Patriarch Anṭūn 'Arīda did not, for obvious reasons, support him. The Patriarch, however, was opposed to Bishāra al-Khūrī, and he was encouraged to believe that Jisr's candidature was a mere manœuvre which would be dropped before the elections actually took place.

The French High Commission, whatever it may have thought of Khūrī, was certainly unprepared to accept a Moslem as President for Lebanon. For them, as Jisr himself was aware, Lebanon stood apart from the Arab countries mainly by virtue of its internationally recognized Christian character. This made it necessary for the President of the Lebanese Republic to be a Christian, especially while the French were there to uphold the Christian claims.[11] Jisr, overestimating the number of Moslems in the country, originally thought he could justify his candidature by having a census organized. The census, carried out on 31 January 1932, proved his estimates wrong. Nevertheless Jisr went on with his campaign, rejecting all pleas to withdraw. Finally, as the time for elections approached, the French High Commissioner Henri Ponsot (1926–1933) decided to take arbitrary action. On 9 May 1932 his deputy summoned Muḥammad al-Jisr to his office and, addressing him as the president of the Lebanese Chamber of Deputies, announced to him the suspension of the Constitution. The Chamber of Deputies was forthwith dissolved and the presidential election indefinitely postponed. On the following day, upon the High Commissioner's request, Charles Dabbās agreed to remain in office as President of the Republic by appointment.

The question of the presidential election was not the only cause for the suspension of the Lebanese Constitution. The behaviour of the Lebanese Chamber was also important. Ever since it was first established in 1926, this Chamber had persistently annoyed the mandatory authorities by overplaying its own constitutional importance in defiance of the French High Commission. The French, in normal circumstances, might have been willing to tolerate such independent behaviour. In 1932, however, the situation in Lebanon was not completely normal. Ever since the beginning of the world depression in 1929, Lebanon had been experiencing economic difficulties which the constitutional Government, engrossed in factional and confessional rivalries, appeared unable to handle. The Lebanese Chamber was too deeply involved in petty politics to be adequately aware of the growing crisis. In these circumstances Henri Ponsot felt justified in dissolving the Chamber and suspending the Constitution. By taking such action, however, Ponsot gave the Christian Lebanese the first serious cause to oppose the Mandate. While the Moslems continued to object to French tutelage on Arab nationalist grounds, the Christian supporters of Bishāra al-Khūrī now openly denounced what appeared to them to be outright French despotism.

From May 1932 until January 1933 President Charles Dabbās, maintained in power by the French High Commissioner, exercised executive authority through a number of Lebanese heads of administration acting as a Council of Directors. Upon the effective resignation of Dabbās on 2 January this Council continued to function as an administrative body under the direction of ʿAbdallāh Bayhum, a prominent Beirut Moslem, who was now appointed Secretary of State. The functions of Chief of State were performed for a short while by an official of the High Commission, M. Privat-Aubouard, who had at one time been governor of Greater Lebanon (*see* p. 164). Finally, on 31 January, the High Commissioner appointed Ḥabīb Pasha al-Saʿd, now aged seventy-five, to succeed Dabbās as President of the Republic, for a one-year term which was later extended to two. Ponsot had meanwhile declared that constitutional life would be restored by stages. Accordingly, before President Ḥabīb al-Saʿd's assumption of office, M. Privat-Aubouard supervised the election of a new Chamber of Deputies of twenty-five members, of whom seven, including Khūrī, Eddé and Dabbās, were appointed by the High Commissioner.

Despite the criticism to which it was locally subjected, the period of non-constitutional government in Lebanon under Dabbās and Saʿd was one of 'consolidation and achievement in the face of grave economic troubles'.[12] It was in fact the politicians rather than the Lebanese people who complained most about the temporary suspension of constitutional life; at the popular level there appears to have been considerable satisfaction with the administrative honesty and efficiency of the government at this period.

> Reductions were made in overgrown officialdom, cuts in salaries imposed, the Gendarmerie and Police reduced. A number of administrative and fiscal reforms were made, Directorates amalgamated, the powers of village headmen defined. The financial crisis forbade the tax reductions for which there was an outcry; but sums were saved for public works, and progress was made in improving port facilities, in agricultural marketing, and in other fields. Cases of discovered corruption were taken to Court; but the slow progress made with these ... showed again the strength of family and confessional influences.[13]

On 1 February 1934, without reference to the Chamber of Deputies, the High Commissioner imposed a Code of Civil Procedure which replaced the still extant Ottoman codes of 1911.

> By a bold stroke of the pen, the mandatory power regularized already-existing judicial practices, procedures, and penalties, reformed the existing judicial organization, and promulgated modern codes.[14]

With the election of the new Chamber of Deputies in 1934 Lebanese political life gradually resumed its course. For three more years, however, no Lebanese government was formed, the administration remaining in the hands of a Secretary of State until January 1937. ʿAbdallāh Bayhum continued to hold this position throughout the presidency of Ḥabīb al-Saʿd. Meanwhile, at the partisan level, the old struggle between Emile Eddé and Bishāra al-Khūrī was renewed with fresh vigour, the partisans of Khūrī now demanding the full restoration of the Constitution and calling themselves accordingly the Constitutional Bloc. As President Saʿd's second term approached its end the Eddé-Khūrī struggle reached its climax, the local French newspaper *L'Orient* waging violent attacks on Khūrī and his powerful business backing while its rival publication *Le Jour*, under the supervision of Michel Chiha, reciprocated with equal venom. At last, in December 1935, it was announced by the High Commission that a new president would be chosen by the Lebanese Legislature to succeed Ḥabib al-Saʿd. The new President was to hold office for a non-renewable three-year term, and the Chamber of Deputies was summoned to meet on 20 January 1936 for the election.

Count Damien de Martel, who had succeeded Henri Ponsot in 1933 as High Commissioner, was personally disinterested in the

Eddé-Khūrī struggle. On the whole, the bitter rivalry between the two Maronite leaders appears to have caused him more amusement than concern. While he may have followed the traditional policy of his office by favouring Eddé, he was certainly not anxious to make a powerful President of him. The High Commissioner appears to have had, moreover, a good opinion of Khūrī. However, when the Lebanese Chamber met for the election, Eddé won over his rival Khūrī with a majority of one vote. This, in Lebanese opinion, was an exact reflection of de Martel's true policy, as it brought to the presidency a weak Eddé who was forced to rely extensively on the French High Commission for his authority.

Upon the election of Emile Eddé as president, Bishāra al-Khūrī remained in the Chamber of Deputies as the leader of an organized opposition. He continued to demand the full restoration of the Constitution, and pressed for the negotiation of a Franco-Lebanese Treaty to replace the mandatory arrangement. Already, in neighbouring Syria, a six-week general strike in Damascus had been followed on 1 March 1936 by the opening of negotiations for a Franco-Syrian Treaty. The Constitutional Bloc, encouraged by the Syrian example, then submitted a memorandum to the Lebanese Chamber of Deputies, on 3 March, demanding that similar negotiations be opened in the case of Lebanon. The French response to this memorandum was encouraging.

Meanwhile, upon his assumption of power, Eddé had dismissed the Moslem Secretary of State ʿAbdallāh Bayhum and appointed in his place a Protestant of Maronite stock, Ayyūb Thābit, who was known to be an outspoken Lebanese Christian nationalist and also a man of scrupulous integrity. In ordinary times the Moslems in Lebanon would have strongly opposed Thābit's appointment. For the moment, however, they were preoccupied with issues which they considered more fundamental. The troubles which shook Syria in the early months of 1936 were echoed in Lebanon, where shops were shut in Beirut and demonstrations organized in Tripoli and Sidon. When the preliminary negotiations for the Franco-Syrian Treaty were started in March in Beirut, the Lebanese Moslems, and particularly the Sunnites, began to clamour again for the union of the Moslem coastal towns and the Biqāʿ with Syria. Consequently, the spring and summer of 1936 in Lebanon was a time of acute nationalist and sectarian conflict, as Syrian unionist groups agitated for their claims with unprecedented vigour, while Lebanese nationalist groups were organized to oppose them.

The Moslem agitation in Lebanon in the early months of 1936 took an important turn on 10 March, when a 'Conference of the Coast' held in the home of Salīm Salām (*see* p. 174), in Beirut, almost unanimously denounced the 'detachment' of Lebanon's Moslem districts from Syria and demanded their 're-integration' in the Syrian State.[15] This 'Conference of the Coast' reflected the opinion of the bulk of Lebanon's Moslems, as an earlier conference by the same name had done three years before. In 1936, however, the conference was attended by members of a newly important group, the Syrian National Party, whose existence the French authorities in Beirut had only discovered in the previous year. This Syrian National Party had been founded in 1932 by Anṭūn Sa'āda, a Greek Orthodox teacher; and among its first members were students and young graduates of the American University of Beirut. When the party emerged into the open in 1935 its Lebanese membership already included several thousands, mainly Greek Orthodox and Protestants with some Shi'ites and Druzes and even a few Sunnites and Maronites. In the manner of the Christian Arab nationalists of the nineteenth century, Anṭūn Sa'āda and his followers believed in a Syrian national identity which transcended all local separatism and confessionalism. Consequently, they agreed with the Lebanese Moslems on the question of union with Syria, urging that Mount Lebanon as well as the coastal towns and the Biqā' be reattached to the Syrian State. In terms of the balance of interests in Lebanon, however, the Syrian Nationalists did not represent a major factor. Christians were generally opposed to their Syrian unionism, while Moslems were suspicious of their reservations with regard to pan-Arabism. For this reason the Lebanese authorities were able to suppress them without difficulty. When they attempted to agitate for union with Syria in March 1936 their leader and a number of his chief helpers were arrested, and for the next three years the Party was subjected to severe repression.

In response to the unionist activity of their Moslem and Syrian Nationalist compatriots, prominent Lebanese Christians had for some years thought of forming a Lebanese nationalist party which would stand for the complete separateness and integrity of Greater Lebanon. Sporadic attempts were made to organize such a party but they met with no lasting success. Finally, in November 1936, the extreme provocativeness of the Moslem unionists in Beirut led to the hasty creation of a Christian youth organization, the *Katā'ib* or Phalanges Libanaises, which immediately proved its efficiency as a force able to counterbalance the unionist agitators. Modelled on the para-military groups then fashionable in Italy and Spain, this organization was ably led by a young Maronite pharmacist, Pierre Gemayel.[16] Its formation was quickly countered by the appearance, in 1937, of the similar if less efficient Moslem para-military organization of the *Najjāda* (or Moslem Scouts). It might be pointed out that the Moslems of Lebanon, by then, had already formed a Moslem Consultative Council whose main object was to co-ordinate the demands of all Moslem sects in the country. Because of this intense sectarian and partisan activity, President Eddé's first year in office was marked by great tension.

Meanwhile, on 9 September 1936, the Franco-Syrian Treaty, closely modelled on the Anglo-Iraqi Treaty of 1930, was signed in Paris. The French now opened negotiations in Beirut for a similar Treaty with Lebanon. By the terms of these Treaties, Syria and Lebanon were recognized as independent and sovereign states, to be recommended for admission to the League of Nations after a preparatory period of not more than three years. The two states were to be allies of France in peace and war, providing her with the military use of specific land, air, and sea facilities. France was moreover to have a privileged position in the two states. The Syrian and Lebanese armies were to be organized under French supervision; the Syrian and Lebanese governments were to seek all technical help and advice from France; the French diplomatic service was to protect the rights of Syrian and Lebanese subjects abroad; and the French ambassador in Damascus and Beirut was to have precedence over all others. In addition, there were detailed provisions regarding currency, the rights of foreigners, the privileges of foreign institutions, and other technical matters. In the case of the Lebanese Treaty, an exchange of notes between President Eddé and the High Commissioner de Martel, added as an annex, specified among other things that the Lebanese

Republic should guarantee the fair representation of all the country's sects in the government and high administration. This item, known after its code number in the correspondence as '6–6 *bis*', was to outlive the Treaty and its annex and continue as a fundamental principle of Lebanese political life.

The text of the Franco-Lebanese Treaty was unanimously passed by the Lebanese Chamber on 13 November, the Moslem deputies joining the Christians in its approval. Outside the Legislature, however, Moslem opinion took the Treaty to be a final confirmation of Lebanon's territorial composition and independent status, and consequently opposed it with vigour. Once the Treaty was approved, trouble broke out in all Moslem districts. There were violent demonstrations and a strike in Tripoli, and anti-Christian rioting in several religiously mixed districts. In Beirut, on 15 November, a particularly serious clash between Christians and Moslems resulted in a number of casualties. It was indeed this last incident which immediately led to the formation of the *Katā'ib* organization as a counterpoise to the Moslem street force in the capital. Meanwhile in the Lebanese Legislature the mood remained unchanged. On 17 November the deputies in the Chamber ratified the Treaty which President Eddé and Count de Martel had signed, the High Commissioner announcing that its terms would take effect from 1937.

By the terms of the Franco-Lebanese Treaty Lebanon, like Syria, was to be admitted to the League of Nations as a fully independent state before the end of 1939. By the late summer of that year, however, the Treaty was still unratified by France. The outbreak of the Second World War on 3 September 1939 indefinitely delayed the implementation of the Treaty. Meanwhile, between 1936 and 1939, Lebanon had been allowed to enjoy three years of constitutional government in which considerable political progress was made. De Martel proclaimed the full restoration of Lebanese constitutional life on 4 January 1937. On the same day, in keeping with the spirit of the Franco-Lebanese Treaty, President Eddé called upon a Moslem deputy, Khayr al-Dīn al-Aḥdab, to form a government.

By 1937 the changed circumstances in Lebanon justified this decision to appoint a Moslem premier. A constitution, a Treaty, and the passage of sixteen years had given ample guarantee to the integrity of Greater Lebanon. Furthermore, the Moslems themselves by now had vested interests in the country; the events of November 1936 had brought into relief the difference in political attitude between those Moslems who were associated with the government and those who were not. Khayr al-Dīn al-Aḥdab himself, once a fiery Arab nationalist (*see* pp. 174–5), had abandoned much of his pan-Arabism since his election to the Chamber in 1934. In April 1936 he had made a parliamentary speech urging the fulfilment of Lebanon's 'national hopes'.[17] When Aḥdab went a step further and agreed to form a government under Eddé, one of the staunchest Lebanese separatists, the Premier's friends were openly critical. Aḥdab, however, was unmoved. 'Should the Arabs decide to unite,' he would say, 'my presence in the Lebanese Serail[18] will not stop them.'[19]

The appointment of Khayr al-Dīn al-Aḥdab as Prime Minister in 1937 set an important precedent in Lebanese government. Henceforth all the premiers of Lebanon were to be Sunnite Moslems, just as all the presidents were to be Maronites. Aḥdab himself held the Lebanese premiership for fifteen months, revising the composition of his cabinet five times to please the Eddé and Khūrī groups in the Chamber. When he finally left office in March 1938 he was replaced by Khālid Shihāb, a Moslem Shihāb emir from Ḥāsbayyā (*see* p. 96) who was in turn followed by the Beirut lawyer 'Abdallāh al-Yāfī. It was while Yāfī was still in office, presiding over his second cabinet, that the Second World War began. Thereupon Gabriel Puaux, who had succeeded de Martel as High Commissioner in January 1939, proceeded on 21 September to dissolve the Lebanese Chamber, dismiss the cabinet, suspend the Constitution for a second time, and confirm Emile Eddé as President and Head of State by appointment. 'Abdallāh Bayhum, as in 1934, was invested with full executive powers as Secretary of State, to be assisted by a French adviser.

To Emile Eddé the presidency he had coveted for so long proved to be a disappointment. Overruled and often slighted by de Martel, Eddé's powers were further curtailed under Puaux, and throughout he had to suffer persistent opposition from François Colombani, the French Chief of Security. In his management of the government the president was faced at every step by obstruction from his old rival Bishāra al-Khūrī. Faced by all these difficulties, Eddé finally ceased to appear in his office at the Government headquarters. The little power that was left to him could easily be exercised from his private home.

By suspending the Constitution and establishing a simplified administration, Puaux in 1939 hoped to stabilize the situation in Lebanon, as in Syria, for the duration of the war. Such stability, however, was precluded by the circumstances of the war. By the spring of 1940 the Allies in Europe were in full retreat as the Germans marched into Denmark and Norway, then Holland and Belgium. By early June, France herself was being invaded; on 14 June the Germans occupied Paris. A week later a Franco-German armistice was signed and France passed under German control, Marshal Philippe Pétain accepting office as Chief of State and establishing a 'collaborationist' régime at Vichy. From London General Charles de Gaulle appealed on 18 June for continued French resistance; by 28 June he had formed a Free French Government in exile, and was recognized by Britain as leader of the Free French. For the time being, however, the resources of the Free French were limited. In the French mandates and colonies it was the Vichy French who remained for the moment in control.

Gabriel Puaux stayed in Beirut for five months after the French surrender. In December 1940 he was succeeded by General Henri Dentz. Meanwhile the wartime food shortage in Lebanon had become serious, and the tottering Eddé régime was unable to handle this crisis. General dissatisfaction with the Eddé-Bayhum Government, encouraged by the President's numerous political opponents, led to widespread rioting in the early months of 1940. At last, in April 1941, Eddé and his Secretary of State were forced to resign. In their place, on 9 April, General Dentz appointed Alfred Naccache,[20] a Maronite judge of known integrity, to take over as Chief of State. A board of four under-secretaries, under the chairmanship of the Sunnite engineer Aḥmad Dā'ūq, was put in charge of the country's administration.

The new arrangement established by Dentz lasted for only a short time. On 8 June, for reasons connected with their general war strategy, British and Free French forces began the invasion of Syria and Lebanon from Palestine. On the same day, in an attempt to secure local goodwill, Allied aircraft dropped thousands of leaflets over the two countries, proclaiming their sovereignty and independence in the name of Free France. The leaflets were signed by General Georges Catroux, de Gaulle's representative in Cairo. Consequently, when the Allies finally occupied Syria and Lebanon towards mid-July, the Lebanese, like the Syrians, looked forward to a rapid termination of French tutelage.

Technically, the French Mandate in Syria and Lebanon came to an end on 8 June 1941, with the Free French proclamation of Syrian and Lebanese independence. General Catroux, who took over authority from General Dentz after the Allied occupation, assumed the title of Delegate-General rather than High Commissioner. On 27 September Catroux formally proclaimed the independence of Syria; on 26 November the independence of Lebanon was likewise proclaimed. Such concessions to local sentiment, however, were not meant for the moment to be truly effective:

> The policy of the French was, in effect, to offer the very minimum towards honouring their promise of independence; to retain all essential control, to hold, and to secure for the future, all that existed of French rights, institutions and privileges, and to postpone until after the war the settlement which must be made to safeguard all these. . . .[21]

Consequently, in the actual administrative arrangements which Catroux introduced into the two countries after proclaiming their independence, he departed little from the earlier mandatory arrangements.

In Lebanon, following the formal proclamation of independence, Alfred Naccache was appointed President of the Republic by the Delegate-General on 1 December. On the same day a Lebanese cabinet was formed under Aḥmad Dāʿūq. This cabinet differed from earlier ones in including a Ministry of Foreign Affairs. In the early summer of 1942 the Dāʿūq Cabinet resigned in the face of a crisis resulting from severe food shortage. A new government was formed by Sāmī al-Ṣulḥ, a member of the influential Ṣulḥ family (*see* p. 174), who had served in high judicial positions since 1920. Meanwhile, immediately upon its proclamation by Catroux, the independence of Lebanon, like that of Syria, had been formally recognized by Britain. Accordingly, in February

1942, Major-General Sir Edward Spears, until then head of the 'Spears Mission' to the Free French movement, was appointed British Minister to Syria and Lebanon. He established his headquarters in Beirut.

The rapid British recognition of Lebanese and Syrian independence, which embarrassed the Free French, reflected the deep concern of Britain for regional security:

> A clear condition of military safety was reasonable popular contentment, which must include political satisfaction, or absence of extreme dissatisfaction. . . . The British concern with defence and security, and their commitment to a Syrian-Lebanese independence . . . necessarily led them towards a politically progressive policy which the French in Syria . . . viewed as indicating all the old bugbears of British interference, designs to extrude and replace the French, and the rest.[22]

In Lebanon, as tension between British and French developed, a large section of Christian opinion, led by the former President Emile Eddé, took the French side. The British, on the other hand, found support not only among Moslem and other Arab nationalist circles but also among the Christian partisans of the Constitutional Bloc, the followers of Bishāra al-Khūrī. Among the prominent members of the Bloc was the Maronite lawyer and former deputy Camille Chamoun,[23] a man widely believed to be connected with British war intelligence. Whatever the true nature of his British connexions, Chamoun was certainly instrumental in maintaining contact between the Constitutional Bloc, to which he belonged, and the British whose forces were still in occupation of Lebanon.

The proclamation of Lebanese independence in November 1941 was followed by a remarkable revival of Lebanese party politics. While Khūrī's Constitutional Bloc developed its connexions with Britain, Emile Eddé re-emerged into public life in 1942 to reorganize his old following as the National Bloc. On the issue of complete Lebanese independence this Bloc showed considerable reserve, preferring to maintain some political ties with France as a guarantee against absorption into a pan-Arab state. To many Christians such an attitude seemed justified, as the Allied occupation of Syria and Lebanon was immediately followed by a powerful resurgence of pan-Arab claims. Against this typical Eddé attitude the Constitutional Bloc took a strong stand, insisting on the complete and unconditional independence of a Lebanon which would take its place as a part of the Arab world. In formulating their policy on this point the leaders of the Constitutional Bloc were encouraged by the appearance of a new attitude among some Lebanese Moslem leaders, notably those of the Ṣulḥ family (*see* p. 174–5), who now spoke of an 'Arab' but fully independent Lebanon. The Lebanese people, these leaders explained, were an integral part of the Arab nation; their country, however, had a character so distinctly its own as to warrant, at least for the time being, complete independence. This formula, preached by the brothers Kāẓim and Taqī al-Dīn al-Ṣulḥ and accepted by their cousin Riyāḍ, was adopted by the Constitutional Bloc as the ideal basis for a Christian-Moslem understanding. The members of the Constitutional Bloc, who were not Arab nationalists, could not accept the suggestion that the independence of Lebanon was in any way a temporary arrangement. But neither side insisted on this point. By the late spring of 1942 the Ṣulḥ formula was already serving as a basis for a vigorous Christian-Moslem alliance, the working principles of which are still known today as the National Pact. On 3 June, while on a visit to Egypt, Bishāra al-Khūrī could state the policy of his Bloc with full confidence:

> Lebanon wants its complete independence within its present boundaries; and we want, on this basis, to co-operate with the Arab States to the greatest possible extent.[24]

Meanwhile, starting in April 1942, General Spears in Beirut began to urge that general elections be held in Syria and Lebanon. The Free French, having recognized the two states as sovereign and independent, had no excuse to reject this suggestion; nevertheless, upon the instructions of de Gaulle, General Catroux managed to postpone action on the matter for several months. Finally, on 25 March 1943, Catroux bowed to British pressure and declared the restoration of the Lebanese and Syrian Constitutions. Earlier, in Lebanon, the Delegate-General had removed President Naccache and Premier Sāmī al-Ṣulḥ from their positions, replacing them in both offices by Ayyūb Thābit, Eddé's former Secretary of State (*see* p. 179). As President of the Republic, Chief of State and Premier, Thābit headed a cabinet of three members which was instructed, after 25 March, to prepare for general elections. For such a delicate mission a less judicious choice than Thābit could hardly have been made. An outspoken partisan of Eddé, the new President began preparing for the elections by fixing the number of deputies to be elected at fifty-four, assigning thirty-two seats to the Christian sects and twenty-two for the Moslems and Druzes. Such a distribution of seats was clearly unjust to the Moslem group, whose numbers in the country justified better representation. Thābit argued, however, that the distribution was perfectly just, as the whole body of Lebanese emigrants, who were mostly Christian, must be included in the franchise. This position the Moslems were completely unwilling to accept. In the face of violent Moslem protests Ayyūb Thābit was at last removed from office on 21 July, to be replaced as Chief of State by a Greek Orthodox lawyer and millionaire, Petro Ṭrād. Thereupon it was agreed to raise the number of seats to fifty-five, giving thirty seats to the Christians and twenty-five to the Moslems and Druzes.[25] This six to five ratio has been maintained ever since, making the number of deputies in the Lebanese Chamber always a multiple of eleven.

The Lebanese elections were held in two stages in the late summer of 1943. They were supervised by President Ṭrād, General Spears, and the new French Delegate-General Jean Helleu. The result was a resounding victory for the Constitutional Bloc and its allies. Once in power, the new Chamber met for the first time on 21 September 1943 and proceeded to elect Bishāra al-Khūrī as President of the Republic by a majority of forty-four votes against eleven abstentions. President Khūrī forthwith called upon his chief Moslem ally, Riyāḍ al-Ṣulḥ, to form a government which would represent the six major sects in the country; the Maronites, Sunnites, Shi'ites, Greek Orthodox, Greek Catholics, and Druzes. Thereupon a new Lebanon emerged into being: a full partnership between the various Christian and Moslem sects in which no one sect alone could determine policy. The sects with the largest representation were the Maronites and Sunnites, represented for the moment by Bishāra al-Khūrī and Riyāḍ al-Ṣulḥ whom everyone recognized as the authors of the National Pact (*see* p. 187).

The new government had no sooner been installed than it opened negotiations with Helleu for the effective termination of the French Mandate. The government's object was the amendment of the Constitution in order to remove mandatory restrictions and secure the transfer of full legislative and administrative powers to its own hands. Furthermore, the French were urgently requested to convert the office of the Delegate-General into an Embassy as soon as possible. Helleu's reply, after consulting the Free French Government now established in Algiers, was discouraging. On 5 November, a message from the Algiers Committee which Helleu transmitted to President Khūrī announced that the French could not admit unilateral changes in the Lebanese Constitution. This, to the Lebanese Government, appeared as open defiance. Consequently, on 8 November, the Chamber of Deputies proceeded to debate and pass a special Bill containing the proposed constitutional amendments. The Bill, unanimously accepted in the absence of Emile Eddé, suggested the removal from the Constitution of all references to the Mandate, the assertion of Lebanon's sovereign status, and the discontinuance of French as a second official language. Once passed, these amendments were immediately countersigned by President Khūrī and published in the official gazette on 9 November, before the French had time to object.

Returning from hasty consultation with the French National Committee in Algiers, Helleu arrived that very day in Beirut to find the constitutional amendments already in force. The Delegate-General, however, was not prepared to accept the accomplished fact. Upon his orders, French Marines and Senegalese troops were sent in the early morning of 11 November to arrest the Lebanese President and his leading ministers in their beds. Forthwith Bishāra al-Khūrī, Riyāḍ al-Ṣulḥ, three other members of his cabinet, and one prominent Moslem deputy[26] were unceremoniously hurried to the fortress of Rāshayyā (*see* pp. 99–100) in the Wādī al-Taym region, where they were kept as prisoners. Meanwhile decrees were issued by Helleu announcing the suspension of the Constitution, the dissolution of the Chamber, and the appointment of Emile Eddé as Chief of State.

The news of Helleu's action fell on the Lebanese public with lightning effect. Immediately the *Katā'ib*, *Najjāda* (*see* p. 181), and other Christian and Moslem parties and organizations forgot their old feuds and came together to establish a unified command and to organize a country-wide strike. In the face of angry demonstrations and riots the French ordered a rigid curfew in Beirut; this, however, only added to the general paralysis of the capital. Meanwhile the two members of the Ṣulḥ Cabinet who had escaped arrest, Ḥabīb Abū Shahlā and Majīd Arslān,[27] withdrew to the nearby mountain village of Bshāmūn and there constituted themselves as a temporary government. At the same time members of the dissolved Chamber, continuing to meet mostly in private homes, decided among other things to abandon the old Lebanese flag and to adopt a new one without the tricolor.[28] The Rump Government of Bshāmūn, backed by the remnants of the Lebanese Chamber, found itself widely supported even among extreme Maronite circles. With open encouragement from General Spears and the local British command, it continued to claim legitimacy from its mountain headquarters, while Eddé in Beirut found himself completely out of touch with the country. The French, faced with an impossible situation, were soon forced to reverse their policy, especially as Britain and the United States were persistently urging them to do so. On 17 November General Catroux arrived in Beirut, sent by the Algiers Committee to deal with the Lebanese situation on the spot. Helleu, who had 'unified the whole Lebanese nation against France in a single night',[29] was immediately recalled from his post. Finally, on 22 November, President Khūrī and his fellow prisoners were released from Rāshayyā and returned to Beirut in triumph. The French Mandate, in effect, was now over.

The political independence which the Lebanese Republic achieved in November 1943 was further extended after January 1944 as one after another the mandatory prerogatives were handed over to the Lebanese authorities. The transfer of these prerogatives, in Lebanon as in Syria, gave the two countries independent control over customs, concessionary companies, press censorship, and public security. By the following year Lebanon, like Syria, was in possession of nearly all the powers and functions of a sovereign government. The French only retained the locally recruited *troupes spéciales*, which remained attached to their own local command. France, however, had not yet given up the idea of replacing her lost Mandate in the two states by special treaties, despite strong opposition from her Allies. On 17 May 1945, nine days after the end of the war in Europe, a body of Senegalese troops arrived in Beirut to reinforce the French army in Syria and Lebanon. The arrival of these troops provoked a violent reaction in both countries, the Lebanese and Syrians assuming that such military reinforcements were being made with the intention of forcing their respective countries to accept treaties with France which would limit their newly acquired independence. In Syria, while the local French authorities made a last attempt at imposing a treaty on the Government, street-fighting broke out in a number of cities, the clashes between the townspeople and the local French garrisons culminating on 29 May with a French bombardment of Damascus. At this point Britain intervened. France, mainly because of British pressure, finally decided to give up the idea of the treaties and to evacuate Syria and Lebanon. The evacuation of Syria was carried out in that same summer. That of Lebanon was not completed before the end of 1946. Meanwhile, on 1 August 1945, the Lebanese *troupes spéciales* were handed over to Lebanon. A few days earlier the Lebanese Government had appointed Colonel Fu'ād Shihāb,[30] a descendant of the former emirs of Lebanon[31], as the commanding officer of its new army.

In securing complete independence in the management of external affairs, the administration of Bishāra al-Khūrī was eminently successful. The French had no sooner withdrawn their last troops from Lebanon than the Khūrī Government took the initiative in restoring good relations with the former mandatory power, making friendship with France an established principle of Lebanese foreign policy. Meanwhile a firm basis for co-operation with the Arab States was also secured. By the Protocol of Alexandria which prepared the way for the formation of the Arab League, the five signatory States (Syria, Jordan, Iraq, Lebanon and Egypt) expressed confidence in Lebanon's general policy and agreed to respect Lebanese sovereignty and integrity within the existing frontiers. The Protocol of Alexandria was signed on 8 January 1944; in the following year, on 22 March 1945, the League of Arab States formally came into being with Lebanon as a founder member. In 1945 Lebanon also became a founder member of the United Nations, and in January 1946 a Lebanese delegation was present at the opening of its first General Assembly in London.

In internal affairs the government of President Khūrī was less successful, its achievement here being mostly limited to the implementation of the National Pact. After 1943, as Lebanon developed firm relations with the neighbouring Arab States, pan-Arab unity ceased to be a serious issue among the Moslems. Arab nationalism remained important; the Lebanese Government, however, found no difficulty in coming to terms with it by adopting a mildly Arab nationalist regional policy. Meanwhile significant and necessary concessions were made to the Lebanese Moslems. In the various offices of government such Sunnites and Shi'ites as were qualified received appointment, reducing the disproportionate number of Christians in public service. The Army Command and the Directorate-General of Security, key positions where the safety of Lebanon was concerned, were by agreement reserved for Christians; otherwise no one was barred from appointment to public office for confessional reasons. Lebanon's Moslems, for the moment at least, appeared to be generally contented. With an effective leader in the person of Riyāḍ al-Ṣulḥ heading the government[32] (*see* p. 188), they felt confident that their interests would receive adequate attention and that no policy would be formulated without their approval.

The shortcomings of the Khūrī Government were mostly on the administrative side, as might be expected in a country where sectarian and family interests predominate. Corrupting influences had been noticeable in Lebanese administration for a long time. During the period of the Mandate, the French High Commission is said to have assisted its Moslem friends in power by making it easy for them to serve their political clients. Whatever the truth of this charge, it is certain that the system of political clients was already well-developed in 1943, particularly among the Moslems. Christian leaders, in emulation, soon gathered their own clients around them; and as such clients were usually found among the city mob, street clashes between Christians and Moslems became frequent in the capital as the interests of sectarian leaders came into conflict. Apart from encouraging sectarian tensions, however, the client system also corrupted the processes of administration, as Christian and Moslem leaders vied with one another in serving their supporters, securing government appointments for some and pressing the claims of others.

In this corruption none were more prominent than some of the president's own relatives and friends.

Criticism of the Khūrī régime became serious in 1947, when the first general elections since independence were held. In these elections, which took place in May, fraudulent means were allegedly used to secure a Chamber favourable to the President. A year later this same Chamber, with a majority of forty-eight to seven,[33] passed a Bill amending the Constitution to permit Khūrī a special renewal of his presidential term. To some Lebanese leaders, including the President's own brother-in-law Chiha (*see* p. 172), such an amendment of the Constitution was in itself a bad thing. It represented, moreover, a threat to the ambitions of other Maronite aspirants. Camille Chamoun, until then the most prominent member of the Constitutional Bloc (*see* p. 186), had since 1943 hoped to succeed Khūrī as President. On the day the Constitution was amended his absence from the Chamber was conspicuous. To him as to his followers, the renewal of Khūrī's term seemed a first step towards the perpetuation of his presidency. Consequently, in the years that followed, Chamoun became the recognized leader of a growing opposition.

Other events in the next few years further affected the popularity of the Khūrī régime. The failure of the Arab States in 1948 to vindicate the Arab cause in Palestine brought discredit to all existing Arab governments, and the Lebanese Government did not escape its share. On 30 March 1949 an angry army overthrew the constitutional régime in Syria, installing Colonel Ḥusnī al-Za'īm in power. The example across the frontier gave heart to the Syrian National Party (*see* p. 180) in Lebanon, which sought to carry out a coup of its own in early July. The attempt, however, was abortive. By 9 July the Party's leader Anṭūn Sa'ada had been summarily tried and shot; six other Party members were later executed, and many more received prison sentences. The supression of the Syrian Nationalists earned Khūrī their bitter enmity. Meanwhile, when the government tried to suppress all organizations of a para-military character, the Moslem *Najjāda* and the Christian *Katā'ib* went over into opposition. After 1949 both organizations reconstituted themselves as political parties, the *Katā'ib* becoming particularly important.

The opponents of the Khūrī régime became more united after

April 1951, when fresh parliamentary elections increased the representation of the opposition in the Chamber. Among the new deputies elected was Pierre Eddé, son of Khūrī's old rival, Emile Eddé, who had died in retirement two years earlier. Another new deputy was Joseph Chader, a prominent Armenian Catholic, who became the parliamentary representative of the *Katā'ib* Party. Eddé, Chader, and five other deputies now formed around Chamoun the nucleus of an opposition bloc which proceeded to ally itself with other dissatisfied elements in the Chamber. Among the members of this Bloc none was more prominent than Kamāl Janbalāṭ, scion of a renowned feudal family and hereditary chieftain of the Shūf Druzes. Janbalāṭ had first been elected to the Chamber in 1943, when he was only twenty-six. In 1948 he was among the seven deputies who voted against the renewal of President Khūrī's term; after that he became the most outspoken member of the opposition. Janbalāṭ, apparently, was motivated partly by idealism, and partly by his resentment at the extensive influence which Bishāra al-Khūrī's brother Salīm had come to exercise among the Shūf Christians. As Chamoun's electoral district was also in the Shūf, it was natural that he and Janbalāṭ should ally themselves against the President's brother.

In 1949, the year Khūrī's second term began, Janbalāṭ organized his, mainly Druze, following as the Progressive Socialist Party, intensified his denunciation of the widespread corruption, and began to agitate for reform. In time many dissatisfied elements in the country grouped themselves around him, including the Syrian Nationalists whose suppression in that year had driven them firmly into opposition. After 1951, when the Chamoun-Janbalāṭ alliance was firmly established, an organized opposition emerged which included among others the *Katā'ib*, the *Najjāda*, the Syrian Nationalists, the Progressive Socialists, and the National Bloc of Raymond and Pierre Eddé. Such a combination could only be a temporary political alliance; nevertheless, its leaders pretended to support a distinct political ideology and called themselves the Socialist Front.

By the summer of 1952 the Chamoun-Janbalāṭ opposition had rallied most of the country around it. President Khūrī's position had grown correspondingly weaker. In the previous summer his old ally Riyāḍ al-Ṣulḥ, while on a visit to Jordan, had been shot dead by a member of the Syrian National Party. While he lived, Ṣulḥ could always be counted upon to form a strong cabinet. He was, moreover, the only man able to control the Moslem populace in times of crisis. After his death it became obvious that no Moslem leader could truly take his place. On 16 September President Khūrī was facing a particularly severe cabinet crisis when the Socialist Front called for a general strike. The Front demanded nothing less than Khūrī's resignation and the complete reorganization of the state. Unable to face the opposition, and failing to secure support from the army, Khūrī finally resigned on 18 September and forthwith went into quiet retirement. Five days later, on 23 September, the Chamber elected Camille Chamoun to succeed him.

On the termination of the Mandate in 1943 the wide powers previously held by the High Commissioner had passed to the Lebanese President, who virtually became his successor. Such powers could easily enable a president to exercise autocratic power. Until 1951, however, the presence of a strong Moslem premier like Ṣulḥ had kept Khūrī's actual power within bounds. When Camille Chamoun succeeded in 1952, the Moslems could boast of no effective leadership. In Tripoli young Rashīd Karāmī had succeeded his late father, ʿAbd al-Hamīd (*see* p. 174), as head of the family, and commanded a large following; but his leadership in that town was disputed by a number of rivals. No true leader replaced Riyāḍ al-Ṣulḥ in Sidon, where a number of weak rivals now disputed the Ṣulḥ succession. Meanwhile, in Beirut, three prominent Sunnites vied with each other for supreme Moslem leadership. Among these Sāmī al-Ṣulḥ, a distant cousin of the late Riyād (*see* p. 185), had probably the largest political following; as a statesman, however, he lacked Riyāḍ's exceptional gifts. A close rival to Sāmī al-Ṣulḥ in popularity was ʿAbdallāh al-Yāfī (*see* p. 183); but Yāfī was reputed to be excessively mild. Of the three Beirut Moslem leaders by far the most forceful was Sā'ib Salām,[34] who only commanded a small political following. With four possible premiers (Ṣulḥ, Yāfī, Karāmī and Salām) to choose from, President Chamoun found himself in a position where he could exercise full power, as he could always change cabinets to suit his policy.

The new President had hardly taken office when his alliance with Kamāl Janbalāṭ came to an abrupt end. As a leader of the Socialist Front which had brought Chamoun to power, Janbalāṭ demanded a large share in formulating the new régime's policy. In particular, he insisted that the former President be brought to trial, and that the dubiously lawful profits of his associates be investigated. Chamoun, however, was unwilling to yield to such demands. The Druze chief, in fact, was systematically ignored as the new President surrounded himself with the former supporters of Bishāra al-Khūrī, who sought favour with the new régime. Consequently, from the very start of his presidency, Chamoun provoked the bitter enmity of Janbalāṭ. Over a period of six years the leader of the Progressive Socialist Party was to denounce the President regularly in his weekly *al-Anbā'*, criticizing every action of his government.

Chamoun's administration, indeed, gave ample room for criticism, often for no fault of its own. On coming to office the new President made an honest attempt to reorganize the government departments. A cabinet of four under Khālid Shihāb (*see* p. 183), drafted laws to re-define the various administrative functions, to reform the electoral system, and to revise judicial procedures.[35] Among other things, the vote was now given to women. In 1954, another cabinet headed by Sāmī al-Ṣulḥ was given extraordinary powers to complete the work of reform. In spite of all these efforts, the main administrative problem in Lebanon remained unsolved. While family and sectarian interests remained predominant, and while politicians sought above everything else to serve their clients, there was little hope of improvement in the efficiency of the governmental machine, no matter what laws were enacted.

The main distinction of the Chamoun régime was in the freedom it secured for public opinion. By 1952, openly authoritarian régimes had already been established in two Arab countries: Syria had been under military rule since March 1949; in Egypt, the Army took over in July 1952. Jordan and Iraq were, in theory, constitutional monarchies, but democratic practice in the two countries was barely more than nominal. Outside the four countries mentioned, in Saudi Arabia and the Yemen, democracy was not known at all. While this situation prevailed in the surrounding area, Chamoun guaranteed full freedom for the Lebanese press. During his six years in office no political party was suppressed; and opposition to his government, though little attention was paid to it, was at least tolerated. Lebanon under Chamoun became a haven of freedom and security and a last bastion of liberalism in the Arabic-speaking world. As the frequent political upheavals in neighbouring countries made investment there increasingly unsafe, capital flowed from these countries into Lebanon during Chamoun's presidency, giving rise to unprecedented prosperity.

The liberal economic policy adopted in Lebanon under the Khūrī régime, and maintained ever since, was to a great extent responsible for the country's prosperity after 1952. Four years earlier, in 1948, the Khūrī Government had established a free foreign exchange and trade system which stood in sharp contrast to the systems of currency and trade controls common elsewhere in the world. Starting in November of that year, the Lebanese pound came to enjoy full transferability. In May 1952, five months before Chamoun took over, the exchange system in Lebanon became completely free. Meanwhile the Lebanese pound, whose high gold coverage was to reach, at the end of 1955, a record of ninety-five per cent of notes in circulation, had become widely reputed for its solid stability. All this encouraged foreign capital movements to Lebanon, the near absence of trade restrictions also bolstering up an import and re-export trade on which Lebanese merchants prospered. Chamoun's Government, towards the end of his term of office, was further to encourage the movement of foreign capital into Lebanon by introducing the guarantee of bank secrecy, which helped make Beirut the leading banking centre of the Middle East.

The unpopularity of the Chamoun régime in some circles was due mainly to the harsh manner in which he dealt with other politicians. Having started by alienating Kamāl Janbalāṭ, the President went on to consolidate his personal supremacy by clipping the wings of all serious rivals. As a result, prominent Maronites were persuaded that Chamoun was bent on destroying their own chances for the presidency. Nor were Chamoun's blows directed only at Maronites. By the end of his fourth year in office, there were few Lebanese leaders whom he had not in some way antagonized. In 1955, when the Maronite Patriarch Antūn ʿArīda died, Chamoun, it was said, expressed strong disapproval of the appointment of Bishop Paul Meouchi[36] as his successor. The new Patriarch, who was politically a supporter of Bishāra al-Khūrī, forthwith joined the resentful politicians in opposition to Chamoun, and his stand with the opposition was certainly embarrassing to the President. Nevertheless, Chamoun could still count, in 1956, on a wide popular support; and he was also backed by the large business class which he favoured. He could consequently afford, for the moment, to ignore the criticism of his powerful political opponents.

It was largely events external to the Lebanese domestic scene which caused the last years of Chamoun's Presidency to be marred by violence and crisis. Between 1953 and 1954, during Chamoun's first years in office, developments of particular importance were taking place in Egypt, where Colonel Jamāl ʿAbd al-Nāṣir gradually superseded General Muḥammad Najīb as master of the Egyptian revolutionary régime. Not content with the control of his own country, President ʿAbd al-Nāṣir soon began to lay claim to leadership of the whole Arab world, receiving wide support in many Arab countries. In Lebanon, the Egyptian leader was widely acclaimed among Moslems, who had never lost their old Arab nationalist yearnings, and who had recently been expressing great dissatisfaction with their lot. Ever since the death of Riyād al-Ṣulḥ in 1951, the Lebanese Moslems had lacked a leader with a country-wide backing. They had hence become steadily more conscious of their reduced influence in the Lebanese State and resentful of the minor role which Chamoun allowed their leaders in the government. Moslem grievances found expression in 1953 in an English-language pamphlet entitled *Moslem Lebanon Today*, which described Lebanese Moslems as a downtrodden majority in a Christian-dominated state. After 1954, there was a growing tendency among these Moslems, particularly the Sunnites, to look towards Egypt for support. In Jamāl ʿAbd al-Nāṣir they saw the long-awaited Arab leader who alone would unify the Arab-Moslem world and vindicate the Moslem claims in Lebanon. Following the general trend, a number of Lebanese Moslem leaders now began to develop their connexions with Egypt, hoping to promote their own local political position by espousing the cause of 'Abd al-Nāṣir. By July 1956, when 'Abd al-Nāṣir nationalized the Suez Canal Company and took over its administration, 'Abdallāh al-Yāfī, Sā'ib Salām, and Rashīd Karāmī had already established themselves as spokesmen for Egypt. Among other Moslem leaders only a few, led by Sāmī al-Ṣulḥ, remained uncommitted to 'Abd al-Nāṣir.

At the time the Suez Canal Company was nationalized, the Lebanese Government was actually in the hands of Yāfī and Salām, the former as Premier and the latter as Minister of State. When the Suez War took place in November, the two Moslem leaders urged President Chamoun to break diplomatic relations with Britain and France, as these Powers had joined Israel in attacking Egypt. To a Lebanese Christian such a course was unthinkable and Chamoun promptly refused the suggestion. Yāfī and Salām thereupon resigned in protest. Chamoun, however, had no difficulty in securing the formation of a new government with Sāmī al-Ṣulḥ as Premier, including General Fu'ād Shihāb as Minister of Defence and Charles Mālik as Minister of Foreign Affairs.

The inclusion of Charles Mālik in the new government was in itself a declaration of policy. For many years ambassador in Washington and delegate to the United Nations, Mālik was well known for his pro-western inclinations. His appointment as Foreign Minister at a time when 'Abd al-Nāṣir was turning to the Communist powers for support indicated the political course which Chamoun intended to take. To Chamoun, the pro-Egyptian agitation which 'Abd al-Nāṣir was already instigating in various Arab States was a distinct and dangerous threat to Lebanon's independence. To secure his country against Egyptian subversion, the Lebanese President sought a guarantee from the Western Powers, mainly the United States. Of such a policy the vast majority of Moslems could not approve; Chamoun, however, was not prepared to take any risks. In March 1957, in the face of Moslem opposition, the Lebanese Government accepted the recently formulated Eisenhower Doctrine. The United States, according to this Doctrine, could use her armed forces to defend any Near Eastern country that so desired against Communist aggression, whether such aggression be direct or indirect. Furthermore, the Doctrine stressed the vital interest of the United States in the independence and integrity of all Near Eastern countries.

Lebanon's acceptance of the Eisenhower Doctrine was understood in Egypt as an act of open defiance. By March 1957, moreover, the Chamoun régime had already antagonized 'Abd al-Nāṣir in other ways. At the time of the Suez crisis, Lebanon had only given half-hearted support to Egypt. The Chamoun administration, besides, was known to be in sympathy with Iraq, the chief Arab rival of Egypt and a member, since 1955, of the Western-sponsored Baghdad Pact. When Lebanon now proceeded to accept the Eisenhower Doctrine, completely disregarding the fact that Egypt strongly opposed it, Lebanese-Egyptian relations became highly strained, reaching almost the point of open breach.

Meanwhile, with the approach of general elections, Yāfī, Salām, and other Moslem leaders began to form an electoral front to oppose Chamoun. By June, a new opposition had been organized, calling itself the National Front and gathering around it all Chamoun's political opponents. Among the adherents of the National Front were Rashīd Karāmī of Tripoli, Kamāl Janbalāṭ of the Shūf, the members of Bishāra al-Khūrī's Constitutional Bloc, and other Christian and Moslem leaders who had been antagonized by the President over the past five years. Chamoun, however, still had a strong following in the country. With Lebanese opinion not divided along strictly sectarian lines, the president could count on the support of a substantial number of Moslems. Among the Christians, a vast majority heartily approved of his foreign policy. The *Katā'ib* party and the National Bloc of the Eddé brothers (*see* p. 194) stood stoutly behind him, as did the Syrian Nationalists (*see* p. 193), who had become active again since Chamoun came to power. In the elections, which were held in the early summer, the supporters of Chamoun won a vast majority. Among the prominent losers were Janbalāṭ, Yāfī, Salām, and the leading Shī'ite chieftain of the Tyre region, Aḥmad al-As'ad. Chamoun, who was suspected of seeking renewal of his presidential term, was forthwith accused of having manipulated the elections for the purpose. The new Chamber of Deputies, it was thought, would before long amend the Constitution to permit his re-election to the Presidency.

Events now followed each other in quick succession. With its chief leaders excluded from the Chamber, the National Front found itself unable to act as an effective constitutional opposition. Some of its leaders, consequently, resorted to terrorist methods. In the Shūf and other Druze districts the followers of Janbalāṭ blew up bridges and blocked roads. In Beirut, bombs were exploded in various quarters with increasing frequency. There were sporadic incidents of violence in various parts of the country, creating a general feeling of unrest; the Lebanese Government, however, tended to ignore these incidents. Meanwhile, in external affairs, polite relations were maintained with Syria and Egypt. On 22 February 1958, when these two states merged to form the United Arab Republic, the Lebanese Government congratulated President ʿAbd al-Nāṣir on the occasion. With the establishment of the United Arab Republic, however, the internal situation in Lebanon degenerated further. While the terrorist activity continued, demonstrations in support of ʿAbd al-Nāṣir became frequent and often violent. Moslem demonstrators clamoured for the inclusion of Lebanon in the United Arab Republic; on one occasion, on 28 March, a Moslem mob trampled the Lebanese flag in the streets of Tyre. As the Chamber was expected to meet in May to renew Chamoun's term, the opposition felt constrained to take more conclusive action. On 8 May an opposition journalist, Nasīb al-Matnī, was murdered in Beirut. The National Front, holding the Government to be responsible, called for a country-wide strike in protest. On 10 May the first serious disturbances occurred in Tripoli; on 12 May an armed insurrection broke out in Beirut. Soon it became obvious that men, arms, and ammunition were infiltrating to the rebel strong-holds from Syria. Meanwhile, on the day the insurrection started in Beirut, a Lebanese frontier post was attacked by armed bands from Syria and the five Christian guards present were killed. Before long the Lebanese Government had virtually lost control over its frontiers, and the insurrection had spread to nearly all Moslem and Druze districts. While the Lebanese army was perfectly capable of crushing the insurrection, General Fu'ād Shihāb was reluctant to do so. In his view the function of the army was not to keep a particular government in power, but rather to protect the country against aggression or, in a crisis, to maintain public order. Hence, when General Shihāb was requested to crush the rebellion, he only agreed to stop it from spreading.

Meanwhile, shortly after the insurrection had begun, Lebanon formally accused the United Arab Republic before the Security Council of having instigated and aided the rebellion against the Government. In late June, United Nations observers were sent to report on the situation. The Secretary-General, Dag Hammarskjöld, himself tried to negotiate a settlement by procuring mutual concessions from 'Abd al-Nāṣir and President Chamoun. The United Nations mission, however, was not successful. With the beginning of summer the Lebanese situation became steadily worse. On 14 July a seemingly pro-Egyptian coup overthrew the Hashemite monarchy in Iraq. President Chamoun, who had already asked the United States Government for help, immediately sent a second message to Washington, saying that if Lebanon did not receive American troops in forty-eight hours his pro-Western régime might be overthrown.[37] The decision in Washington was promptly taken. By the evening of 15 July warships and transports of the American Sixth Fleet had landed the first batch of Marines near Beirut.

The arrival of American forces in Lebanon did not put an end to the insurrection in the country, although it did stop effective outside intervention. In the weeks that followed, the Lebanese Moslem rebellion, cut off from the outside world, lost much of its pan-Arab character and began to appear more as an internal movement. This it was, to a great extent, from the beginning. While the lower-class Moslem, envious of the superior lot of the lower-class Christian, may have frequently confused his aspiration for a better life with the ever-present Moslem yearning for Arab union, leaders of the insurrection in Beirut, Tripoli, and elsewhere were thinking more in terms of a change of government. This was certainly the attitude of Kamāl Janbalāṭ in the Shūf, and of those among the Christian leaders who supported the rebels. From the beginning, the insurgents had demanded the immediate resignation of Chamoun. The President, however, stood firm, declaring that he would only leave office on 22 September, the last day of his constitutional term. Sāmī al-Ṣulḥ, still Premier, stood firmly by him, defying his own sect and insisting on the constitutional principle involved. On 5 June his Government announced that the Chamber of Deputies would meet in late July to elect a new President, thereby assuring the opposition that Chamoun would not renew his term. This, however, did not appease the rebels who still called for Chamoun's immediate resignation.

On 16 July, one day after the landing of the first American Marines in Lebanon, US Under-Secretary of State, Robert Murphy, arrived in Beirut as President Eisenhower's special political representative, with instructions 'to do everything possible to restore peace and tranquillity to the Government and to assist President Chamoun in so doing'.[38] Murphy forthwith proceeded to meet with Chamoun as well as with pro-government and opposition leaders, trying hard to secure agreement from both sides on a compromise solution. By now it was clear that the happiest solution would be to have General Shihāb elected as President. The General's stand throughout the crisis had won him the respect of the Moslems. Among the Christians the approval was far from unanimous; many Christians, however, could understand the delicacy of the General's position and his determination not to involve his army in politics. Consequently, on 31 July, the Lebanese Chamber elected Emir Fu'ād Shihāb, who had just resigned his army command, as ninth President of Lebanon. Shihāb now prepared to succeed Chamoun in September. Meanwhile, the insurrection in the country continued, although with an apparently reduced vigour.

The departure of Camille Chamoun from office on 22 September was followed by what was probably the most violent phase of the crisis. On the day President Shihāb took over power, the Lebanese Broadcasting Station announced the formation of a new cabinet headed by a former rebel leader, Rashīd Karāmī, and composed mostly of elements favourable to the National Front. The new premier forthwith declared that his cabinet had come to 'harvest the fruits of the Revolution'. Karāmī's statement immediately provoked an uproar among the Christian groups, and particularly among the *Katā'ib* party which now assumed the Christian leadership. The disappearance of a prominent *Katā'ib* journalist on the following day, reportedly kidnapped and killed by the Moslem rebels, was immediately followed by a Christian general strike which completely paralysed the country. Attacks and reprisals between the Christians of the *Katā'ib* party and the Moslem rebels accompanied the strike, causing the situation to deteriorate into almost a sectarian war. Clearly, the Karāmī

Government could not hope to rule Lebanon at all without the *Katā'ib* party and the pro-Chamoun group being represented in it. Hence, on 14 October the establishment of a new Karāmī cabinet of four members was announced, two Sunnite ministers representing the rebel side and two Maronite ministers[39] representing the originally 'loyalist' side. The slogan 'no victor, no vanquished', earlier chosen to end the crisis, now became the formula for peace.

With the end of the 1958 crisis, the Lebanese situation returned almost immediately to normal. Contact between the Christians and Moslems, never abandoned even at the height of the crisis, was resumed without difficulty, and the original pattern of Lebanese political life was soon restored. Fu'ād Shihāb, as president, soon proved eminently successful in several respects. By allowing Moslems a fairer share in the government, he was able during his first two years to reduce much of the earlier Moslem resentment against the Lebanese State. As a Lebanese Christian, Shihāb feels that no Moslem can be as loyal to Lebanon as his Christian compatriot unless he is also as contented. Consequently, he has paid much attention to the depressed areas of the country, which are mainly inhabited by Sunnites, Shi'ites, and Druzes. Where politics are concerned Shihāb's personal attitude has been strictly constitutional; he has also strongly resisted a growing tendency among leading army officers to interfere in government. In other respects, however, he has met with serious obstacles. Like Chamoun in 1952–54, Shihāb has been attempting, since he took over power, to improve the country's administration; so far he has only met with limited success. While he himself sets a perfect example of personal disinterest, the politicians with whom he has to deal take an entirely different attitude, complicating by their conflicting ambitions the work of successive governments.

In the early summer of 1960, barely two years after Shihāb took over power, the eleventh general elections since 1920 were held in Lebanon. Considering the general situation in the surrounding Moslem world, the event was particularly significant. In a region where military dictatorship had become the rule, the Lebanese Republic, because of its peculiar nature and problems, could still afford the free practice of constitutional life.[40]

NOTES

INTRODUCTION

1. A mutesarrifate (Arabic *mutaṣarrifiyya*) in Ottoman administration was a subdivision of a vilayet, or province, which differed from the more ordinary sanjak in being administered by a mutesarrif with special powers.
2. I have rounded the official figures to the nearest five hundred. The total population of Lebanon in 1956, accordingly, was 1,410,000.
3. Because they accept as valid the imamate (leadership) of 'Alī's descendants through his son Ḥusayn to the twelfth generation.
4. The name *Ḍanniyya* (correctly *Ẓanniyya*), like *Bāṭiniyya*, was commonly used for the various esoteric Shi'ite sects, notably for the Isma'ilites or 'Seveners' who only accept as valid the imamate of the first seven imāms. *See* footnote 3 above.
5. The term Syria, as used here, denotes the geographic region including Lebanon, Palestine and Transjordan as well as the territory of the modern Syrian Republic.
6. According to the last official population figures (for 1956), there were 68,700 Armenian Gregorian, 14,600 Armenian Catholics and 13,600 Protestants.

CHAPTER I: THE SHIHĀB EMIRATE

1. Turkish *kâhya*: steward.
2. Volney, *Voyage en Egypte et en Syrie*, new edition (Paris, 1959), p. 227. The translation is mine.
3. Volney (*op. cit.*, p. 234–6), who visited Lebanon in the days of Emir Yūsuf, thought the Emir to be Druze.
4. *Ibid.*, p. 243.
5. In 1773 'Ali Bey was killed in battle as he led his troops to Egypt to regain his lost position.

CHAPTER II: THE REIGN OF BASHĪR II: 1788–1840

1. Shams was the mother of Bashīr's three sons: Qāsim, Amīn, and Khalil. After her death, Bashīr married the Circassian slave-girl Ḥusn Jahān, who bore him two daughters: Saʿdā and Suʿūd. So fond was Bashīr of his daughter Saʿdā that he was nicknamed after her, Abū Saʿdā – a nickname by which he is still popularly known.
2. Asad J. Rustum, *Calendar of State Papers from the Royal Archives of Egypt relating to the Affairs of Syria* (Beirut, 1940–43), II, pp. 69–70.
3. Christians and Jews in Moslem states did not normally serve in the army, which was the preserve of the Moslems. A special poll-tax which they paid was presumed to entitle them to military protection, and was later re-interpreted as a commutation payment in lieu of military service.
4. A *khalwa* is a Druze religious retreat.

CHAPTER III: THE END OF THE EMIRATE: 1840–42

1. Salmān was later blinded, in 1828, at the orders of Bashīr II.
2. Adel Ismail, *Histoire du Liban du XVIIe siècle à nos jours; IV, Redressement et déclin du feudalisme libanais, 1840–60* (Beirut, 1958).
3. Malcolm H. Kerr, *Lebanon in the Last Years of Feudalism*, 1840–68; *a Contemporary Account by Anṭūn Ḍāhir al-ʿAqīqī, and Other Documents* (Beirut, 1959), p. 3.
4. Yūsuf Muzhir, *Taʾrīkh Lubnān al-ʿāmm* (Beirut, 1900), p. 569.
5. Technically, Salīm Pasha and his successors were the Pashas of Sidon, but after 1840 their residence was established in Beirut.
6. Ihdin in the Bsharrī district, Bʿabdā in the Beirut coastal district, and Jazzīn in the Shūf are among the leading Maronite towns in Mount Lebanon; Zahleh, with its largely Greek Catholic population, is the leading Christian town in the Biqāʿ.

CHAPTER IV: THE DOUBLE KAYMAKAMATE: 1842–58

1. ʿUmar Lutti Pasha, known in Lebanon as ʿUmar Pasha al-Namsāwī (the Austrian), was born Michael Lattas in 1806, and later adopted the name ʿUmar upon embracing Islam.
2. Charles Henry Churchill, *The Druzes and the Maronites under Turkish Rule, from 1840–60* (London, 1862), pp. 66–7.

3. *Ibid.*, p. 67.
4. Adel Ismail, *op. cit.*, p. 193.
5. Father Maximilien Ryllo, known in Lebanon as Būnā Mansūr, first arrived in Lebanon in 1837. He was an instigator of the Christian rising against Ibrāhīm Pasha in 1840, and later of the 1841 troubles. In the summer of 1841 the French Consul in Beirut requested his immediate withdrawal from the country.
6. Adel Ismail, *op. cit.*, pp. 180–1.
7. Charles Henry Churchill, *op. cit.*, p. 72.
8. Adel Ismail, *op. cit.*, p. 183.
9. Charles Henry Churchill, *op. cit.*, pp. 75–6.
10. Colonel Churchill reports rumours that Shiblī al-ʿAryān surrendered to the Turks after he had been bribed by the Turks to betray his countrymen and their cause. Charles Henry Churchill, *op. cit.*, p. 79.
11. The proposal for the double Kaymakamate in Lebanon was first considered at a meeting of the ambassadors with the Ottoman Foreign Minister in Istanbul on 27 May, and it was initially decided upon at a similar meeting on 15 September. Asʿad Pasha was then sent to Lebanon to study its practicability and it was finally decided to adopt the proposal on 7 December.
12. Aḥmad Arslān was one of the Druze chiefs placed under arrest by ʿUmar Pasha.
13. The Janbalāṭs, ʿImāds, Abū Nakads, Talḥūqs and ʿAbd al-Maliks.
14. For the text of this agreement see Adel Ismail, *op. cit.*, pp. 212–215 fn.
15. Technically the district, regularly farmed out by the Ottomans to the Lebanese emirs, had never formed an integral part of the Lebanese feudal domain.
16. The feudal domain of the Abū Nakads consisted of the Manāṣif (originally part of the Shūf) and the neighbouring Shaḥḥār district, of which the main town was ʿAbay.
17. A purse equalled 500 Turkish piastres.
18. Charles Henry Churchill, *op. cit.*, p. 83.
19. *Ibid.*
20. The al-Saʿd family was a branch of the al-Khūrī family who were the sheikhs of Rashmayyā in the Jurd. Ghandūr's father, in the second half of the eighteenth century, had served Emir Yūsuf Shihāb, and was hanged with him in Acre.
21. Charles Henry Churchill, *op. cit.*, p. 84.
22. Yūsuf Karam (1823–89), a Maronite chief of Ihdin, later gained wide recognition as a champion of the Lebanese Christian cause.

23. Ālay, now well known as a summer resort, was, at the time, the principal town of the upper Gharb and the seat of the Talḥuqs.
24. Charles Henry Churchill, *op. cit.*, p. 91.
25. *Ibid.*, p. 92.
26. Previously each *wakīl* was responsible to the kaymakam of his own sect.
27. Charles Henry Churchill, *op. cit.*, p. 110.
28. *Ibid.*, pp. 109–10.
29. From a letter by Yūsuf Karam addressed to Patriarch Būlus Masʿad, quoted in Yūsuf Muzhir, *op. cit.*, I, p. 604.

CHAPTER V: LEBANON IN TURMOIL: 1858–60

1. Charles Henry Churchill, *op. cit.*, pp. 122–3.
2. A *shaykh shabāb* was a village strong man, so called because he depended for his power on an armed following of young men (Ar. *shabāb*). The *shaykh shabāb* himself was not necessarily a young man; he was more frequently middle-aged.
3. Charles Henry Churchill, *op. cit.*, p. 45.
4. Al-Aqīqī, as translated by Malcolm H. Kerr, *op. cit.*, p. 45.
5. *Ibid.*, p. 47.
6. *Ibid.*, p. 49.
7. Thus spelt in the published translation.
8. Al-Aqīqī, as translated by Malcolm H. Kerr, *op. cit.*, p. 53.
9. The Bayt-Mirī affray of 30–31 August, 1859. Charles Henry Churchill, *op. cit.*, p. 132, states that 'the original cause was a quarrel between a Druze and a Christian boy'. Both versions find support in other sources.
10. Malcolm H. Kerr, *op. cit.*, pp. 55–7.
11. Henry H. Jessup, *Fifty-three Years in Syria* (New York, 1910), I, p. 166.
12. Spelt ʿAun in quotation from Malcolm H. Kerr – see Note 11 and p. 88.
13. Henry H. Jessup, *op. cit.*, p. 165.
14. Charles Henry Churchill, *op. cit.*, p. 137.
15. *Ibid.*, pp. 138–9.
16. Dayr al-Qamar.
17. Janbalāṭ.
18. Henry H. Jessup, *op. cit.*, p. 167.
19. Iskandar Abakāriūs, *The Lebanon in Turmoil, Syria and the Powers in 1860; Book of the Marvels of the Time Concerning the Massacres in the*

Arab Country . . . translated by J. F. Scheltema (New Haven, 1920), p. 66.
20. *Ibid.*, pp. 67–8.
21. Henry H. Jessup, *op. cit.*, pp. 168–70.
22. Quoted in footnote in the translation of Iskandar Abkāriūs, *op. cit.*, p. 58, fn. 56.
23. Henry H. Jessup, *op. cit.*, p. 173.
24. Charles Henry Churchill, *op. cit.*, p. 147.
25. *Ibid.*, pp. 142–3.
26. Iskandar Abkāriūs, *op. cit.*, p. 80.
27. *Ibid.*, p. 83.
28. *Ibid.*, p. 78.
29. *Ibid.*, Appendix II, p. 198.
30. Charles Henry Churchill, *op. cit.*, p. 159.
31. *Ibid.*, p. 162.
32. *Ibid.*, p. 163.
33. *Sitt*, in spoken Arabic, is the equivalent of the English 'Lady'.
34. Charles Henry Churchill, *op. cit.*, pp. 163–4.
35. *Ibid.*, p. 165.
36. According to other sources, it was sent as a trophy not to Saʿīd Janbalāṭ, but to Salīm Shams who was staying with him.
37. Charles Henry Churchill, *op. cit.*, pp. 170–2.
38. E. L. Porter, *Five Years in Damascus* (London, 1855), II, p. 279.
39. Charles Henry Churchill, *op. cit.*, p. 182.
40. Iskandar Abkāriūs, *op. cit.*, pp. 95–7.
41. Ḥusayn Abū Shaqrā, *Al-Ḥarakāt ī Lubnan* (n.p. 1952), p. 131. This work is the only available Druze account of the 1860 disturbances in Lebanon, related by a contemporary.
42. This according to a contemporary Druze source (*see* fn. 43). *Ibid.*, p. 131.
43. Iskandar Abkāriūs, *op. cit.*, p. 118.

CHAPTER VI: GOVERNMENT OF MOUNT LEBANON: 1860–1920

1. See Chapter VII on the Lebanese cultural awakening of the time.
2. Philip K. Hitti, *Lebanon in History*, p. 447.
3. *Lubnān; mabāhith ʿilmiyya wa ijtimāʿiyya*, edited under the direction of Ismāʿīl Ḥaqqī Bey (Beirut, A.H. 1334).

4. A project to establish a port for Mount Lebanon in the bay of Junieh was long discussed, but never carried out.
5. Bilād Bishāra is the hilly region to the south-east of Sidon, a part of Jabal 'Āmil; the swamp region of lake Hūla is in northern Palestine, and now part of Israel; Marj-'Uyūn is a region in the southern Wādī al-Taym. For 'Akkār, *see map*.
6. M. Jouplain, *La question de Liban; étude d'histoire diplomatique et de droit international*, second edition (Junieh, 1961), pp. 544–5. The translation is mine.
7. See Kamal S. Salibi 'Islam and Syria in the Writings of Henri Lammens' in Bernard Lewis and Peter Holt, *Historians of the Middle East* (London, 1962), p. 341.
8. M. Jouplain, *op. cit.*, p. 545. The translation is mine.

CHAPTER VII: THE LEBANESE AWAKENING

1. Volney, *op. cit.*, p. 241. The translation is mine.
2. *Ibid.*
3. Kamal S. Salibi, 'The Maronite Church in the Middle Ages and its Union with Rome', *Oriens Christianus*, XIII (1958), pp. 92–104.
4. Kamal S. Salibi, *Maronite Historians of Mediaeval Lebanon* (Beirut, 1959), p. 23ff.
5. *Ibid.*, p. 89ff.
6. Volney, *op. cit.*, p. 226. It must be remembered that Volney, a product of the French enlightenment, was strongly anti-clerical.
7. Kamal S. Salibi, *op. cit.*, p. 91.
8. *Al-majma' al-iqlīmī al-ladhī 'aqadahu fī Jabal Lubnān . . . Baṭriyark ṭā'ifat al-Siryān al-Mawārina al-Anṭākī . . . sanat 1736 . . .* (Junieh, 1900), pp. 526–7, 535, 546. The translation is mine.
9. For the schools established in Lebanon in the eighteenth century see Philip K. Hitti, *Lebanon in History from the Earliest Times to th Present* (London, 1957), pp. 401–2, 417; George Antonius, *The Arab Awakening* (Philadelphia, 1939), pp. 37–8; Ismā'īl Ḥaqqi, *Lubnān . . .* pp. 465–6.
10. Assaad Y. Kayaṭ, *A Voice from Lebanon, with the Life and Travels of Assaad Y. Kayat* (London, 1847), pp. 7–8.
11. *Narrative and Report regarding Lebanon Schools, superintended by John Lowthian, Esq., of Carlton House, Carlisle; Mr Elijah George Saleebey, Mount Lebanon; and his brother Mr Soloman Saleebey.* (Printed gratuitously, in Britain, 1856), p. 8.
12. *Ibid.*, pp. 7–8.

13. George Antonius, *op. cit.*, p. 38.
14. Bernard Lewis, *The Emergence of Modern Turkey* (London, 1961), p. 51. *Ibid.*, p. 50, gives a brief account of the development of printing in the Ottoman Empire. The development of Arabic printing, with particular reference to Lebanon, is summarized in Philip K. Hitti, *op. cit.*, pp. 456–8.
15. George Antonius, *op. cit.*, p. 38.
16. For the names of the Maronite scholars and writers of the eighteenth century and their works see Georg Graf, *Geschichte der Christlichen Arabischen Literatur* (Vatican City, 1944–53), III, pp. 383–476.
17. For the literary revival of the eighteenth century among the Melchites of Syria see Georg Graf, *op. cit.*, III, pp. 127–59 (for the Greek Orthodox), pp. 172–256 (for the Greek Catholics). Notice the polemical nature of much of the literature cited, the larger literary output of the Greek Catholics, and the number among those who wrote in Lebanon.
18. Albert Hourani, 'The Fertile Crescent in the Eighteenth Century' in *A Vision of History; Near Eastern and other Essays* (Beirut, 1961), p. 50.
19. *Ibid.*, pp. 51–2.
20. Georg Graf, *op. cit.*, III, pp. 251–4.
21. *Ibid.*, III, pp. 244–51.
22. *Ibid.*, III, pp. 242–4.
23. *Ibid.*, IV, pp. 303–5. After 1840 Buṭrus Karāma accompanied his master to exile, first in Malta and then in Istanbul where he was employed in his last years in the Ottoman chancery.
24. *Ibid.*, IV, pp. 294–5; Philip K. Hitti, *op. cit.*, pp. 392–3.
25. The term 'Syrian' here denotes an inhabitant of geographic Syria, usually a Christian (*cf. Suriens* in Crusader usage); the use of the term was mainly by Christians.
26. The italics are in the original.
27. Assaad Y. Kayāt, *op. cit.*, pp. 34–6.
28. Philip K. Hitti, *op. cit.*, pp. 454–5.
29. (K.S.), 'Islam', *Current Affairs Bulletin* (Sydney, Fe. 1962), Vol. 26, No. 8, p. 118.
30. Asad J. Rustum, *Bashīr bayn al-Sulṭān wa'l-'Azīz* (Beirut, 1956–57), pp. 230–1.
31. George Antonius, *op. cit.*, p. 39.
32. Asad J. Rustum, *op. cit.*, pp. 231–2.
33. Isaac Bird, *Bible Work in Bible Lands; or, Events in the History of the Syrian Mission* (Philadelphia, 1872), p. 312.

34. *Ibid.*, p. 319.
35. *Ibid.*, pp. 318–19.
36. *Ibid.*, p. 319.
37. *Ibid.*, p. 346.
38. *Ibid.*, see also 'al-Bustānī' in *The Encylopaedia of Islam* (original edition).
39. *Ibid.*, pp. 357–8.
40. *Ibid.*, pp. 312, 319–20, 322–3, 346.
41. *Ibid.*, pp. 358–61.
42. See N. N. Lewis, 'Churchill of Lebanon', *Journal of the Royal Central Asian Society*, XL (1953), pp. 217–23.
43. For the story of these schools see *Narrative and Report regarding Lebanon Schools*, passim.
44. *Ibid.*, pp. 14, 16–17.
45. For the history of the schools established by the Ṣalībī brothers and John Lowthian in Lebanon see *Report on the Lebanon Schools, with Treasurers' Accounts*, 1856–68.
46. Starting in 1860 the school at Sūq al-Gharb was used to train teachers for the other schools, in an effort to meet the problem of the shortage of teachers.
47. *Report on the Lebanon Schools* . . . (1868), p. 6.
48. *Narrative and Report Regarding Lebanon Schools*, p. 18.
49. *Report on the Lebanon Schools* . . . (1860), p. 6.
50. Henry H. Jessup, *op. cit.*, pp. 383–4. Ilyās Ṣalībī retired first to England, then returned to spend his last years in Lebanon where he died in 1891.
51. *Ibid.*, pp. 508–21.
52. For the Catholic, Greek Orthodox and Moslem schools in Lebanon, as well as for al-Dāwūdiyya, see Philip K. Hitti, *op. cit.*, pp. 445, 448–50, 453–61; Ismā'īl Ḥaqqī, *Lubnān* . . . pp. 470–1, 476–7; George Antonius, *op. cit.*, pp. 44–5; Henry H. Jessup, *op. cit.*, p. 812; *Awrāq Lubnānīyya*, I (Beirut, 1955), pp. 52–6, 153–6.
53. Ismā'īl Ḥaqqī, *Lubnān* . . . pp. 478–9.
54. Bernard Lewis, *op. cit.*, p. 124.
55. N. A. Faris, 'Lebanon, "Land of Light" ', *The World of Islam; Studies in Honour of Philip K. Hitti*, ed. by James Kritzeck and R. Bayly Winder (London, 1959), p. 349.
56. John Alexander Thompson, *The Major Arabic Bibles, their Origin and Nature* (New York, 1956), pp. 20–7.
57. Henry H. Jessup, *op. cit.*, p. 483.
58. *Ibid.*, p. 484.
59. *Ibid.*, p. 484.

60. For Yāzijī, Bustānī, Asīr, and their contemporaries see Philip K. Hitti, *op. cit.*, pp. 461–9.

CHAPTER VIII: GREATER LEBANON

1. For the text of this agreement see George Antonius, *op. cit.*, Appendix B, pp. 428–30.
2. See the McMahon Correspondence in, *ibid.* Appendix A, pp. 413–17.
3. Stephen Hemsley Longrigg, *Syria and Lebanon under French Mandate* (London, 1958), p. 53.
4. Gallicized form of Iddī.
5. Gallicized form of Shīḥā; Michel Chiha, a prominent author and intellectual, wrote mainly in French.
6. Quoted by Pierre Rondot, *Les Chrétiens d'Orient* (Paris, 1955), p. 252.
7. Stephen Hemsley Longrigg, *op. cit.*, p. 171.
8. *Ibid.*
9. The Khūrī family were feudal sheikhs of the Maronite sub-district of Rashmayya. *See* Chapter IV, fn. 20.
10. A well-known Lebanese writer in French. His name, as spelt here, is the Gallicized form of the Arabic Qurm.
11. Iskandar Riyāshī, *Qabl wa Ba'd* (Beirut, n.d.), p. 111.
12. Stephen Hemsley Longrigg, *op. cit.*, p. 204.
13. *Ibid.*
14. George Grassmuck, and Kamal Salibi, *A Manual of Lebanese Administration* (Beirut, 1955), p. 9.
15. Actually there was no 'Syria' before 1920. The geographic entity generally referred to as Syria had, until the end of the First World War, consisted of three Ottoman vilayets, of which that of Damascus was sometimes called the 'vilayet of Syria'.
16. Gallicized spelling of Jumayyil.
17. Bishāra al-Khūrī, *Ḥaqā'iq Lubnāniyya*, I (Harissa, 1960), p. 200.
18. The government headquarters in Beirut.
19. This according to Iskandar Riyāshī, *op. cit.*, p. 161.
20. Gallicized spelling of Naqqāsh.
21. Stephen Hemsley Longrigg, *op. cit.*, p. 321.
22. *Ibid.*
23. Gallicized form of Kamīl Sham'ūn. Chamoun first became a deputy in 1934.
24. Bishārā al-Khūrī, *op. cit.*, I, p. 245. The translation is mine.
25. For current population estimates in Lebanon (*see* p. 000).

26. ʿAbd al-Ḥamīd Karāmī of Tripoli. *See* p. 174.
27. A Greek Orthodox and a Druze respectively.
28. The Lebanese flag has since consisted of three horizontal stripes red-white-red, with the cedar emblem on the middle stripe.
27. Georges Catroux, *Dans la Bataille de Mediterraneé* . . . (Paris, 1949), p. 414, quoted by Stephen Hemsley Longrigg, *op. cit.*, p. 333.
30. Spelt in this manner for consistency; he actually spells his name Chehab.
31. He is actually a descendant of Emir Yūsuf.
32. He held the premiership continuously from September 1943 until January 1945, and from December 1946 until February 1951.
33. Actually the vote was unanimous, with forty-six deputies present. Of the nine absent only seven were opposed.
34. Son of Salīm Salām (*see* p. 174).
35. The legislative decrees of 1953.
36. Gallicized form of Būlus al-Mʿūshi.
37. Richard L. Miller, *Dag Hammarskjöld and Crisis Diplomacy* (New York, 1961), p. 178.
38. *Ibid.*, p. 186.
39. Pierre Gemayel, head of the *Katā'ib* party (*see* p. 181) and Raymond Eddé, head of the National Bloc (*see* p. 194).
40. This final passage of the book was written in February 1963, during Shihāb's term which did not end until September 1964. Since then the twelfth general election has been held (Spring of 1964), and the new Chamber has elected a new President, the lawyer and former journalist, Charles Helon (Ḥilū), to succeed Shihāb.

BIBLIOGRAPHICAL NOTES AND SUGGESTIONS FOR FURTHER READING

THIS BOOK is based mainly on original sources: traditional histories, family histories, memoirs, books of description and travel, documentary material, and contemporary accounts of events. There has been, indeed, little study in the field of modern Lebanese history on which the writer of a general book on the subject can rely. One exception is the work, in Arabic, on the period of Ibrahim Pasha's rule in Lebanon and Syria (1832–40) by Asad Rustum, *Calendar of State Papers from the Royal Archives of Egypt relating to the Affairs of Syria* (Beirut, American Press, 1940–3). Another is a study of social, economic and political changes in Mount Lebanon during the first half of the nineteenth century by William R. Polk, *The Opening of South Lebanon, 1788–1840; a Study of the Impact of the West on the Middle East* (Cambridge, Mass., Harvard University Press, 1963), which appeared after the manuscript of the present book was ready for the press. Other studies in English on the history of Lebanon in the nineteenth century include translations from Arabic, with notes, of two contemporary accounts of the period of civil disturbances, 1840–60. The first is by J. F. Scheltema, *The Lebanon in Turmoil, Syria and the Powers in 1860; Book of the Marvels of the Time concerning the Massacres in the Arab Country by Iskandar ibn Ya'qūb Abkāriūs* (New Haven, Yale University Press, 1920). Scheltema, in his notes, shows a lack of sympathy with the traditional Christian interpretation of the Lebanese massacres. The second of the two translations is by Malcolm H. Kerr, *Lebanon in the Last Years of Feudalism, 1840–68; a Contemporary Account by Anṭūn Ḍāhir al-'Aqīqī, and Other Documents* (Beirut, American University, 1959). Kerr's introduction to 'Aqīqī's account is a good summary of the events of the period.

While some specialized studies in the field of modern Lebanese history do exist, no connected and detailed general work on the subject has been written in any language. The book of Philip K. Hitti, *Lebanon in History* (London, Macmillan, 1957), surveys the history of Lebanon from prehistoric to modern times. The survey, however, is rapid, and concerned more with the general regional history in which Lebanon was involved than with the intimate history of the country. A much earlier work by Henri Lammens, *La Syriei précis historique* (Beirut, Imprimerie Catholique, 1921), gives a coherent account of the internal development of Lebanon in the context of the general history of Syria as a region. Two years before the appearance of Professor Hitti's *Lebanon in History*, there appeared the first volume of another general work on the subject in French, planned in six volumes, by Adel Ismail, *Historie du Liban du XVIIe siècle à nos jours; le Liban au temps de Fakhr-ed-Din II (1590–1633)* (Paris, Maisonneuve, 1955). Three years later Ismail published the fourth volume of his work under the subtitle *Redressement et declin du feodalisme libanais (1840–1860)* (Beirut, Harb Bijjani, 1958). Unlike the well-balanced first volume, the fourth volume, relying heavily on French archival material, has a strong pro-French bias. The second and third volumes of Ismail's work, dealing with the period 1633–1840, have not appeared so far, nor have any volumes subsequent to the fourth been published as yet.

On the history of Lebanon since the First World War, the most important work is that of Stephen Hemsley Longrigg, *Syria and Lebanon under French Mandate* (London, Oxford University Press, 1958). Longrigg carries his history down to 1946. The book of Albert Hourani, *Syria and Lebanon; a Political Essay* (London, Oxford University Press, 1946), gives an analysis of the general situation of Lebanon and Syria as these two countries emerged from mandatory status to independence. Hourani's book has since gone into a second edition, but has not been brought up to date. An account of developments in Lebanon since the time of the Mandate is found in a book by Nicola Abdo Ziadeh, *Syria and Lebanon* (London, Benn, 1957).

To the reader interested in current Lebanese affairs, the works of Pierre Rondot are of the first importance. His *Les Institutions Politiques du Liban* (Institut d'Études de l'Orient Contemporain, 1947) is a standard work on Lebanese politics, which he has since supplemented by a number of articles on the subject. Another work by Pierre Rondot, *Les Chrétiens d'Orient* (Paris, Peyronnet, 1955) throws light on the intellectual and political attitudes of Lebanese Christians and the effect these attitudes have had on Lebanese and regional politics

Where the modern intellectual history of Lebanon is concerned, the recent book of Albert Hourani, *Arabic Thought in the Liberal Age, 1798–1939* (London, Oxford University Press, 1962) is indispensable. On the administration of Lebanon under the Mutesarrifate the standard work is still Vital Cuinet, *Syrie, Liban et Palestine; Géographie admini-*

strative, statistique, descriptive et raisonnée (Paris, Ernest Leroux, 1895). On the government and administration of the Lebanese Republic, the descriptive study by George Grassmuk and Kamal Salibi, *A Manual of Lebanese Administration* (Beirut, American University, 1955) is currently being brought up-to-date for a second edition.

No general books on the sociology, economics, or social and economic history of Lebanon exist so far. Some specialized studies, however, can be recommended. Of the sociological studies on Lebanon, a book of interest is by John Gulick, *Social Structure and Culture Change in a Lebanese Village* (New York, Wenner-Gren Foundation for Anthropological Research, 1955). The book of Yusif Sayigh, *Entrepreneurs of Lebanon: the Role of the Business Leader in a Developing Economy* (Cambridge, Mass., Harvard University Press, 1962), is perhaps the best book so far on Lebanese economics. Another book to be recommended on the subject is by Arthur E. Mills, *Private Enterprise in Lebanon* (Beirut, American University, 1959).

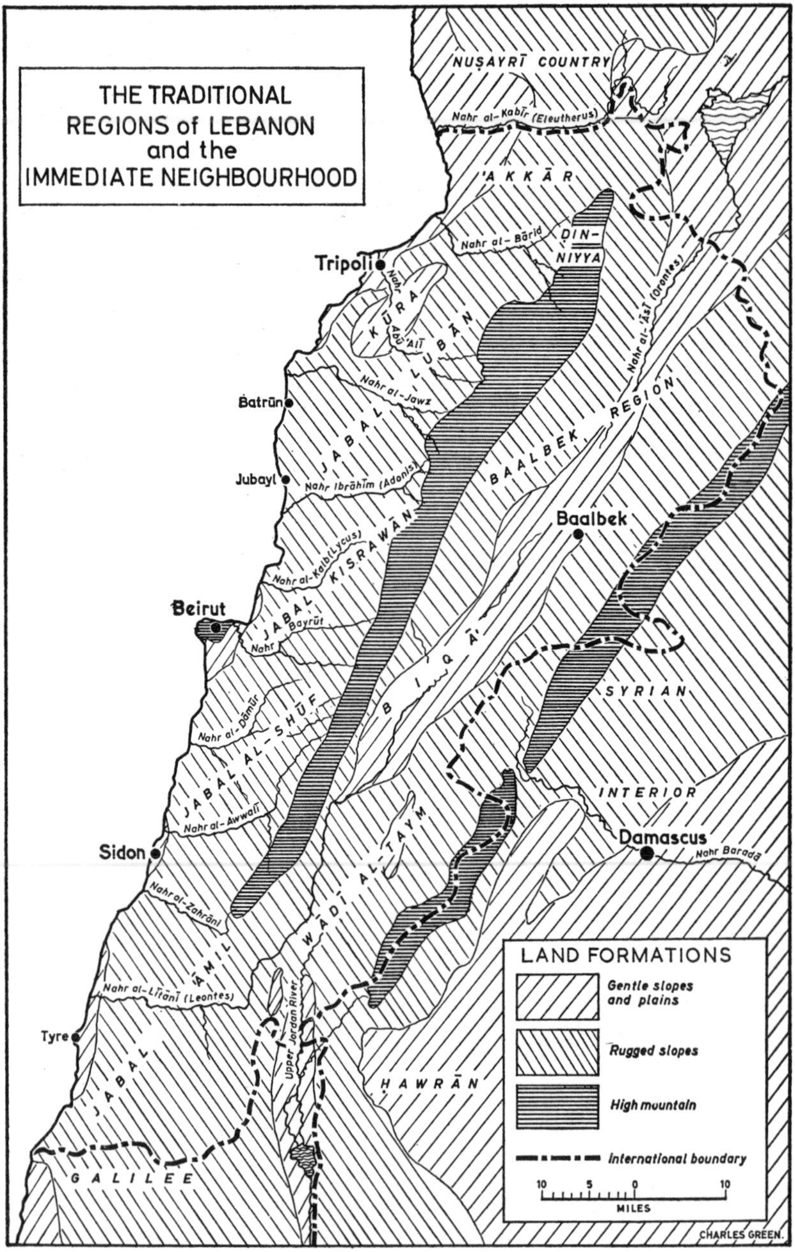
THE TRADITIONAL
REGIONS of LEBANON
and the
IMMEDIATE NEIGHBOURHOOD
NUṢAYRĪ COUNTRY
Nahr al-Kabīr (Eleutherus)
'AKKĀR
Nahr al-Bārid
DIN-
NIYYA
Tripoli
Nahr
Abū 'Alī
KŪRA
LUBNĀN
Nahr al-'Āṣī (Orontes)
Nahr al-Jawz
Batrūn
JABAL
BAALBEK REGION
Jubayl
Nahr Ibrāhīm (Adonis)
Baalbek
Nahr al-Kalb (Lycus)
KISRAWĀN
JABAL
Beirut
Nahr Bayrūt
BIQĀ'
SYRIAN
Nahr al-Dāmūr
JABAL AL-SHŪF
INTERIOR
Nahr al-Awwalī
WADĪ AL-TAYM
Damascus
Nahr Baradā
Sidon
Nahr al-Zahrānī
'ĀMIL
Nahr al-Līṭānī (Leontes)
Upper Jordan River
Tyre
JABAL
HAWRĀN
GALILEE
LAND FORMATIONS
Gentle slopes and plains
Rugged slopes
High mountain
International boundary
10 5 0 10
MILES
CHARLES GREEN.

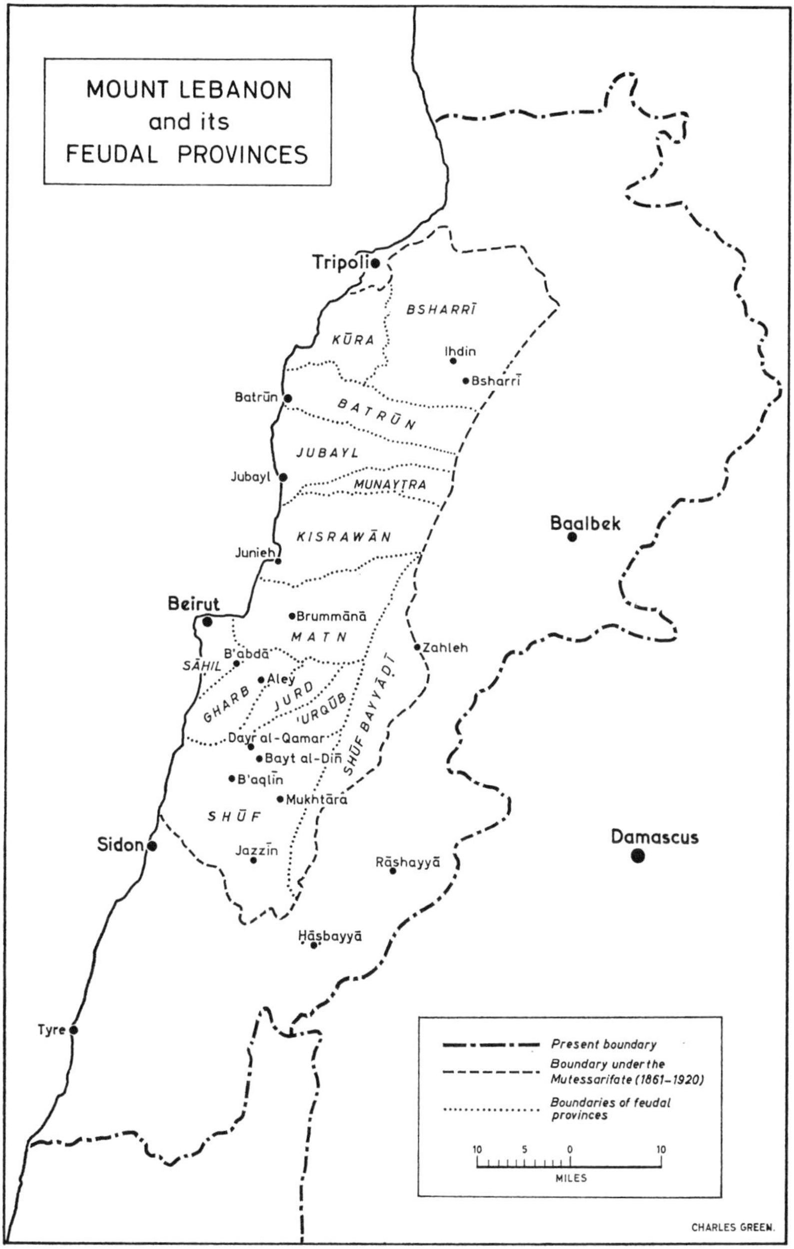
MOUNT LEBANON
and its
FEUDAL PROVINCES
Tripoli
BSHARRĪ
KŪRA
Ihdin
Bsharrī
Batrūn
BATRŪN
JUBAYL
Jubayl
MUNAYTRA
KISRAWĀN
Baalbek
Junieh
Beirut
Brummānā
MATN
Zahleh
B'abdā
SĀHIL
Aley
JURD
GHARB
'URQŪB
SHŪF BAYYĀDĪ
Dayr al-Qamar
Bayt al-Dīn
B'aqlīn
Mukhtāra
SHŪF
Sidon
Damascus
Jazzīn
Rāshayyā
Hāsbayyā
Tyre
Present boundary
Boundary under the Mutessarifate (1861-1920)
Boundaries of feudal provinces
10 5 0 10
MILES
CHARLES GREEN.

INDEX

I.